T0151220

I take great pleasure in applauding the advent of the Ubu Repertory Theater Publications. Devoted to bringing English versions of important contemporary dramatic works from French-speaking countries, this program could not be more important or timely when institutions such as the Eugene O'Neill Theater Center and the Milwaukee Repertory Theater have begun to embrace and espouse the cause of this key element of cultural exchange.

It is particularly important to realize that the plays chosen for translation and publication are not part of any specific genre, but rather are eclectic and are selected to inform the English-speaking public of the scope and richness of present-day French-speaking playwrights.

I cherish the hope that this marvelous project will spark a renaissance in professional collaboration between our French and English-speaking theaters and foster greater understanding between diverse national groups.

George C. White, President
Eugene O'Neill Memorial Theater Center

UBU REPERTORY THEATER PUBLICATIONS

PREFACE

To publish a collection of political plays in the summer of 1990 opens up a fine sense of the possible: this past year has seen such upheavals that the very idea of politics has changed as seismically as have the Eastern European states. No one foresaw these changes; our consciousness, formed by 45 years of Cold War, hasn't begun to assimilate them, let alone figure out exactly what happened and what it will mean. But clearly the effect on theater will be enormous—most obviously in Europe, but also in countries like China, where popular unrest has been defeated, and, with some luck, here in America. Everywhere the idiom of dissent has been associated with the kind of authoritarian socialism that is now in retreat.

So far, the Eastern European revolutions—particularly Czechoslovakia's—have only sharpened American awareness of the painful difference between their cultural world and ours. Perhaps soon they will start to inspire us. Meanwhile, we'd do well to take a lesson from Ariane Mnouchkine's *Mephisto*. Theater people in the United States, including critics, tend to pat themselves on the back for their liberalism (if they are mainstream) or their radicalism (if they think of themselves as avant-garde). They rarely question their own roles vis-à-vis state and corporate power. They hardly ever juxtapose one kind of theater with another ethically, the way the official theater and the dissident cabaret are opposed in *Mephisto*. They—we—have forgotten what used to be easily understood: when an artist collaborates with power, what happens isn't just selling out or buying in but something much more consequential than ordinary careerism; it's never a simple refusal to take sides. When artists stop dissenting they end up with a society against whose repressions they are defenseless.

From Aimé Cesaire we can learn, again, how to make theater out of immediate political history, and from Jean-Pol Fargeau we can learn how to look back on the slaveholding, colonial roots of our country and trace their effects in racism and rage; in Wendy Kesselman's work we can see how unfamiliar even the most familiar of old revolutions looks when reinterpreted by feminism; in Sylvain Bemba's play, the canonical work of one civilization is metamorphosed through the struggles of another. All these attempts—recreating history, narrating it through the silenced voices of women or black people, viewing the dominant culture through the eyes of those it has dominated—address questions as urgent now as when the plays were written. And they address these questions in many ways, but never naturalistically.

The superficially realistic prose play of psychology and domesticity, which has been taken over by mainstream theater, television, and film, is useless. Certain techniques of antinaturalism, those radical forms which a generation ago we thought led inevitably to a radical outlook, have also been taken over; they now are comfortably used by MTV, by commercials, by yuppified formerly experimental genres. These forms can still be used, but warily. Only true simplicity and true complexity haven't been appropriated by commerce—simplicity because it's the nature of commercial art to manipulate, and complexity because its nature is to avoid ambiguity and the urge to stop and think. A straightforward grip on the ambiguity of history can lead to plays in poetry, to epic theater, to performance art, and to forms still unknown.

I hope this book inspires American readers to connect theater with politics again, to think about the stage as a space for public discourse about public issues.

—Erika Munk

BEMBA
CÉSAIRE
FARGEAU
KESSELMAN
MANN/MNOUCHKINE

THEATER
& POLITICS

an
international
anthology

Preface by ERIKA MUNK

Ubu Repertory Theater Publications
Françoise Kourilsky
Catherine Temerson
General Editors

Printed in the United States of America
1990
Library of Congress Catalog Card Number: 90-70691
ISBN 0-913745-32-4

CONTENTS

Sylvain Bemba

BLACK WEDDING CANDLES FOR BLESSED ANTIGONE

**Translated from the French by
Townsend Brewster**

(A drama in three acts and fourteen tableaux
inspired by Sophocles' *Antigone*)

This English translation of *Black Wedding Candles for Blessed Antigone* was given its first public reading at Ubu Repertory Theater, in memory of Townsend Brewster, on April 15, 1990, with the following cast:

Margaret Bintu	**Kim Brockington**
Dorothy Mela, Figure in Black with a Scythe, Jamaican Make-up Woman	**Benja K.**
Melissa Yadé	**Melody Cooper**
John Abiola	**Paul Knowles**
Titus Saint-Just Bund	**Stanley Earl Harrison**
Griot, Officer	**Mathew Idason**
Second Figure in Black, Stage Hand, Creon, New Leader of the Amandian Republic, Official	**Donald Lee Taylor**
Narrator	**Scott Williams**

Directed by **Randy Frazier**

SYLVAIN BEMBA was born in Sibiti, Congo in 1934. He began his literary career in 1953 as a sports writer, receiving a prize a year later. In 1955 he became an editor of the journal *Liaison* and started publishing short stories in *Le Petit Journal* in Brazzaville. Bemba became well-known in his country for his news and sports reports, his editorials, and his radio broadcasts; he also held an administrative position in the Ministry of Information. He is the author of two award-winning plays, *L'Enfer c'est Orfeo* (1969) and *L'Eau dormante* (1972), as well as *L'Homme qui tua le crocodile, Tarantelle noire et diable blanc, Un foutu monde pour un blanchisseur trop honnête*, and, in 1987, *Qu'est devenu Ignoumba le chasseur?* He has also published four novels (*Rêves portatifs, Léopolis, Le Soleil est parti à M'Pemba*, and *Le dernier des Cargonautes*) and a history of Congolese music from 1920 to 1970.

TOWNSEND BREWSTER was a playwright, librettist, lyricist, poet, translator, and critic. Three of his comedies, *Please Don't Cry and Say "No," Arthur Ashe and I*, and *The Girl Beneath the Tulip Tree*, were produced Off-Broadway, as was his verse translation of Corneille's *Le Menteur*. Ubu commissioned many translations from him. These include Bernard Dadié's *Monsieur Thôgô-gnini*, which is available through Ubu Repertory Theater Publications, and Maxim N'Debeka's *Equatorium*, included in Ubu's anthology *Afrique*. He also translated Senouvo Agbota Zinsou's *The Singing Tortoise*, which was produced during the 1988 Ubu International Festival, and Emmanuel Genvrin's *Etuves* and *Black Slavery*, which were given a staged reading at Hunter College Little Theatre as part of Ubu's 1989 festival "Homage to the Revolution." Mr. Brewster was listed in both *Who's Who in Theater* and *Who's Who in America*. He had just completed his translation of *Black Wedding Candles for Blessed Antigone* for Ubu at the time of his death, on February 1, 1990.

FOREWORD

No fitting tears or solemn rites avail
To quench the flames of rekindled memory...
nor quasi-official whitening of indelible shrouds
nor use of some Satanic rubberstamp
to obliterate remembrance
and reinter dead heroes.

    With *Leopolis* I tried, novelistically, to bring back to life the man I have described as "the first patrician of the African independence movements."

    According to André Malraux, in "L'homme précaire et la littérature," Sophocles' immortal work—a work created long before Christ and today the heritage of all mankind—was once absent from human memory for nearly a thousand years. And it is because it is truly, as they say, in the public domain that I have tried, very humbly and with great respect, to use it in a theatrical fiction. It bears the still-open wound of the memory of the man who is still mourned by the youth of Africa— and, indeed, the world—as the second Lumumba of our half century.

    Antigone's blood wedding, through the contraction and wordplay of the author's imagination, became, in French, *Noces posthumes de Santigone* (literally, *Posthumous Marriage for Santigone*), which the play's English translator has rendered, poetically, as *Black Wedding Candles for Blessed Antigone*.

    The work is dedicated to the Conseil National des Lettres, which made it possible by making a grant to the author, who was at the time living in Limoges for health reasons; to the Festival International des Francophonies, which enabled the author to work and to live in conditions propitious to "creation"; and to the Théâtre International de Langue Française, which gave the author a foothold so that his voice could be heard in France.

I would like to express my deep gratitude to Madame and Monsieur Jean-Pierre Juillard for their warmth and hospitality and to his friends Régine and Jacques Colombier for their kind hearts. Thanks go to Professor Sergio Zoppi, who translated the play *Qu'est devenu Ignoumba le chasseur?* into Italian. I also wish to express my gratitude to my long-time friend M.N., who criticized the first draft of the manuscript with his usual clear-sightedness and impartiality, which stem from his exemplary probity. Lastly, I wish to thank Miss Béatrice Princelle, who prepared the manuscript with great professional skill and friendly cooperation.

"Do not cry.
Walk proud!
He died face down.
Turn him over...
If his belly is hard
It means he met death standing."

—*Tchicaya u Tam'Si*

"For yourself, lift your thoughts to heaven.
What merits this life? Naught, save contempt.
Happy when danger fraught,
And self forgot."

—*Giacomo Leopardi*

"Everything ends," said the Ho master.
"Everything ends; you are wandering even now
through tomorrow's ruins."

—*Henri Michaux*

"Time does not exist where nothing kills itself."

—*Jean Mazeaufroid*

"Be braver than you've ever been.
A man who has not known trials cannot stand firm.
One's ears must be boxed and made to ring with the
din of woes and penitence...."

—*Thomas Munzer*

CHARACTERS

The parts can be played by seven or eight actors, divided into two groups. The first group is comprised of specific characters who play the same roles throughout the play, namely, the roles of:

MARGARET BINTU, *Amandian student, 25*
DOROTHY MELA, *Amandian student, 25*
MELISSA YADÉ, *who plays Antigone, Amandian, 22*
JOHN ABIOLA, *Amandian citizen, 40s*
TITUS SAINT-JUST BUND, *appearing successively as the Patient, the First Silhouette during the storming of the palace, and the silhouette of the Young Soldier who appears in a vision to Melissa Yadé*

The second group includes all the other, interchangeable, roles:

THE GRIOT
THE FIGURE IN BLACK WITH A SCYTHE
THE SECOND FIGURE IN BLACK, WHO LATER PLAYS THE PHYSICIAN
THE SIGHTSEERS IN THE PUBLIC PARK
THE STAGE HAND
THE JAMAICAN MAKE-UP WOMAN, 50
THE SECOND, THIRD, FOURTH, AND FIFTH SILHOUETTES DURING THE STORMING OF THE PALACE
THE REPORTERS
CREON
THE OFFICER
THE NEW LEADER OF THE AMANDIAN REPUBLIC
SOLDIERS
THE OFFICIAL

The actors in the first group should play the parts in the second group by changing costume, voice, and movement.

Prologue

(Enter the Griot. He may wear a mask to help differentiate him from other roles He will play without one.)

GRIOT: A memory of forgotten pain. Pain for the man I remember I was. I've forgotten the remembrance since they shot my memory full of holes. To make me forget I remember him. And you who insanely seek refuge in oblivion no longer remember me. You've all forgotten me, you whose cushioned slumber goes unracked by diurnal fits of coughing. I remember forgotten pain because it bleeds. Being shot full of holes keeps my memory intact. I read the past in the lines of my left palm. Images swirl in those of my right. We have here the chronicle of my...of his...of your...of our memory.

Act I, Tableau 1

(A female students' room, in companionable disorder. Various objects are strewn about. A large British flag covers a great portion of the wall, on which a photograph of Michael Jackson is no less prominent. There are a group of dolls in African costume. Rounding out the decor is a piece of batik artwork. Dresses hang in a wardrobe. There is radio music, along with which one of the young women is singing while the other is tidying the place. Both students wear Afro wigs and négligées.)

MARGARET BINTU: Wasn't that party a blast last night! That Gloria is lucky to have a father so rich he can give her whatever she wants. And you see who showed up.

DOROTHY MELA: Did I see! I was part of the receiving line. I welcomed a healthy assortment of swells: movie stars, here and there a diplomat or two, British as well as African.

MARGARET BINTU: And just think, Gloria wanted to stick me with the check when I had my heart set on working with the musicians.

DOROTHY MELA: I know what you mean. That hunk, Jimmy, was the DJ. They can't throw a party without him. No one can touch him when it comes to picking exactly the right music to set rooms rocking.

MARGARET BINTU: Jimmy's a wiz.

DOROTHY MELA: If he's anywhere near as talented in the sack, you're a happy woman.

MARGARET BINTU: As of last night.

DOROTHY MELA: Provided Jimmy leaves you a little time for your play.

MARGARET BINTU: Especially June 23. The local papers report nothing else. In the street, in cafés. There's never been such excitement. Yes indeed, it's like the return of the prodigal son.

DOROTHY MELA: *(with irony)* I take it you mean Richard Cooper.

MARGARET BINTU: *Sir* Richard Cooper, knighted by the Queen and considered to be one of the three greatest directors in Great Britain.

DOROTHY MELA: *(acidly)* Fine and dandy.

MARGARET BINTU: *(running with it)* And there's more. Sir Richard Cooper cancelled some fabulous engagements. He'll celebrate his seventieth birthday here in the city of his birth.

DOROTHY MELA: *(intrigued in spite of herself)* What's he like? An old geezer? A sage?

MARGARET BINTU: He doesn't show his age. Full of life. Somewhat on the order of Gregory Peck. He looks at you, and you feel the tide flow from the shore of your belly. Our big men on campus? Their tails stay between their legs when this gentleman's around. You should have attended at least one rehearsal.

DOROTHY MELA: Thanks a lot. What's more, I'm not attending the performance either.

MARGARET BINTU: Dottie, darling, you can't do this to me. This is my first Sir Richard Cooper production—

DOROTHY MELA: But Buchanan started it off, and he's the one who sacked me in favor of that snip, Melissa Yadé, my understudy for the past four years.

MARGARET BINTU: You'd been quite ill. Your lungs.

DOROTHY MELA: Enough of that! I'm no tuberculosis case. You, yourself, saw my X-rays. Anyway, who needs lungs to act? What it takes is heart, guts, and sex. It didn't take Buchanan quite long enough to forget that, one after another, I'd played Saint Joan, Phèdre, Juliet, and Mother Courage.

MARGARET BINTU: Four great roles for one great actress.

DOROTHY MELA: Buchanan nipped all that in the bud. Ah, to receive the seed of the great playwrights and, as a mother, to carry yourself in your womb and emerge as a newborn child! There's nothing more wonderful than that. Melissa's robbed me of that great hope.

MARGARET BINTU: Be a good sport. Think of Melissa as our little sister. Then you'll be really proud of her. She's given up on sleep and barely takes the time even to eat. Often, you see her roaming the moors like a ghost. Do you know what Sir Richard says about her?

DOROTHY MELA: *(passionately)* I don't want to know. Even not knowing gashes my throat like a cactus spine. *(after a pause)* I'm stifling in this room. I'm going out to get some air.

> *(Exit Mela. After a short pause, there is a knock at the door. Bintu rushes to the mirror to repair, as much as she can, her disheveled state. She opens the door to admit John Abiola, an elegant man who is quite sure of himself and who enjoys hearing himself talk.)*

ABIOLA: Where's Dottie?

BINTU: Gone out for a walk.

ABIOLA: Fine! Fine! *(He rubs his hands together.)* Let's make the most of her absence by catching up on our love life.

BINTU: You're really into pipe dreams. Have I ever given you the least encouragement?

ABIOLA: Since when do we men need encouragement? I have a variety of approaches. *Blitzkrieg,* troop maneuvers, war of attrition.

BINTU: And you expect my cooperation?

ABIOLA: I expect an honest explanation. You always run for cover. Rehearsals here, rehearsals there. Where do I fit in?

BINTU: We might as well be frank. Yorkshire's not that far away, and it's where you have a wife and child. Said wife is English. I have no problem with that, but neither am I keen on being your wife in this particular port. As for filling in twice a month—

ABIOLA: I don't believe in being rigid. I'm always for leaving doors open just in case.

BINTU: And I'm always for knowing exactly how things stand.

ABIOLA: When a pretty woman says "No," it means she loves someone else.

BINTU: That's none of your business.

ABIOLA: Aha! I've struck a nerve, eh? Well, little lady of my heart, let's pass the peace pipe right now. We could start with your offering me a drink.

(Bintu bestirs herself to get two glasses.)

A lot of whiskey and a splash of Coke, if you've got any.

(They clink glasses as Abiola examines the room with a critical eye.)

It's not bad, your little pad. Just the right amount of the woman's touch, intimate but not to excess. But one thing in this room does astound me, the British flag.

BINTU: Rather like your wife. Or hadn't you noticed?

ABIOLA: All right, I'll accept that. But I carry a Gold Nugget passport. I don't think of myself as one of your white-skinned Blacks.

BINTU: A black-skinned White, then?

ABIOLA: A Gold Nugget man and proud of it.

BINTU: Congratulations! Gold Nugget barely scrapes along by passing the hat to the rest of the world. An excellent reason, I grant you, for feeling proud.

ABIOLA: Excellent or poor, my country remains my country.

BINTU: I completely agree. The Good Guys are in. They proved they were top-drawer by declining to roll out a nice little banana-peel carpet for the Bad Guys. Long live the ways of the Old West! Long live the rodeo, where the cowboy is thrown no sooner than he's on horseback. Meanwhile, everything disappears, and our peasants are starving to death. You might call them our Indians.

ABIOLA: Since the events of June 2, things are changing.

BINTU: What do you mean?

ABIOLA: Admittedly, the old problems are still with us, but there's now a new way of dealing with them. I sense a renewal of hope in the hearts of our countrymen.

BINTU: The wordmen certainly know their craft, but I've heard the song before. They're telling us to fall in step. I don't much like it.

ABIOLA: You exaggerate.

BINTU: Come on, Abiola, open your eyes. The time is past for dreaming. Eight hours of sleep, all right. But two years?

ABIOLA: I'm not asleep, I assure you. I'm simply giving the present régime a chance.

BINTU: That's your choice. But I've been burned. It will never happen again.

ABIOLA: Some day, you'll take a more objective view of the matter.

BINTU: Put your money on any horse you please. As for me, though your "Djibund" is a sweetheart, he's just not my type. When I hear a snake charmer playing, I cover my ears.

   (Abiola makes an "I-give-up" gesture.)

Act I, Tableau 2

(A public park, with pasteboard cutouts of trees with detachable leaves of the same material. Enter two figures in black. One of them carries a scythe. They wheel in a bed on which a patient is lying. Enter the Griot.)

GRIOT: Death keeps records and does his accounts. He would like to advance the passage of time to collect his arrears. But he lacks the power to do so. Nothing accelerates the Sun's course; no one speeds the natural pace of events.

(Exit without having been seen by the two figures in black.)

FIGURE WITH THE SCYTHE: *(speaking on the telephone to someone invisible)* Hello! Hello! The Shadow here.... The Repository of the power of the Shadow Master speaking. Is God there? I know God doesn't have an unlisted number. I assume He has a machine... Please tell Him I've been after someone for the past four years, that I'm giving up on the victim as a figment of my imagination who'll take his own sweet time entering the Kingdom of the Dead. *(To his partner as he throws up his hands)* What can I tell you? I've hung up. God seems not to be paying the least attention.

SECOND FIGURE IN BLACK: But He always keeps His promises.

(Noises off of persons in conversation)

I told you this was a public park.

FIGURE WITH THE SCYTHE: We'll come back on the stroke of midnight, when no one will disturb us. Let's go.

(Exit both, pushing the bed. When they have gone, enter some sightseers, who stroll about fanning themselves, one with a handkerchief, one with a hat. A woman crosses the stage carrying a parasol. Enter John Abiola; he crosses the stage and sits on a bench. He is fanning himself with a newspaper. After a while, he is alone onstage. Enter Melissa Yadé.)

ABIOLA: And here I thought I had it made. That I was top dog. Now I have to face the fact that my chances with Margaret Bintu are dead and buried. Maybe I'd have had better luck with her roommate, Dottie.

(During this speech, a young woman has crossed the stage without having noticed Abiola. She sits on a park bench across the stage from him. They have their backs to each other.)

It's an F in strategy for me today. They say that, on St. Helena, Napoleon ceaselessly refought the Battle of Waterloo. So let me see. *(He counts on his fingers.)* One: Hang in there without seeming to. Feign indifference. Two: Adopt a wait-and-see attitude. Three: Limit our conversation to polite exchanges of small talk. Four: Determine the adversary's weak spot by concentrating on her interests, shunning intellectual topics like the plague. Five: Having aroused the antagonists interest, instead of pressing my luck, temporarily abandon the field to let her heart grow fonder.

(Melissa Yadé gets up and paces back and forth. She is greatly perturbed. The stage darkens. A color slide

of an applauding audience is projected. There is a tape of a lengthy ovation interspersed with shouts of "Melissa!" "Antigone!" "Melissa!" "Antigone!")

OFFSTAGE VOICE: Seven curtain calls for Melissa Yadé tonight. What a triumph for this young Black actress! The audience gave her a standing ovation. The stage is literally buried in flowers. All circuits are tied up with reporters calling in their stories to London. There's never been anything like it. Sir Richard Cooper, who's standing at Melissa's side, raises her hand to acknowledge the acclamation. I'm going to let you listen as the audience goes wild.

(As the lights come up, Melissa is weeping for joy.)

MELISSA: Four years. Four years. I've waited four long years in Dorothy Mela's shadow. Four years of champing at the bit. Four years on the pill to keep from getting big with all the dreams to which human nature is susceptible. Four years of vile consorting with the Devil. Yes, yes, ah, yes, I confess, confess to nightly orgies of pride, anger, and envy, which have all been my companions. May God forgive me for all the evil I've wished on Dorothy Mela. *(Her voice rises an octave.)* Dorothy Mela, the sole obstacle between me and the acme of delight.

(John Abiola has leapt to his feet upon hearing this female voice filled with acerbity and bitterness. He walks around his bench and hesitantly approaches Melissa.)

Here on Earth, everything withers; everything fades. Only the victors' laurels are evergreen.

ABIOLA: *(aside)* What's wrong with that woman? She's speechifying as if this were Hyde Park.

MELISSA: *(as before)* If only I can sustain the fire till June 23, especially so as not to let Sir Richard Cooper down since he's the one who's formed me. As the star, I must be on fire; I must burn and give myself entirely over to my public to devour like fresh bread. *(with increasing exaltation)* I must engulf the theater in flames that will spread to the walls of Birmingham, itself. The audience must—*(Suddenly aware of a human presence, she turns round to see Abiola.)* Who are you? What do you want?

ABIOLA: That name you were speaking just now. It belongs to someone whose place I've just left, Dorothy Mela. You'll have to admit it's a striking coincidence.

MELISSA: I don't understand. Are you some kind of warlock? There's no way I could have spoken about Mela to you since I've never seen you before in my life.

ABIOLA: Don't get excited. John Abiola at your service. *(He bows.)* An honest citizen, I assure you, who has nothing to do with warlocks.

MELISSA: Are you African?

ABIOLA: Gold Nugget.

MELISSA: Gold Nugget? I can't believe my ears. Is your watch running?

ABIOLA: *(looking at his wristwatch)* My watch? Er...yes, I believe so. It's about 8 P.M.

MELISSA: And I maintain your watch stopped at the turn of the century. The country you call by that name was, at that time, a veritable gold mine. Now it doesn't turn out an ounce of dust.

ABIOLA: You've completely bewildered me. *(He thinks*

for a second.) I know. You're from Amandla. Is that it?

MELISSA: In time, you'll bring yourself up to date. A glance at your passport might help.

ABIOLA: Forgive me. Habit, you know. And this new name is only two years old.

MELISSA: Yet it's inscribed in the history of our people. Three young cadets swore one day, here on British soil, to change the course of events in their native land. A somewhat insane oath, but, nonetheless, they succeeded. *(with a touch of bombast)* Amandla! I speak your name as a tribute to Freedom!

ABIOLA: No doubt about it, you're an Amandian. What's your name?

MELISSA: Melissa Yadé.

ABIOLA: *The* Melissa Yadé?

MELISSA: Yes. I'm, as you put it, *the* Melissa Yadé.

ABIOLA: Of course, I know you by name, as the fiancée of President Titus Saint-Just Bund. I...I...I hope I've displayed the proper respect. Let me assure you I have the deepest admiration for our President. He's fully earned the sobriquet Chief Justice. What a man! I still remember his inaugural speech and his byword, "Strive for justice through just means."

MELISSA: What you have just said warms my heart. Too many of our compatriots have judged him hastily without taking into account...without trying to understand the Chief Justice.

ABIOLA: It's true our fellow citizens have mixed feelings. All the same, there's greater understanding of him today. You no longer hear as you used to in the beginning "Just another fancy talker like Muhammad Ali. And, one day, he'll split his throat!" I'm not going to pretend an amount of mistrust doesn't persist. Some are suspicious of the President's charm. "Too smooth to be genuine," they say. Speaking for myself, however, I sincerely admire him.

MELISSA: He asks nothing for himself. He thinks only of others. Those few words sum up Titus. He's chosen Lawrence of Arabia for a model as regards sense of duty and self-sacrifice.

ABIOLA: That's strange. Because Lawrence of Arabia wasn't exactly a revolutionary.

MELISSA: He was the most scrupulous of men. He restored a soul, a land, a sovereignty to a people previously dispersed. And, more importantly, directed the world's attention to the way men, once roused, can realize their dreams. But, for Titus, an even greater inspiration is Thomas More.

ABIOLA: Ah, yes, the famous Utopian. It takes all kinds to make up this world. I was saying to Bintu just this afternoon that it's good to have an occasional dream. How else can new ideas come into being? We must live. And live the good life. I like to dance, to party. Bintu told me about a play she's going to be in. The theater's a great way to relax. You have a lot of fun that doesn't get you into any trouble. It would be wonderful if I could be there to cheer her on. The problem is the price of the ticket.

MELISSA: If that's all it is, I can get one for you.

ABIOLA: Perfect! And, with your connections, nothing could be simpler. Thanks a lot!

Act I, Tableau 3

(The same public park as in the preceding scene. Obsessive snare-drum rolls are punctuated with occasional bass-drum booms. The intermittent cawing of crows completes the instrumentation of this weird music. The two Figures in Black with the Patient, who is stretched out on the rolling bed, enter. The Patient looks out at the audience. Brief spasms convulse him. Suddenly, there is total silence. Then the opening strains of Saint-Saën's "Danse macabre" burst forth. As if they had been waiting for this signal, the two Figures in Black execute a few grotesque dance steps. Enter the Griot.)

GRIOT: "La Danse macabre" issuing from the deeps of time. Masters or slaves, emperors or subjects, rich or poor, true believer or skeptic, weak man or strong, greybeard or babe, the dead of past generations cavort. No matter who they were, they're caught up in the whirlwind of tomtoms and join the infernal quadrille. *(He withdraws to the side of the stage to listen.)*

FIGURE WITH THE SCYTHE: At last, the long-awaited music. The prelude to the final voyage of our young cadet; stricken with a terminal illness, for months, he's been trundled from hospice to hospice.

SECOND FIGURE IN BLACK: Some months after his latest return to his native land, he's a fire borne on the wings of a fever, hovering like an eagle among the highest temperatures. The biggest men in medicine have, only with great difficulty, these peaks all but inaccessible to science. "Irreversible" is the word for the cadet's condition. But he hangs on to life. He hangs on like the Devil.

FIGURE WITH THE SCYTHE: His resistance beats me. He's somehow survived the malarial fever that's been devouring him, stifling him with an asphyxiating cloak of cinnabar red.

SECOND FIGURE IN BLACK: Which he's managed to tear away in his memorable struggle against you, Prince of Shadows. You've had no greater success in trying to envelop him in a tunic of gold and purple tailored for him from dead leaves.

FIGURE WITH THE SCYTHE: It's true he slipped through my fingers last fall. Then I expected him at the crossroads after his next relapse.

(They both go to the backdrop and remove the representation of green foliage; they hang death's heads in place of the leaves as a snowfall covers them.)

Winter's here at last. The Patient has fought valiantly. It's time this long journey came to an end. We must bring him the ciborium full of balm to torment his soul in full flight.

SECOND FIGURE IN BLACK: Patience....Just a little patience, great prothonotary of funerary rites. Wait for Father Time to make his way down the waiting list—

FIGURE WITH THE SCYTHE: Not another interruption! What I want to know is, what kind of game are they playing? I show up last summer. They tell me I'm too early. Mounted on their caracoling steeds, the North, East, South, and West Winds intervene once more come autumn to keep me from completing my task.

SECOND FIGURE IN BLACK: Those who weigh souls have found this young man to have a moral weight greatly exceeding the norm. They wish to allow some respite to devote to the work of serving humanity.

FIGURE WITH THE SCYTHE: Let them find someone else, God damn it! This man belongs to me. I have the word of the Horsemen of the Four Winds who draw the chariot of Fate.

SECOND FIGURE IN BLACK: Every one of those Horsemen has charge of earthly concerns for one of the seasons. This time, it was the turn of Harnattan, the African who bestrides Capricorn. He personally requested this respite.

FIGURE WITH THE SCYTHE: Africa, they're making you wait, while anguished with thirst, day by day, flake by flake, memories of you crumble. The voices of your parched ancestors calling for libations of blood become less and less audible.

SECOND FIGURE IN BLACK: In the Africa of today, we fill the ancestors' calabashes with wine pressed from the most scrupulous of those who adore the Absolute, those able to dedicate themselves to a cause with total self-abnegation. This sacrifice takes place on the topmost step of the altar consecrated to the Sun God of Freedom. That's where you find the presses that draw from Man the wine of the choicest vintage.

FIGURE WITH THE SCYTHE: *(with great sarcasm)* I see they demand a very good year. And they hope to find it in this whippersnapper who's not yet dry behind the ears. Ha! Ha! Ha! I'd thought I'd heard them all.

SECOND FIGURE IN BLACK: You underestimate Titus Saint-Just Bund. You may be sure he'll flourish in death because of the life he's led and that his name will live on after that life is spent.

(The strains of the "Danse macabre" are heard once more. One by one, the Figures in Black unhook the death's heads from the trees, replacing them with leaves, while a spectacular dawn breaks on the horizon. The Patient, who throughout the preceding had not stirred, now leans on one elbow. The Second Figure in Black helps him, the Figure with the Scythe having exited with the rise of the Sun.)

PATIENT: Where am I? Just a moment ago, I was swathed in harshest winter's swaddling bands...Have I crossed over?

SECOND FIGURE IN BLACK: Not yet. Here on Earth, you still have before you a rocky road strewn with obstacles. The royal road reserved for heroes.

PATIENT: Damn being a man of Destiny! What good does it do in Africa? The springs of the African soul have run dry; our shores have been polluted by the torrent of the white man's money. A total defoliation afflicts our culture. Empty, empty are the granaries of honor that enabled the ancestors to stand firm.

SECOND FIGURE IN BLACK: It's up to your generation to reverse all that, to start new springs flowing, to water new fields, to fill new granaries.

PATIENT: I no longer have the strength. All I have now is an overpowering weariness and a secret attraction to someone who somewhat resembles you.

SECOND FIGURE IN BLACK: *(He crosses the stage and picks up a multicolored glass ball.)* In this ball, I can read the future. What will happen is already written in the stars. *(adopting a prophetic tone)* I see three men on a mountaintop. They will bear the tablets of the

New Commandments for Africa. Two of them will, in the end, let their tablets fall. Only one will continue to bear his burden. The two others will throw him from the top of the cliff. *(His eyes pop. He screams. The ball becomes increasingly heavy. He perspires profusely and sets down the ball with the utmost care. He looks haggard.)*

PATIENT: What's the matter? What's happening to you? What have you seen?

SECOND FIGURE IN BLACK: *(still under the spell of the vision)* It's always too late to tear out your eyes when the future, with a stormy hand, is writing its decrees in lightning on human destiny.

PATIENT: Could you recognize those three men?

SECOND FIGURE IN BLACK: Their lineaments are blurring in my mind. I retain scraps of what was written on the tablets. Give me a moment to collect my thoughts. Ah, I have it. The first commandment: No salvation, no future for Africa except in rampant insanity. Second commandment: Death to that useless beacon stuck to the back of the neck and therefore lighting only the road already traveled. Third commandment: Let lunatics run things. You see where sane men have gotten us.

(Brief blackout.)

GRIOT: *(down center)* In the days to come, will there ever be a time that will reveal the pelt of a future of the past? Who knows? In the meantime, mariners of the good ship ploughing the seas dianoia, hoist the sails and tack to sail before the wind toward Africa, toward Vangu. A change of venue, a changed complexion.

PATIENT: *(yawning as he sits up in bed and rubs his*

eyes) Have I been dreaming? The vise has loosened its grip on my breast and my brow; now I feel almost buoyant.

SECOND FIGURE IN BLACK: *(disrobing to reveal a physician's white and, around his neck, a stethoscope)* What a relief to see we've snatched you back from the jaws of death! The thermometer shows we've licked this thing.

PATIENT: *(bitterly, as he sits on his bed)* I'm out of danger, you say? Yet I'm still in the midst of death. Must one man survive at the cost of so many others? What's my life against those of thousands of my people? Why save one life the cost of the majority? It's better to sleep through life than to suffer the cruel decrees life looked in the face. Enfold me once more in your arms that I long for, monstrous visions of the night. Just now, it was four years ago, and I was back in Europe. It was winter. A terrifying sight of death's-head trees lined the street. No sign of life as far as the eye could see, aside from the silence of hollow eyes in the infinite void. By the way, what's today's date?

SECOND FIGURE IN BLACK *(as a Physician)*:   June 4.

PATIENT: It's still a long time till June 23. I'm assuming there'll be no postponement.

SECOND FIGURE IN BLACK *(as a Physician)*:   On the contrary, I have everything to fear from an illness of such long standing. Four years ago, in England, it nearly did me in. I need a reprieve until June 23.

SECOND FIGURE IN BLACK *(as a Physician)*:   Will that date be significant for you? For our country?

PATIENT: For a young woman now living in Birmingham, it will be a red-letter day.

Act II, Tableau 1

(Feverish activity in the wings. A number of persons move to and fro, one carrying a flat, another, an urn, and others, various props. With exaggerated gestures, they converse, argue, make points, and come to terms with loud bursts of laughter and slaps on the back. Printed on a large sign are the words "TONIGHT, THE PURE SPEECH SOCIETY'S PRODUCTION OF THE ANTIGONE OF SOPHOCLES, TRAGEDY IN FIVE ACTS DIRECTED BY SIR RICHARD COOPER, FIRST CITIZEN OF THE CITY OF BIRMINGHAM, THE CITY OF HIS BIRTH, DOCTOR OF LETTERS OF THE UNIVERSITY OF BIRM-INGHAM." Enter Abiola.)

ABIOLA: *(Elegantly turned out in a frock coat and holding a top hat in his right hand, he addresses a stage hand who crosses the stage carrying some apparatus.)* Hey, there! May I have a word with you, Sir? Yes, I mean you. I need a bit of information. Can you tell me where the dressing rooms are?

STAGEHAND: Whom do you want to see? And about what?

ABIOLA: Margaret Bintu. I'm down from Coventry.

STAGEHAND: Go down the left corridor; then turn right till you come to the plaster statue of the Nike of Samothrace, the girl with her arms knocked off, that is. Then turn right just before you get to the loggia. You'll see the actors' dressing rooms, with their names on the doors in big felt-trimmed letters. Margaret Bintu's dressing room is the next one after Melissa Yadé's.

ABIOLA: Did you say, "Melissa Yadé"? She's the one who got me the ticket for this play. But what's Melissa Yadé doing here?

STAGEHAND: *(condescendingly)* Well, well. She got you the ticket, and you're asking me who she is? You're really from the sticks. I don't know what's up in Coventry. But here, in Birmingham, Melissa Yadé's a rising star. Do you know dozens of reporters have come from London, and other cities, too, to cover this story? And that tonight will be televised? Who's the cause of all this commotion? No one but Melissa Yadé, who'll be playing Antigone. A Black ball of fire endowed with a diamond tongue. No, those aren't my words. It was Sir Richard Cooper who spoke them.

ABIOLA: *(having forgotten to tip the Stagehand and heading at a brisk pace toward the dressing rooms)* Damn! Melissa's playing Antigone?

STAGEHAND: *(watching Abiola exit)* That guy's not wrapped too tight. I should have asked him for his papers. *(suddenly alarmed)* Only a loony would show up at four wearing a frock coat for a seven o'clock curtain. Oh, God! If he's one of her boyfriend's enemies, I'm up the creek. I didn't even get his name. *(putting two fingers into his mouth, he gives a shrill whistle and starts to run after John Abiola, who has already exited.)* Sir! Stop! Stop!

Act II, Tableau 2

(Melissa's dressing room. Melissa is surprised to see Abiola.)

MELISSA: What are you doing here?

ABIOLA: You're the one who got me the ticket.

MELISSA: It's not four o'clock yet.

ABIOLA: I was firm with the stage doorman. It's no easy thing to say "No" to someone dressed like an English gentleman, who, moreover, says he's made a special trip from Coventry.

MELISSA: Generally, they don't let anyone in. *(Enter the stagehand, bursting in like a madman and panting loudly. As he catches his breath, he glares fixedly at Abiola.)*

STAGEHAND: Excuse me for disturbing you. I...I... see you know each other.

MELISSA: This gentleman is a compatriot living in Coventry.

STAGEHAND: So he told me when he asked me to direct him to Margaret Bintu's dressing room. All kinds of thoughts ran through my head. Again, please excuse me.

(Exit.)

MELISSA: *(disappointed)* You're here to see Bintu? Her dressing room's right next to mine.

ABIOLA: Forgive me, Melissa. I swear I didn't know.

MELISSA: You didn't know what?

ABIOLA: That you were an actress, that you were a star.
   Antigone? I can't get over it. You'll be up on that
   stage; I'll be in the audience. I know I'll be rubbing my
   eyes, and like Doubting Thomas, I'll be consumed
   with the desire to touch you to convince myself you're
   real.

MELISSA: *(thoughtfully)* The day before yesterday, we
   were speaking of Thomas More. Now another Thomas
   suddenly comes to mind. One who was also assassinated,
   also Archbishop of Canterbury, also canonized. Are we
   living in the times of the Thomases?

ABIOLA: I still can't get over it. You're Antigone.

MELISSA: Not quite. There are centuries between the
   two of us. In the past few months, I've embarked upon
   a long journey in search of her. Moving toward her
   isn't enough. We must intermesh. The audience must
   feel what's taking place onstage is a current event. Can
   Antigone have heard my call and come to meet me
   halfway along the vastness of time? *(with fervor)* Mr.
   Abiola, I see it all before my eyes. If she and I can join
   forces, I'll come out ahead because of the current I flow
   with, and thanks to whom the miracle will occur.
   Waterwoman, I shall rise from my riverbed to engulf
   my public awaiting me on the shore.

ABIOLA: *(still under her spell)* You express yourself so
   eloquently. I see I'm going to have a wonderful time
   tonight. *(looking around him)* Wow! Your dressing
   room's knee-deep in flowers. Knee-deep in flowers.

MELISSA: Unknown admirers except for the names on
   their cards.

ABIOLA: They've shown me up because I didn't think of doing likewise. I didn't know the Antigone would be you.

MELISSA: You're entirely forgiven.

(Enter the Make-up Woman.)

MAKE-UP WOMAN: Excuse me. I thought Melissa was in here by herself. Another fan has sent this gigantic bouquet.

MELISSA: *(looking around)* There's not one empty vase. But you'll simply have to find me one to hold these magnificent red roses.

(The Make-up Woman hands her a small envelope. Melissa opens it excitedly, and, uttering a cry, sinks down into an armchair.)

ABIOLA: *(running to her and taking the card)* The queen of spades! A nasty trick! If I could get my hands on the one who sent it! *(to the Make-up Woman)* Miss, will you be good enough to get rid of these poisoned flowers?

(Exit the Make-up Woman with the enormous bouquet in her arms.)

You mustn't give it a second thought. The world is full of lowlifes of every description.

MELISSA: *(recovering)* If he really believed he'd be attending my funeral tonight,.... *(Mechanically, she wipes her brow.)* What's going on inside me? It's not that I'm a coward, Mr. Abiola, let me assure you of that. It's more that...all of a sudden, I'm terrified that whatever's going to happen is going to happen to him.

ABIOLA: To whom?

MELISSA: To Titus. Rumors about an impending conspiracy in Vangu are rampant in England. A conspiracy against Titus Saint-Just Bund.

ABIOLA: *(no less alarmed, but striving for an air of detachment)* Such rumors are nothing new. Certainly, the Chief Justice knows all about them.

MELISSA: But he never pays them any mind. His excessive faith in human nature will someday be his undoing. *(more and more upset)* What's about to happen? The wall of anguish has suddenly crumbled inside me, freeing mountainous waves of darkness to benight my soul.

> *(The transition to Tableau 3 should be prepared for so that placing a paper screen will divide the stage partially or totally into two sections, thereby making possible, with the aid of music and lighting, the change to a set until the end of the preceding tableau. All this should take place with no break between the words "to benight my soul" and the rest of Melissa's speech that follows.)*

From time to time, he telephones me, not so often as I might like. He always says the meager officer's pay he lives on, though he's now Chief of State, isn't enough to cover frequent long-distance calls.

> *(With perfect synchronization, the telephone rings exactly at this point. Melissa picks up the receiver and listens for a second; then her eyes open wide in astonishment.)*

Speak of angels, and you hear....It's a call from Vangu. The call's coming through London. Hello,...

hello. With whom am I speaking? Francis Ikokuh? Strange, I hear a frightening anxiety in his voice. What's going on? Mr. Abiola, take the receiver. What's that I hear?

ABIOLA: *(taking the receiver)* No doubt about it. Those are automatic rifles. Hello,...hello,...Ah, that's better. Someone's speaking.

VOICE OFF: Don't hang up. The President will be here in a minute. He's gone to supervise the resistance. Don't get excited. He has the situation well in hand.

(As Melissa collapses to the floor, reenter the Make-up Woman; she and Abiola rush to her assistance. Music in a stormy Wagnerian vein, punctuated with clangorous cymbal clashes, plays as loudly as possible. Simultaneously, the screen has been removed to reveal the rear half of the stage, glaringly lit; the downstage area is immediately plunged into darkness. Then a lighting especially designed for Tableau 3 will take over.)

Act II, Tableau 3

(Bursts of automatic rifles that never let up. Pantomime of five Silhouettes of armed men in uniform. Ever on the alert and intently listening, they move about in all directions, come together, and then disperse. They need not be identifiable; it is more important to hear their exchanges. Their voices should reveal calm assurance tinged with an edge of humor along with the predictable tension; their irony suggests their scorn of danger and their professional familiarity with situations of this kind.)

FIRST SILHOUETTE: This is the countdown, friends. All that matters now is proving we've got balls, balls and guts. Deep down, I've always known everything that's happening would happen, and still I'm not ready for any of it. I've deceived myself with the false hope of the sleeper who thinks he can hold back the dawn by keeping his eyes closed. It's dumb to be caught napping like this.

SECOND SILHOUETTE: Hey, Chief Justice. Aren't you overstating the case a little? From the very start, everyone's said your two buddies would screw you in the end. You wouldn't listen. Now, you're nothing but a dope in deep shit.

FIRST SILHOUETTE: *(bursting out laughing)* Hey, hey! You might say I'm being told off. To give you some of your own back, you and your bitch of a bleeding heart make me take you for virgins at their first communion.

SECOND SILHOUETTE: Virgins! Communion! Tell your men we're standing our ground. When I deal with punks, my machine gun's always at the ready, and, if that's not enough, my pistol is, too. As I was saying before, a royal screwee, that's what you are, Chief Justice. All you wanted was your people's good? Fine. But when payday rolled around what did you give them? Funny money. Your hangers-on would come up with no more than a weak imitation of your stabs in the right direction.

THIRD SILHOUETTE: A bad lot, your team. I hear back in England they were closer than a dog who's just laid his bitch. Well, where are they now, those goddamned Rambos? Where are your punks? Maybe you think thcy're messing their pants. No way! Those unfrocked revolutionaries have gone over to the other side.

FOURTH SILHOUETTE: You want proof? Try telephoning them. They've taken a powder instead of keeping it dry.

FIRST SILHOUETTE: Ikokuh, Get me Melissa in Birmingham.

FIFTH SILHOUETTE: I did that half an hour ago.

FIRST SILHOUETTE: Half an hour ago? The poor girl. She must have hung up by now.

SECOND SILHOUETTE: Pressed to the point of forgetting his dearest darling's waiting on the line three thousand kilometers away? You need some Valium, Chief Justice—or, rather, Just-Ass.

FIRST SILHOUETTE: Shit! I wanted to wish her all the best before she went on. This is a great day for her. How wonderful that she's playing Antigone!

THIRD SILHOUETTE: Ha, Chief Justice, you're a laugh with your backstage gossip. It's completely off the wall, right? And your cutlure and your goddamned snootiness, you can shove them where the Good Lord split you.

SECOND SILHOUETTE: Meanwhile, you're slipping ever so easily into the depths of Hell because the Chief Justice has neither understood nor learned from history. He didn't know how to pick his friends. I'm here to tell you history thumbs her nose on those who don't learn where to stick thumbs for plums.

FIRST SILHOUETTE: I can't deny I've been a jerk, a patsy. According to a Russian proverb, "A hundred years living, a hundred years learning, you'll still die a blockhead." In the belief that I was using just procedures, I behaved like the granddaddy of all lunatics for six whole months. An embargo on baby food and one on Novocaine. The people hailed this protection of mother's milk and our frail pharmaceutical industry. Then came the blockade. Zowie! No more ships landed at Vangu. No more manufactured products. The big squeeze. I didn't know what to do.

SECOND SILHOUETTE: Not doing anything, O.K. But how come you didn't say anything? Why this sudden failure to communicate with the people? Especially since no one's better in bed with them than you are.

FIRST SILHOUETTE: What could I have told them? What is there to say when a malaria epidemic is decimating your people? When another unidentified plague is doubling the infant mortality? What answer can you give to public opinion that accepts them both as punishment visited on us for having taken you-know-what measured?

THIRD SILHOUETTE: It was no time for a wait-and-see policy. All through the land, false prophets were multiplying like seven-year locusts, proclaiming the end of the Republic of Amandla.

FIRST SILHOUETTE: I couldn't be everywhere. I couldn't do everything at once. That's why I had a staff. At least, I thought I had one. When things are going well, any leader has dozens of followers in his wake. Now, I realize they were man-eaters, crocodiles who start with your shadow and then devour your body and soul. *(A deflagration interrupts him.)* Uh-oh! There's the big bass drum out there, and we're going up against it with pop guns. Our position will soon be untenable.

SECOND SILHOUETTE: We'll fight to the bitter end. The sons of bitches. They've trained a battery of ten-pounders on us. That means the Salvador Allende Elite Corps was too much for them by themselves.

FOURTH SILHOUETTE: And now for the second fall of Santiago, with this palace standing in for Moneda. Let's get set to take our place in history.

THIRD SILHOUETTE: Don't count on it. History can be a whore who opens her legs to all comers.

FIRST SILHOUETTE: Fine! But I've heard enough. I must get back to my office. If there's a shred of power left, that's where to find it. But, whatever happens, I've no regrets about the way I've lived my life. My loyal companions, I have something crazy to say to you. I love you as you've loved me.

SECOND SILHOUETTE: No question of it. I know a last farewell when I hear one. Get going. We'll follow you to your office to pay our last respects. *(He laughs.)* A funny thing's occurred to me. Chief Justice, if you could live your fucking life over again,....

FIRST SILHOUETTE: The dumbest question ever! What's done is done. That's all there is to it.

SECOND SILHOUETTE: On the chance that one of us gets out alive, have you any last words for posterity, Chief Justice?

FIRST SILHOUETTE: Big deal! I don't give a damn for what they'll do with my body because they'll never be able to shit on my spirit.

> *(The cannon's roar is now followed by the equally recognizable sound of falling rubble, an indication that the palace is undergoing a systematic bombardment. There is a blackout and a heavy silence. The stage lights up briefly to show the five Silhouettes differently arranged, striking elegant poses. The orchestral version of the "Confutatis" or the "Dolorosa" from the Mozart* Requiem *follows.)*

(Melissa's dressing room. A number of persons are bustling about the actress, who finally comes to. John Abiola, who is still on the telephone, looks at his watch and resigns himself to hanging up. The downstage area, darkened during Tableau 3, has returned to its previous lighting.)

ABIOLA: *(with great authority)* Ladies and gentlemen, are there any reporters among you?

(Murmurs of assent)

In that case, I am about to announce, with the permission of Melissa Yadé—if she will consent—

(Affirmative nod from Melissa)

That events of the greatest significance are, at this very moment, taking place in Vangu, the capital of Amandla.

A GROUP OF REPORTERS: *(surrounding Abiola and speaking all at once)* Has there been a *coup d'état?* Does Titus have the situation under control? A tribal war? How many dead? 5,000? 10,000? *(Still surrounding Abiola, the Reporters start off.)* Sir, will you please come with us to the press room?

(Exeunt Abiola and the Reporters.)

MELISSA: *(alone, turning her back to the audience and facing upstage, where a spotlight is shining on a Silhouette completely covered with a white cloth, which, when removed, reveals a young soldier smiling as he extends his arms toward Melissa)* Titus! Titus! Titus!

(Enter the Make-up Woman, who runs to help Melissa. The spotlight has gone out and Silhouette has disappeared.)

The President is dead!

(The Mozart Requiem *bursts forth anew, the "Lachrymosa." Melissa weeps.)*

Polynices will die twice today. Once in Vangu this afternoon and once again this evening before the play even begins.

MAKE-UP WOMAN: He's dead, you say? But how do you know? What are you going to do?

MELISSA: I mean to go on tonight no matter what. I must go on so that he won't stop living in the memory of men. I must go on because he did the next best thing to being at my side by telephoning me this afternoon. I must go on to join forces with the men and women who, for more than twenty-three hundred years, have pointed out the road to high standards by way of dignity and honor in the face of direst adversity. I must go on tonight to offer my voice to those who will never hear his. I must keep my eyes dry so that his vision will remain clear in the other world. I must be strong for fear he be weakened.

MAKE-UP WOMAN: I'm from Jamaica, and you have all my sympathy. *(dreamily)* What kind of man was this one just murdered miles away that he can kindle such a light in your eyes, who can fortify your heart with such courage and strength of will and your soul with such hope? Who can he have been who, on another continent, has given you a child that need not be born because you, yourself, have just been reborn?

MELISSA: What can I say of Titus Saint-Just Bund? His
   conquerors will certainly vilify his name and stain it
   with mud. Since the world heard the first cockcrow,
   mankind hasn't changed. An enemy's dead body
   smells sweet in their nostrils. Still Africa, Amandla,
   will always remember one thing. Other than
   Lumumba, no one but Saint-Just Bund lit a lamp to
   try to see clearly in the dark cave of our doubts. Till the
   end of his life, he stood firm at the point where human
   concern and human destiny come face to face.

ACT II, TABLEAU 5

(A stage. Creon is seated on his throne. A few steps below are the Guard, who also acts the part of the Chorus Leader, and Antigone.)

CREON: Apparently, my timing couldn't be improved upon.

GUARD: I bring before you, Sire,
This girl whose crime is burying the dead.
She's yours to punish as her seed demands.

CREON: You've apprehended her. But how and where?

GUARD: She dug the dead man's grave. Need you know more?

CREON: You know whereof you speak, I trust,
And speak it truly.

GUARD: With these very eyes, I saw her. Am I clear and making sense?

CREON: *(to Antigone)* And you, with hanging head and downcast eyes,
Do you admit to having done this thing?

ANTIGONE: I so admit; there's nothing I'd deny.

CREON: I ask you, "Did you know of my decree
Forbidding such an action?" Yes or no?

ANTIGONE: How could I not have known? It was proclaimed.

CREON: And still you dared to break the law?

ANTIGONE: Because the ban was not decreed by Zeus.
Your strongest laws will never have the power
As you are mortal, ever to eclipse
The changeless though unwritten writs of Gods,
And, though you judge my deed a deed of madness,
It well may be a mad man deems me mad.

CHORUS LEADER: A graceless father's likewise
graceless daughter,
She will not yield to unrelenting Fate.

CREON: She recognized her overweening when
She broke the law and scruples not at all
At further overweening as she dares
To boast about and revel in her crime.
She'll be the man that I'll no longer be
If such a sin of pride goes unredressed.

ANTIGONE: Will such redress extend beyond my death?

CREON: Your death will do. No reason for extremes.

ANTIGONE: Then why delay? For nothing you can say
Is worth my hearing any more than what
I'll say can bring delight to you. To give
My brother funerary rites, of all
Things glorious, this is the greatest glory.
And those who hear my words would all agree
If only fear did not enforce restraint.
But now, as always tyranny is free
To do and say whatever it desires.

CREON: No son of Cadmus entertains such thoughts.

ANTIGONE: Such thoughts are those they think but dare
not utter.

CREON: You feel no shame at being out of step.

ANTIGONE: There is no shame in honoring a brother.

CREON: No evil man deserves a good man's due.

ANTIGONE: But, in the Underworld, is such the rule.

CREON: No enemy becomes a friend through death.

ANTIGONE: My ways are those of love and not of hate.

CREON: Your ways are Love's? Go join and love the Dead.
But, while I live, no woman shall prevail.

Act II, Tableau 6

(Antigone is alone onstage. It is immediately evident that the throne Creon had previously occupied is vacant. The Guard/Chorus Leader has also exited. A tape of repeated bursts of applause plays. Antigone bows several times to an imaginary audience. She is now dressed completely in black and wears a black veil. Enter the Griot.)

GRIOT: Beginning three months ago, and on each of the subsequent nights, the extraordinary saga of the Pure Speech Society has unfolded, a saga widely covered and documented by the aggregate of the British press. With one or two exceptions, every city in the land has vied for the honor of welcoming this remarkable personality, who has become the company's soul, its ambassador, its star, the one who has taken on the responsibility of vigilantly safeguarding what she terms "the wounded memory" of her heroic husband. This African woman of Amandla burns with the flame of all our unsatisfied demands and embodies the brutalized conscience of her country. By a special dispensation from the highest authority of the Church, this celebrated actress has received the right to become the wife of the man who loved her and whom she loves so that she may legally bear the name Mrs. Melissa Yadé Bund in the eyes of God and of Man. *(announcing)* Ladies and Gentlemen, Mrs. Melissa Antigone Bund.

(the sound of prolonged applause)

MELISSA/ANTIGONE: Dear friends, I am deeply touched by your support of the cause of Amandla in the person of your humble servant, who will strive to live up to it in every particular. I pay tribute to the press and thank them for having joined in to make my battle their own.

Nevertheless, I am not the female Billy Graham, as certain British newspapers have dubbed me. The well-known American clergyman preaches in the name of God; whereas I am fighting in the name of a mere man who loved Africa, who loved his country, who loved freedom. I am fighting for the restoration of this man's honor. Our company's tour has come about thanks to the spontaneous solidarity of all my colleagues, notably my compatriots John Abiola and Margaret Bintu, and with the quiet and effective backing of Sir Richard Cooper. Tonight is the first time the London public is watching us. Ten performances have been scheduled here in the captial. I proclaim it loud and strong: Despite all their cannons, the powers that be in Vangu do not frighten me. Despite all their death threats, I shall never renounce my Amandian citizenship. I shall continue to demand what I have never ceased demanding for the past three months: an Amandian passport in order to return to Vangu to insure my husband's decent burial. I know that you love freedom. Help me; help your Antigone to attain hers in her native land.

Act II, Tableau 7

(John Abiola, Dorothy Mela, and Margaret Bintu. At curtain, Bintu is packing a valise. Mela is standing; Abiola is seated.)

DOROTHY MELA: *(beginning in a noncommittal voice)* Bintu, you won't be the only one going with Melissa. One of our compatriots is here to see you. She's come for the express purpose of going back with you.

MARGARET BINTU: Is it Fanta? Nafia? Yanou? Let me see, is there someone I've forgotten?

DOROTHY MELA: Thanks to her family connections, she's been able to get a passport and an exit visa.

MARGARET BINTU: You still haven't told me who she is.

DOROTHY MELA: For her, this trip will be an atonement. What happened this past June 23 opened her eyes. Our compatriot felt nothing but hatred for Melissa, her detested rival, who had robbed her of everything on Earth, beginning with Titus. On the night of June 23, do you know what this young woman did? She shut herself up in her room, unhooked the receiver, and drew the curtains. Then she performed the contemptible Black-Mass ceremony, holding in her hands a portrait of Melissa she had already punched full of holes during the previous weeks.

MARGARET BINTU: *(at the point of hysteria)* But who is she? Who?

DOROTHY MELA: It was midnight. She had headed for the city's Catholic cemetery. The gate was locked. She prowled around it; it was morning before she returned to the city. Sometimes Destiny reveals itself to us in the most commonplace guises. That morning, it took the form of a newsboy. *(Changing her voice, she imitates the newsboy.)* "Get your *Morning Star*! President Titus Bund assassinated! Read all about it! Get your *Morning Star*!" The woman fainted dead away; when she came to, she was in a hospital, babbling so incoherently that they held her several days for observation.

(Bintu and Abiola draw nearer to Mela.)

Where Titus is now, our wretched little stories of jealousy and spite are ridiculous. Her eyes opened by the tragedy in Vangu, the woman, as long as she lives, will never forgive herself for having sent to Melissa's dressing room, on June 23, an enormous bunch of red roses with the queen of spades in place of her card.

ABIOLA: A piece of dirty work worthy of a demon!

DOROTHY MELA: How could she atone for this sacrilegious act? How could she redeem herself in Melissa's eyes? Since she wasn't able to follow your troop on its tour, she had to content herself expressing her contrition and repentance to Melissa in long letters.

MARGARET BINTU: Melissa has kept these letters, all signed "Your unknown big sister." During our tour, rereading these letters would set her weeping. Their mysterious writer has so far concealed her identity.

DOROTHY MELA: Do you know the last thing she said to me? Today, she no longer has the slightest reason to maintain her anonymity. Ah, *(with her hand on her heart)* if only Melissa would forgive me!

MARGARET BINTU: *(full of emotion, throwing herself into the arms of Mela)* Mela! Oh, Mela!

ABIOLA: *(stupefied)* Her "unknown big sister"! I'm absolutely floored. It hit me right here. *(holding his solar plexus)*

MARGARET BINTU: It will come as a great relief to Melissa! She's received expressions of sympathy from everyone else. That of her "unknown big sister" will serve to crown the extraordinary rocket display of solidarity. You see, Abiola, there's more to politics than the tricks of bad guys and cutthroats, as you recently put it at a memorial for President Titus Bund.

ABIOLA: *(still in control of his emotions, the heedless character of the beginning having matured as a result of the events in which, in spite of himself, he has taken part)* Even "the unknown big sister" won't make me change my mind. Prizefighting is the continuation of politics in the ring, politics, the misshapen image of that sport. In other words, the complete opposite of the noble art in which it's forbidden to hit the opponent when he's down. In prizefighting, at least, you always wear gloves; whereas, in politics, you sometimes take them off.

ACT III, TABLEAU 1

(Enter the Griot.)

GRIOT: Ladies and Gentlemen, you've seen these actors, you've seen these wondersmiths in London. Now, they've left their sets, their stage behind. Antigone, one of those witches of the theater, has gotten on her broomstick and flown toward the continent of mystery, Africa, where legends thrive. It seems that I, the Griot, have competition from this doohickey. *(He points to a set next to him, which is actually a stylized representation of a screen on which is a cartoon face, with two arcs for eyes, a line for a nose, and oblique lines for teeth.)*

This is the new Mamiwata, the female spirit who is absolute ruler of liquidity and who catches her lovers in nets woven of her pictures, only to drag them to the bottom of the stream to gobble up their souls. Reportedly, she's stronger than I am. That remains to be seen. Oh, no doubt, they've been looking forward to my burial for a long time, ever since the moon surrendered her nocturnal light to this seductive appliance and all but signed the death warrant of nighttime get-togethers. But I have yet to have my last say.

VOICE OFF: Ladies and Gentlemen, we have begun to Vangu, the Capital of the Republic of Amandla, where we are due to arrive at 6:55, local time. The ground temperature is 38 degrees centigrade. We draw to the attention of British subjects in particular, a certain number of measures taken by the Government of Amandla. It is strictly forbidden to pronounce in public or in private the name "Titus Saint-Just Bund" and the sobriquet "Chief Justice," to allude, directly or indirectly, to the being who might have borne such a name or nickname, as his existence has been officially crossed out of the administrative archives of the country. All periodicals published in Great Britian must remain on board; likewise, all photographic, taping, and filming equipment must be left at the airport's customs house. Unconditionally forbidden is the Thomas De Quincey essay "Murder as One of the Fine Arts," all the works of Sophocles, and those books treating Greek tragedy, the books of Thomas More, as well as references to the word "utopia." Magistrates are forbidden to wear powdered wigs, as is everyone to drink tea in public or in government buildings or to play British music on public squares, in dance halls, or other night spots. Note that the ban on English-language films does not include those from America unless the director of the film is British, nor does the ban apply to British actors directed by Americans. Practitioners of safe sex are hereby warned to use condoms manufactured outside of Great Britian; British prophylactics are strictly forbidden. Finally, citizens of Amandla answering to the names of Titus, Just, Justin, Justinian, and to the family name of Bund are reminded that their country will look upon them as undesirable until they have undergone a change of identity.

GRIOT: One might compare Amandla to a virgin who thinks she can ward off rape by swaddling her private parts in an armory of petticoats. Or to a dark room in dread of electric lights, or to a safe scared to death someone will steal the combination without which it is totally naked. In this former British colony, which is one of the poorest nations on Earth, the balance of trade will surely improve once they've exported this list of bans. Notwithstanding, we mustn't lose sight of the fact that a man is dead, murdered and stripped of his past and his present. They plan to strip him of his future and to erase his name from the collective memory. In the Africa of our ancestors it was recommended that the poison and the antidote, the disease and the cure, good and evil, knowledge and ignorance, truth and falsity all cohabit in the same village so that the one may serve as the counterweight for the other. "Death to the mad so that the wise may live wisely in this age of ages," such is the one-sided credo carved on the pediment of the new African temple. Fine! Wisdom, when it's African, is prodigious.

Act III, Tableau 2

(Margaret Bintu and Dorothy Mela in a room in Vangu.)

MELA: I was out of my mind with worry when you didn't come back. I haven't touched a bite of food since yesterday.

BINTU: No matter how long you must chew, the Devil's unwilling guests must always keep up their strength.

MELA: Now that you're here, I'll be able to. Where did they take you?

BINTU: No way of telling in the dead of night and blindfolded to boot. All I can tell you is they questioned me for ages. I felt stripped naked. They're pretty well informed about us down to the smallest details, as well as what John Abiola and his friends are up to in England.

MELA: It's a bloody shame. It won't be long before we're out of the frying pan...

BINTU: They've already grilled me for almost two hours.

MELA: But why did they start with you? Did they give you any particular reason?

BINTU: They were asking the questions.

MELA: The worst thing of all is not knowing what their game is. It's like being shut up in the dark. If there's a cat, you can't tell whether it's grey.

BINTU: There are plenty of cats, and we're the mice. And it's anything but easy to stay one step ahead of the police mentality.

MELA: Do you mean they broke you? That you cracked? Tell me, did they torture you?

BINTU: Not the way you mean, but it amounts to the same thing. They're extremely polite, gracious, you might say, but, all the same, there's violence there, although in its frozen state.

(Mela disappears behind a screen set up for that purpose at the beginning of the tableau. At the same time, lights go up on a small office. At Stage Center is a chair. A lighting change indicates the following is a flashback. During this rapid change, an officer has taken his place in the chair.)

OFFICER: I hope my men haven't roughed you up. You must try to overlook a tad too much zeal on the part of these hastily promoted youngsters. Our orders were to treat you as befits your station, no matter what your London friends may have told you. Giving way to partisan biases, manipulated by enemies of the Republic, these theater types are spreading slander abroad, making it obvious they're in cahoots with British intelligence.

BINTU: I don't know whom you mean.

OFFICER: The first time I saw you, I said to myself, "She's of the stuff that makes for good citizens and patriots."

BINTU: Then I don't see why you've arrested me.

OFFICER: What's that you're saying? This is merely a simple interview.

BINTU: So I see.

OFFICER: There's bitterness in your voice. Haven't you been free to come and go as you please since your return?

BINTU: *(sarcastic in her growing excitement)* Just like an animal in the zoo. No chains. Fed and housed. But in a cage. Fine freedom that is!

OFFICER: You're spouting the same propaganda as your friends. You disappoint me.

BINTU: What friends? I've only the one who made the trip with me.

OFFICER: Waiting won't do Miss Dorothy Mela any harm. It's been four years since your last return to Vangu.

BINTU: Every year, we've waited for an exit visa, but the country's been in a prolonged state of crisis, you see.

OFFICER: Thank you, Miss Bintu, for having reminded me that you've come here without the necessary papers your country's government issues.

BINTU: I find it strange you're not questioning me about why we've come to Vangu.

OFFICER: All in good time.

BINTU: What have you done with the late President's widow?

OFFICER: We've informed both your family and Miss Mela's of your arrival in Vangu.

BINTU: Is this your roundabout way of blackmailing me? Because, if so—

OFFICER: Very interesting. Exactly what every egghead says when his conscience isn't clear. Blackmailers are figments of your imagination.

BINTU: *(furious)* How can you say such a thing? Was June 23 a figment of my imagination?

OFFICER: No need to ruffle up your feathers like a mother hen whose chicks are under attack. Flying off the handle doesn't suit you. Leave it for the cocks.

BINTU: By which you mean the "pricks" ever rising to the occasion for the cause of male supremacy.

OFFICER: Mind your manners, Miss Bintu. For the time being, I must put an end to this interview. We'll meet again, Miss Bintu.

(There is a brief pause during which the officer exits as Dorothy Mela resumes her position of the opening of the tableau. The lighting is now also that of the opening of the tableau.)

MELA: If you wanted to frighten me, you've succeeded perfectly. What's going to become of us?

BINTU: Our heads are in the lion's mouth. The real disaster is not being with Melissa. We'll fight for her no matter what.

Act III, Tableau 3

(An elaborate setting. It is dreamlike, as in some of the paintings of the Congolese artist Gotene. Masks are visible everywhere, and the deliberately diffused lighting provides an uneasy ambience for the ensuing conversation. Clangorously in the background, scores of voices intone a song that may from time to time be amplified, but the words of which nonetheless remain indistinguishable. In the eyeholes of the masks, green lightbulbs are inserted, and, on a level with their mouths, little loudspeakers are concealed. The man displays great uneasiness during the following dialogue, whereas the woman is in full control of herself and her emotions. The Griot stands motionless at one side of the stage. A shadow envelopes the man and the woman. Their features are indistinguishable; we recognize the woman's voice.)

GRIOT: The news of the return to her country of the Woman in Black has spread throughout the land. There are those who receive it joyfully who do so with great uneasiness. Heretofore, it had been feasible to quell one's conscience. Heh! Heh! Heh! No conscience, no sleepless nights in beating the thorny bushes of remorse, right? The vinegar of duty had chased away the flies. Honey had attracted them back. These flies now fly to vie with one another at informing on such of their neighbors who resist becoming sheep. The new baa—baa—baattle cry is "ask no questions and fight your way back to the rumbling stumbling obesity that got done in by the recent diet of strict morality imposed by you-know-who, damn his eyes! The living-Bride-of-the-Dead-Groom came here to resurrect corpses. To shake up benumbed consciences. To fire up those whose heads are wan on the outside and worm-eaten within. Heh! Heh! Heh! *Alleya!* The view from the back of the neck doesn't impress me, because all it sees is where we've already been. Burdened with choosing between honor and gold, we disdained the first to wallow in the glitter of the latter. Heh! Heh! Heh! *Alleya!* Karibi's gold has thickened our tongues and left us paraplegics. Ha! Ha! Ha! Hee! Hee! Hee! *Alleya!* That Lady in Black, she's one hell of a guy, eh?

(Exit.)

NEW LEADER: I've been looking forward to this meeting for a long time.

MELISSA: I've unfailingly told all your emissaries I'd find your presence distasteful, that I had no wish to see you. I'm doing so now only through having no choice or voice in the matter.

NEW LEADER: I've come here tonight as a suppliant. I bear all your abuse with humility.

MELISSA: This interview makes my flesh crawl. Be good enough to cut your unwelcome visit short.

NEW LEADER: I spoke of humility. I'm ready to humble myself before you, to grovel at your feet like a puppy dog. I impose no conditions.

MELISSA: Your soldiers' thick boots have already done so for you.

NEW LEADER: Has anyone disrespected you for even one minute of one day? It would have cost him dear if he'd done so.

MELISSA: You expect my thanks?

NEW LEADER: The foreign press has acknowledged the comfort of your surroundings.

MELISSA: You'd previously imprisoned my whole family.

NEW LEADER: An unfortunate misunderstanding.

MELISSA: That resulted in the death of my younger brother.

NEW LEADER: Your parents haven't been mistreated.

MELISSA: Torturers usually plead ignorance. Such was not the case with this abomination.

NEW LEADER: Your brother was extremely nasty to the police. He wouldn't answer any of their questions. When he would open his mouth it was only to defame the Government and make ridiculous accusations and threats. A report was drawn up.

MELISSA: Dead men don't make rebuttals.

NEW LEADER: According to the B.B.C., there's a handful of hotheads who're trying to stir up trouble. Your friends need only the excuse of a show of government force to invade us once again. I won't give them the satisfaction.

MELISSA: You've already slaughtered the innocent.

NEW LEADER: I've already said I'd accept your insults with all humility.

MELISSA: I haven't uttered a single insult. I'll not say so much for the one who's insulted the grief of a woman, of a sister restrained from attending her brother's funeral.

NEW LEADER: You need only have asked.

MELISSA: I ask nothing of you but the one thing that has become my sacred obligation.

NEW LEADER: Let the dead bury the dead.

> *(Red spotlights illuminate the stage. The New Leader's words are immediately drowned out by the nasal laughter of those whom the African tradition, under Judeo-Christian influence, has designated "devils," that is to say, those who inhabit the next world while maintaining close contact with the living. The laughter of the Dead bursts forth from the loudspeakers hidden behind the voiceless mouths of the masks. This spectral charivari lasts long enough for the New Leader to feel considerable discomfort; he shakes his head like a puppet, and in great anguish covers his ears.)*

Forgive me. It must be fatigue. I'm overworked. Sometimes, there's a ringing in my ears. All these responsibilities weigh me down.

MELISSA: Isn't there a heavier weight on your conscience?

NEW LEADER: I heard laughter, or rather....perhaps voices singing.

MELISSA: Voices singing? Why not, since there are five thousand of them outside not far from here who've taken part in my brother's funeral? They know I'm shut up in this villa.

NEW LEADER: A mere handful. Your foreign-press friends have swollen your head by inflating the numbers. They make a mountain out of a molehill.

MELISSA: A handful like the Judicialists?

NEW LEADER: Well, well. So you know the name adopted by those who support the Other.

MELISSA: What Other? Hasn't he a name?

NEW LEADER: Dead men.... (*Thinking better of it, he abruptly breaks off.*) Since you're so well-informed, I'll get right to the point. On the side of the mountain overhanging the city, a handful of diehards has seized the Army's main ammunition dump. These lunatics have been threatening for months to blow Vangu sky high.

MELISSA: On the radio, on television, and in your newspapers, they're on the point of caving in. But their strength of will will never cave in. So, in the dark of night, you negotiate with them. Proverbially, in the dark of night, you can't see your hand in front of your face. Still, doesn't the left hand know what the right one is doing?

NEW LEADER: The more important issue of the country is at stake. Your arrival screwed everything up; those wild-eyed radicals see you as a flag to rally 'round.

MELISSA: Oh, I see. So I've earned my stripes with the fighters.

NEW LEADER: The fighters?

MELISSA: Obviously, I mean the fire fighters who want to come to terms with the arsonists.

NEW LEADER: For your country, it's a matter of life and death.

MELISSA: I've no intention of moving in between the Devil and the deep blue sea of your politics.

NEW LEADER: Whether you like it or not, you're a citizen of Amandla. Your country's in grave danger. You're the only one who can get us out of this mess. I'm making a solemn appeal to your conscience. This morning, my emissary was the Archbishop.

(The Woman gets to her feet and paces slowly.)

Do not reject my offer. I ask you to consider it carefully. It's a matter of life and death.

(The Woman continues pacing.)

I wish to save the Republic of Amadla from further ordeals. Our battered nation now longs only for peace, that it may lick its wounds and devote its time to altering its underdeveloped state.

(Pause. The Griot comes Down Center.)

GRIOT: In the land of the ill-sighted, they neutered the Sun. Our nights became deserts with breasts dry of the milk that suckles the stars. Souls crack and dreams fray to tatters of unslaked desires. Who then will come to resow the seed of man in man? On cold hearths, how can we warm the agonized hearts to bake the bread of hope?

(He leaves the stage and goes down the middle aisle of the auditorium.)

NEW LEADER: Words! More and more words! Damn poetry! Time is standing still. The future's threatening to cave in about our ears.

(A spotlight abruptly focuses on the Griot among the audience.)

GRIOT: This discussion lasted almost all night long. That Lady in Black, she's one hell of a guy, eh! She's a real ball of fire, as they say. Ho! Ho! Ho! Hee! Hee! Hee! *Alleya!*

(The spotlight goes out on the Griot. The stage action resumes.)

NEW LEADER: You're passing on giving the Archbishop his answer? Very well, I bow to that decision. There's something more important than all our problems, than all our hates, than all our fears. It's our country. Never forget that.

MELISSA: Your words are of our country, but my loyalty is to our native soil. I am, I remain, I shall die an Amandian. As for you...*(She dismisses him with a contemptuous gesture.)*

NEW LEADER: When I came here tonight, I wasn't expecting a heartfelt welcome. You hate me with all your being. Of the two of us, who is wrong? Who is right? Only time will tell.

MELISSA: You poor slob. You didn't think twice about groveling before me. You deserve nothing but contempt. If I were a hater, I'd put this country through fire and slaughter. You know that's something I won't do, that I'd never do.

NEW LEADER: *(for the first time, showing signs of relief)* The night's on its last legs. The time for goodbyes is almost here. Ah, I think back on our old days in Birmingham. The years of our youth seem to be so far away, and yet, I sometimes fancy I can reach out and touch them.

MELISSA: All well and good. But weren't there others besides us two? Some of us sold our youth to the Devil for thirty pieces of pound sterling.

NEW LEADER: *(with a deep sigh)* Nothing is simple, my dear. We aim at one thing, and life imposes something entirely different on us. Buffeted by opposing winds, we are sometimes the playthings of Fate.

MELISSA: Ah, so we offer the blind forces in evidence and wash our hands like Pontius Pilate. Fate's great *Symphony in F Major.* How much ballast did you throw overboard to set your balloon inflated with the hydrogen of your personal ambition a-soaring?

NEW LEADER: I repeat, there's more to it than that. Life is more complex....In the meantime, will you do me the honor of accepting this token? *(He offers her an envelope.)*

MELISSA: *(Having leapt to her feet, she speaks in a harsh tone.)* I'm not for sale! What do you think your money can buy? My grief? My tears of blood? My sleepless nights? A flight of vultures wheels above the ruins of the country. A tempest hovers over Vangu. And, if I have undertaken to silence this symphony of thunder and lightning, it is as a patriot, not as a prostitute. Don't press your luck, dung heap!

NEW LEADER: *(stricken)* Let me assure you my intentions were...were.... Very well, let's forget it.

MELISSA: Tomorrow morning, I shall see the Archbishop to arrange for my husband's burial. I ask nothing further. Tomorrow evening, I shall go back to London. But not empty-handed. I'll be taking this.

NEW LEADER: What is it?

MELISSA: This book by Thomas More, found in the Palace debris. I'll not reveal how I came by it. It's a holy relic, because it's stained with blood.

NEW LEADER: Stained with blood?

MELISSA: The blood of Titus Saint-Just Bund!

(The terrifying sound of something that falls with a crash or that caves in underground is heard. The hollow eyes of the masks are suddenly lit with green light. Simultaneously, offstage voices echo the words the woman has spoken.)

OFFSTAGE VOICES: THE BLOOD OF TITUS SAINT-JUST BUND. THE BLOOD OF TITUS SAINT-JUST BUND!

NEW LEADER: *(leaping to his feet)* Do you hear those voices? Do you hear them? Do you hear them?

MELISSA: I hear nothing.

NEW LEADER: I do. I hear them. They shiver my conscience from top to bottom.

OFFSTAGE VOICES: *(repeatedly)* THE BLOOD OF TITUS BUND! THE BLOOD OF TITUS BUND! THE BLOOD OF TITUS BUND!

(The Man utters a piercing shriek and collapses. Immediately, Silhouettes bearing rifles emerge from all sides in great excitement.)

A SOLDIER: *(addressing the woman menacingly)* What's happened? What have you done to him?

(The other soldiers point their rifles at the woman.)

If you've so much as touched a hair on his head, you're a dead man.

MELISSA: I'm a woman, girls: I see you're as ready to shake in your shoes as this hotshot warming the floor.

(She points at the man lying on the floor, as a soldier continues approaching her.)

Hands off, no one lays a hand on Antigone.

(She assumes an air of regal authority. The soldiers draw back as she walks slowly forward to the wings. She turns towards them one last time.)

By the way, when he comes to, don't forget to give him this message. Tell him from Antigone that these words completely comprise my strength. "My ways are those of love and not of hate."

(Exit. Blackout.)

FINAL TABLEAU

(Rigged out with an African mask, the Griot, who is carrying a voluminous piece of luggage, lines up with other passengers, preparing to board. A security official is examining the passports of those who are leaving and subjecting their papers to the utmost scrutiny before stamping them in an exaggerated manner. The entire scene should have a satirical cast, and the official may even wear a clown mask.)

OFFICIAL: *(dealing with the man in the African mask)* You don't have a passport! You've got your nerve!

GRIOT: *(Stagily)* I am of all lands and all ages. I am the nameless traveler. I change complexion at will. Like cats, I have nine lives, the difference being that I can relive mine infinitely.

OFFICIAL: Have you gone through customs? Have you anything to declare?

GRIOT: Oh, a stage character or two. Some leading roles, others less prominent and some bit parts. They're all in my big bag. I hear them all grumbling, "a six-hour delay!"

OFFICIAL: A necessary precaution. A bomb threat on this British Airline flight. This is the third time I've had to search all the passengers and their luggage as well. *(He suits his actions to his words.)* Aha! An emperor with enough gold trimming for one of the magi. Could it be Bokassa? You say it's Creon? And this sorry guard with the spooky mug, isn't he Bob Denard or some gun-totin' Katanga? Hm, Hm. Gary and Corypheus, Leader of the Chorus, from the Salvation Army no doubt. *(He continues his search*

and his sudden show of great respect becomes visible.)
Antigone, a great lady in all our eyes, and she's still
wearing her wedding-funeral gown and veil.

EPILOGUE

GRIOT: Ladies and Gentlemen, boarding time. The
engines are on. Hee, Hee, Hee, Hoo, Hoo, Hoo,
Alleya! Alea jacta est. The die is cast. . . . Don't take off
your cap, Security Guard. You look enough like a
flight commander today. Passengers, take your places,
get back in line, please. . . . Show me your seat
numbers.

(He seats the Actors.)

Please pay close attention to the announcement.
Antigone is invited to the forward cabin. Immediate
take off.

*(The woman in the black gown and veil moves to
take a place by herself in one of the front-row seats.
The Griot turns to the audience, while the sound of
an airplane takeoff is heard and a screen conceals all
the "passengers." The Griot is holding something
in his hand.)*

Who left this cassette with me? In such a crowd it's
hard to remember.

*(He puts the object into a cassette player, and we
hear the voice of an actress the audience has come to
know.)*

VOICE OF MELISSA YADÉ: One, two, three, . . . testing.
One, two, three, . . . testing. This is Melissa Yadé
speaking. Perhaps for the last time. Well or poorly,
I've played my part. I've refused any sort of

compromise with anyone who dare not face themselves in the mirror of their conscience over which they choose the limbo of forgetfulness. . . .

GRIOT: *(as if continuing Melissa's address)* "Each hour wounds and the last one kills." And time continued on board the plane, and time went by heavy with vague threats. And then...and then the abrupt cessation of any contact with the London Control Tower. Hours of anguish and fruitless effort as the plane went down, sinking more than eight hundred meters under the waves...They still have not found the black box. Accident or murder? Nobody knows. Even buried alive in her steel sarcophagus with 130 other passengers, Melissa-Antigone shines forth from the deeps of her ocean-necropolis like a supernova that showers all its fire into the troubled dreams of orphaned nights. No superhuman diver has been able to bring up to the surface our memories adorned with twisted starfish. But, I'll say this, the memory of the people will one day rise again.

—Limoges, August 28, 1988

ᔐ

Aimé Césaire

A SEASON IN THE CONGO

Translated from the French by Ralph Manheim

AIMÉ CÉSAIRE was born in Martinique in 1913. He is
world renowned as a poet, dramatist, and essayist.
Césaire was one of the founders of the review *Tropiques,*
which was instrumental in establishing the use of
surrealism as a political weapon. Collections of his
poetry include *Cahier d'un retour au pays natal* (1939),
Les Armes miraculeuses (1946), *Soleil cou coupé* (1948),
Corps perdu (1950), *Ferrements* (1960), *Cadastre* (1961),
and *Moi Laminaire* (1982). Césaire's plays are recognized
as among the most important French-language works of
the 1960s. His first play, *Et les chiens se taisaient* (1956),
was a poetic work; the three subsequent plays—*La
Tragédie du roi Christophe* (1963), *Une Saison au Congo*
(1967), and *Une Tempête* (1969)—allowed him to reach a
broad audience and were written partly under the
influence of Jean-Marie Serreau, who directed them. *A
Season in the Congo* was premiered at the Théâtre de
l'Est Parisien in October 1967, revived at the Théâtre de
l'Odéon, and produced at the Théâtre National de la
Colline in Paris in the fall of 1989. *La Tragédie du roi
Christophe* was produced at the Montreal World's Fair
and *Une Tempête* was produced in Tunisia, Avignon,
and Paris. *A Tempest* is available through Ubu
Repertory Theater Publications. In 1969, Césaire was
awarded the International Literary Prize "Viareggio—
Versilia" for his life's work. He is mayor of Fort-de-
France, Martinique and represents Martinique in the
French Assembly.

RALPH MANHEIM is one of the most distinguished
translators from the French and German. He has
translated all the fiction of Günter Grass, Louis-
Ferdinand Céline's *Journey to the End of the Night* and
Death on the Installment Plan, and Peter Handke's *Slow
Homecoming, Sorrow Beyond Dreams,* and *Repetition.*
Manheim's translations for the theater include Bertolt
Brecht's *The Threepenny Opera* (with John Willett),
Mother Courage and Her Children, The Good Person of

Setzuan, The Caucasian Chalk Circle, and *The Resistible Rise of Arturo Ui*; Günter Grass's *The Plebeians Rehearse the Uprising,* which was produced by the Royal Shakespeare Company; Peter Handke's *The Long Way Round,* published by Methuen, London, and produced by the National Theatre Workshop; and several plays by Slawomir Mrozek, including *Vatzlav.* His translation of Aimé Césaire's *The Tragedy of King Christophe* was published by Grove Press in 1969.

CHARACTERS

THE SALESMAN (LUMUMBA)
MOKUTU
MAMA MAKOSI
BASILIO
GENERAL MASSENS
KALA LUBU
MPOLO
HAMMARSKJÖLD
CROULARD
ISAAC KALONJI
HÉLÈNE
PAULINE LUMUMBA
OKITO
TZUMBI
TRAVÉLÉ
MSIRI
MATTHEW CORDELIER
THE SANZA PLAYER
TWO BELGIAN POLICEMEN
THE VOICE
A MAN
FIRST WOMAN
SECOND WOMAN
TWO JAILERS
THE WARDEN
FIVE BANKERS
A BAKONGO TRIBESMAN
FOUR RADIO VOICES
ZIMBWÉ
THREE SENATORS
AMBASSADOR OF THE GRAND OCCIDENT
VOICE OF CIVIL WAR
THREE MINISTERS
THE BISHOP
A PILOT
GHANA
A MERCENARY
ONLOOKERS
SOLDIERS
A GROUP OF GIRLS

ACT 1
SCENE 1

(African quarter of Leopoldville... Natives are gathered around a salesman who is making a speech. Beer is being dispensed from a stand. Two Belgian cops are looking on rather suspiciously.)

SALESMAN: Friends, the white men have invented a lot of things and brought them here to our country, good things and bad things. I won't stop to talk about the bad things today. But take it from me, friends, one of the good things is beer. My advice to you is to drink. Drink and drink some more. Come to think of it, do they leave us free to do anything else? If we get together, we end in jail. Hold a meeting? Jail. Write an article? Jail. Try to leave the country? Jail. And more of the same. But you don't have to take my word for it. Use your own eyes. I've been talking to you now for a good fifteen minutes, and their cops don't interfere... I've been doing the country from Stanleyville to Katanga, and their cops haven't bothered me! Why? Because I'm selling beer. Yes, you could say that here in the Congo a mug of beer is the symbol of all our rights and liberties.

But not so fast. Same as there are different races in one and the same country—that's right, even in Belgium they have their Flemmings and their Walloons, and everybody knows there's nothing worse than the Flemish—there are different kinds of beer. Different races and families of beer. And I've come here to tell you about the best of the lot: Polar Beer.

Polar, the freshness of the poles in the heat of the tropics. Polar, the beer of Congolese freedom! Polar, the beer of Congolese friendship and brotherhood!

ONLOOKERS: Sure! But I've heard that Polar makes a fellow impotent. Takes away your *ngolo*. What do you say to that?

SALESMAN: That's a mean crack, citizen. If I wanted to give you a mean answer, I'd tell you to lend me your wife or sister for a few minutes.

(Laughter in the crowd.)

ONLOOKER: Ho, ho! He's got what it takes.

SALESMAN: But why not ask those girls over there, those lovely little girls; we'll put it up to them. What about it, girls? You with the beaming smiles, you with the smooth snake bellies: you tell us what's what.

THE GIRLS: *(singing)*
Women smooth as mirrors
Bodies without guile
Honey fritters,
Hair a shimmering water.
Two ripe and flawless
Papayas for breasts.

(Applause in the crowd.)

FIRST BELGIAN COP: Not bad, his spiel. He's got a tongue in his head.

SECOND BELGIAN COP: I suppose so. But it's got me worried. That beer mug of his is a grab bag. You never know what he's going to pull out of it next. I've got a mind to ask him a question or two.

FIRST BELGIAN COP: Watch your step. We can't interfere with the sales of Polar Beer. Don't you know who owns Polar?

SECOND BELGIAN COP: How should I? All I know is that that nigger's dangerous.

FIRST BELGIAN COP: You're young. Just listen to me. The Minister's behind Polar...That's right...The

Minister for the Congo! Knocks you for a loop, eh? But that's how it is. So now you see what's what. Come on, let's have a glass.

SECOND BELGIAN COP: Suits me. But let's take that saleman's name...Something tells me we're going to need it.

FIRST BELGIAN COP: Don't worry. We've got it. It's on file. His name is Patrice Lumumba.

SECOND BELGIAN COP: And what about him over there? Is he on file too?

FIRST BELGIAN COP: Oh, he's only a sanza player. Harmless. But a nuisance. He's everywhere all at once. Like a fly. And always buzzing.

SANZA PLAYER: *(sings)*
Ata-ndele...[Sooner or later...]

SCENE 2

(Waiters and customers moving about. They are setting up an African bar. Meanwhile a voice rises off-stage, growing louder and louder.)

THE VOICE: Hear, hear! The buffalo is wounded. Plugged full of bullets, he's at the end of his strength. He's gone mad. Who's the buffalo? The buffalo is the Belgian government. And now that the buffalo's wounded, he's threatening us right and left. What do you say? You going to let his threats get you down? The buffalo is a brute. Are you afraid of his brutality? Of his heavy tread? This is the song of our ancestors:

> The buffalo has a heavy tread,
> A heavy tread, a heavy tread.
> If you see him, don't be afraid of his heavy tread,
> His heavy tread, his heavy tread.

(The bar has been set up. Glaring lights. Small tables. Men and prostitutes are moving about.)

FIRST WOMAN: *(singing)*
Come, don't be afraid.
I'm not a married woman.
I married too soon.
I thought there was nobody else.
Oh, if I'd only known!

(Approaching a table full of men.) Really, Congo people have no manners. Men drinking beer all by themselves while a poor girl dies of thirst.

A MAN: *(whistles)* And what a girl! Say, boys, she's high octane. Move over, friends, there's plenty of room. Sit down, baby, sit down.

SECOND WOMAN: *(approaching)* Hey, girls, help! Help! I've had an accident. I'm losing my *jikita*. Those

Belgian waistbands are no good. Rotten cork, that's all they are. Damn Belgians, they cheat us every way they can.

A MAN: They cheat us, they exploit us; that's right, lady-o, they exploit us. Black people are just too trusting.

FIRST WOMAN: *(stripping)* I've solved the problem. I've given up the *jikita*. The *jibula's* the dress for me.

MAN: *(laughing)* More like undress. Take it easy, sister. The slightest move in that get-up unveils the thighs. And plenty more. Hee, hee! Plenty more.

SECOND WOMAN: Is that any way to talk to a lady? It's free, isn't it, so why complain? Ah, men are getting stingy and mean. Anyway, I'm sick of it all. *(Singing.)*

Listen, friends,
God gave us mothers,
Mothers who kill us for money,
For money and more money.

(Enter Mokutu in European dress. He looks like a pimp.)

MOKUTU: Boys and girls, howdy! I've got news for you. The Belgians have arrested Patrice, they wouldn't listen to reason. They've taken him to Elisabethville in handcuffs, and meanwhile the politicians are sitting around the table in Brussels, deciding the fate of the Congo. If those African politicians had any guts, they'd boycott the conference until Patrice is released.

MAN: Well, that's one way of looking at it. But isn't the fate of the country more important than the fate of one man?

MOKUTU: Oh, oh! Have we got Belgians around here? Black Belgians? Tell me, friend, did you ever stop to think that the fate of the country might depend on the fate of one man?

MAN: Okay, okay. But what are we going to do? Do you want us to storm the Elisabethville prison with our bare hands?

MOKUTU: Christ, how do I know? Just do something. Anything you can do in the Congo today is a step toward the revolution. Do what you like. As long as you do something.

SANZA PLAYER: *(his voice rises off-stage and sings the hymn of the Kibanguists)*

> We are the orphan children,
> Dark is the night, hard is the way.
> Almighty God, who's going to help us?
> Father Congo, who's going to give us a hand?

FIRST WOMAN: I suggest we go into mourning for six months. That's what you do when you lose a member of the family, and I call Patrice a member of the family.

MOKUTU: Don't make me laugh. Is that any skin off the Belgians' ass?

SECOND WOMAN: I say we go on strike and parade with our banners. All our organizations, the Lolita Club, the Dollar Association, the Free Woman, marching up and down with our flags—yellow, green, and red— that'll put their eye out.

MAMA MAKOSI: [*the Mighty Madame*] Baloney. No mourning, no strike. Work is work. We'll work. Harder than ever. We'll raise bail. The buffalo likes money. He feeds on money. And Patrice will sit at the table in Brussels with the rest of them. I have spoken.

MOKUTU: Friends, I've got to leave you now. Do what your hearts tell you. Anything you do for Patrice is good. Thank you.

SANZA PLAYER: *(stands up and sings; the song is taken up by the crowd)*

When the rainy season comes,
War will come too,
The season of red blood.
The buffalo's strong and the elephant's strong.
Where can we hide?
Their science doesn't tell us.
The buffalo will fall,
The elephant will fall,
They'll feel the heavy hand of God.
The blood-red season's coming.
The season of our freedom.

Scene 3

(Elisabethville prison.)

FIRST JAILER: *(on the phone)* Hello, yes, sir... Certainly, sir...

SECOND JAILER: What is it, boss? Bad news?

FIRST JAILER: It's the warden. He's on his way over. Something about Mister Patrice Lumumba.

SECOND JAILER: What a pest he turned out to be! I've seen a lot of prisoners in my time, but take it from me, there's nothing worse than an eggheaded nigger.

FIRST JAILER: You can say that again. Who does he think he is? He's even started writing poetry. Since when do baboons write poetry? All right, bring him in, we'll get him into shape to see the warden.

(While the Second Jailer goes out and returns with Lumumba, the First Jailer reads.)

Get a loud of this!

"Congo, and then the white men came
Raping your women and making
Your warriors drunk.
But the future will bring deliverance.
The banks of the great river will be yours,
Yours this land and all its riches,
Yours the sun in the sky."

Where does he get that stuff about the sun? I knew they wanted our houses and our women. Now they even want our sun...Oh, so there you are, you bastard. Ungrateful dog! So His Nibs writes poetry. Just tell me this, you baboon, who taught you how to read? Couldn't have been the no-good Belgians, could it? All right, I'm going to give you a little poetry in the ribs. *(He hits Lumumba.)*

SECOND JAILER: You don't know the half of it. Look what I found in his cell. The manuscript of an article protesting against his imprisonment. Claims it's illegal—that's what they all say. Demands to be set free so he can attend the Round Table conference in Brussels. Signed: Patrice Lumumba, president of the NCM.

FIRST JAILER: That's rich. *(He hits Lumumba again.)* So His Blackness wants to go to Brussels, eh? And what would you say to the king if you saw him? What would you say to the Bwana Kitoko?

SECOND JAILER: *(hitting Lumumba)* I guess he wants to be a minister! *(He laughs.)* His Excellency, the baboon!...His Excellency.

FIRST JAILER: Maybe so. But he'll have to eat King Kala first. Easy there, son. Don't rough him up too much. The warden'll be here any minute. Hm. Here he comes.

(Enter the Warden.)

THE WARDEN: Mr. Lumumba, I bring you good news. Yes, believe it or not, occasionally a warden has good news for a prisoner: I've just received word from Brussels. His Excellency the Minister for the Congo has decided to release you. He wishes you, as president of the NCM—the National Congo Movement, as you call it—to attend the Round Table conference. I have been instructed to do everything in my power to help you prepare for the trip. There's a Sabena plane for Brussels tomorrow. You are free, Mr. Lumumba. Bon voyage, Your Excellency!

THE JAILERS: Good grief! *(They bow.)* Bon voyage, your Excellency!

(The Sanza Player passes, singing:)

Kongo Mpaka Dima. [Be watchful, brothers, the Congo is moving.]

Scene 4

(A sign is lowered from the grid, saying: Brussels, Conference Room. The antechamber of a room in the palace. Four or five men, caricatures of bankers—dinner jacket, top hat, big cigar—are pacing about. Indignation and panic; they have just heard through indiscretion that at Lumumba's request the Belgian government has set the date for Congolese independence at June 30, 1960.)

FIRST BANKER: We're screwed. A government of traitors has given away our empire.

SECOND BANKER: They've set the date for independence.

THIRD BANKER: They've knuckled under to that baboon.

FIFTH BANKER: Chin up, gentlemen. Chin up, I say. You've got to wed the spirit of the times. I don't say love her, it's enough to wed her. There's nothing so frightening about this independence.

FIRST BANKER:
What's this? You shrug your shoulders at a blow
That will disrupt the state and dam the flow
Of our finances. Good Lord, this will make
Belgium a third-rate power, a Liechtenstein!

FOURTH BANKER:
Your attitude is dangerous. Do you mean
It, or is that a sample of your wit?
I'm a plain man, and I'll speak straight
From the shoulder. When ruin threatens a great state,
It's not the time for liberal ideas.

FIFTH BANKER:
My friend, when ruin threatens a great state,
The only good ideas are bold ideas.

FIRST BANKER:
    We've heard enough of your obscurities.
    Come to the point. If you have got some plan,
    Let's hear it. Speak up. Make some suggestion, man.
    Don't stand there looking wise.

SECOND BANKER:
    That's telling him. Have you a policy?

FIFTH BANKER:
    Policy? Hm. That's maybe too much said,
    But some ideas have shaped up in my head.
    No credit due. It's normal after twenty
    Years in the tropics, time to find out plenty.
    To handle savages, there are two ways:
    One is the club, but that's seen better days.
    The other is the purse.

FIRST BANKER:
    Go on.

FIFTH BANKER:
    All right, I'll spell it out. Just pay attention.
    What do their leaders want? They want to be
    Presidents, ministers, living in luxury.
    In short, the purse! High-powered cars,
    Villas, high wages, cushy bank accounts.
    Spare no expense. Just grease their palms and stuff
    Them. The investment will pay off.
    You'll see, their hearts will melt. And presently
    Those smirking, smiling politicians will be
    A special class between us and their people.
    They'll hold the people down provided we
    Tie them with bonds—well, maybe not of friendship,
    That's out of date in this sad century—
    But knots and tangles of complicity.

FIRST BANKER: Bravo! Good man! We're with you.

CHORUS OF BANKERS: Hurrah! Hurrah! Three cheers
    for independence.

SCENE 5

(Leopoldville. The crowd is celebrating independence. Atmosphere of friendly good nature. The "Independence Hot-cha-cha" is heard.)

A WOMAN: How's Dependa going to get here? By car? By bat? Or by airplane?

FIRST MAN: She's coming with the little white king, Bwana Kitoko. He's bringing her.

SANZA PLAYER: Listen to me, citizens. Nobody's bringing us Dependa. We're taking her.

THE BAKONGO TRIBESMAN: It's all the same. Maybe they're giving us Dependa and maybe we're taking her, but one thing is sure: Now that we've got her, we're going to send all those Bengalas back to their villages. The Bengalas are wrecking the country.

FIRST MAN: Watch your step, sir. Don't try to provoke us. If you ask me, it's pretty nice of us to put up with a Bakongo president, to let a Bakongo rule us. By rights a river man should have the job. Jean Bolikango! That's the man! Hurrah for Jean Bolikango!

MPOLO: That's enough, gentlemen. Calm down. Let's not have tribal quarrels. That's just what the colonialists want. Divide and rule, that's their motto. We've got to stop being Bengalas, Bakongos, and Batetelas. From now on we're all just plain Congolese, free, united, and organized. Let's all drink a good glass of beer to our unity. Be my guests, gentlemen.

FIRST MAN: Good idea. But the question is: what kind of beer? I only drink Polar.

SECOND MAN: Primus is my brand.

THIRD MAN: Primus, the queen of beers. That's King Kala's brand.

FIRST MAN: It's Polar for me: the freshness of the poles in the heat of the topics.

MPOLO: Let's drink to peace. To every kind of peace, peace in our hearts, peace between tribes, peace between the different brands of beer. Drink, gentlemen, Polar or Primus, it's all the same. So long as we drink to the Congo!

ALL: Here's to the Congo! *(They sing the "Independence Hot-cha-cha.")*

SCENE 6

(Somewhere in Leopoldville. Basilio, King of Belgium, and General Massens, Commander of the Congolese militia, standing before the curtain.)

BASILIO: Not so long ago this barbarous people lay stunned beneath the heavy fist of Stanley, of Boula Matari, the Rock Crusher, as they call him out here. We took them in hand. Yes, Providence entrusted them to our care, we fed them, cared for them, educated them. The independence I am granting them today will show whether we have succeeded in bettering their nature, whether our efforts have been rewarded. Freedom will put them to the test. Either they will set all Africa an example, as we ourselves have done in Europe: the example of a united, self-respecting, hardworking people. In that case the emancipation of our wards will redound to the eternal glory of Belgium. Or else the barbaric root, nurtured in the moldering depths, will regain its noxious vigor and stifle the good seed sown for the last fifty years by the untiring devotion of our missionaries. In that case...

GENERAL MASSENS: In that case?

BASILIO: We'll see about that when the time comes, Massens. Meanwhile, let's put our trust in human nature.

GENERAL MASSENS: Your Majesty, these experiments bear witness to your generosity, your genius. But you know how I feel about it. I have my doubts...However, if such is your sovereign will, I have only one recommendation. Make it clear to them that you have given them this freedom—this hashish that intoxicates them with such deplorable visions—and that they haven't conquered it. Perhaps they are not too obtuse to grasp the big difference between a right they have earned and the gift of your Royal Munificence.

BASILIO: Don't worry, Massens. I will make that very clear. But here they are.

(The curtain rises, disclosing Lumumba, Kala, other Congolese delegates, and, in the background, the Congolese crowd.)

KALA LUBU: *(President of the Congolese Republic, to Lumumba)* Mr. Mayor, oh, I beg your pardon, Mr. Prime Minister, I mean. The essential thing, in my opinion, is that this ceremony should pass off smoothly, that we observe the proprieties. The rules of good manners demand it, the rules of politics as well. This is no time for complaints and recriminations, for high-sounding—or low-sounding—words. Childbirth is never painless; that's the law of nature. But when the child is born, everyone smiles. Today I want to see a Congo wreathed in smiles. But here's the King. *(Addressing the crowd.)* All together now, Long live the King!

THE CROWD: Long live the King! Hurrah for Bwana Kitoko! Hurrah for King Kala!

(The crowd waves little flags with the sign of the kodi, *a shell pierced with a sword, emblem of the Abako, Kala's political organization. Firecrackers are set off. A group of black children led by a bearded missionary sing a song in the style of the* Vienna Sängerknaben.)

BASILIO: I shall be brief. A word in pious recollection of my predecessors who were the guardians of this country before me, and first of all of Leopold, the founder, who came here not to take, not to dominate, but to give and to bring civilization. And a word of gratitude to all those who built up this country day by day—at the cost of untold hardships. Glory to the founders! And glory to those who carried on their work. And now, gentlemen, I give you this State, the work of our hands. We are a nation of engineers and manufacturers. I can say without boasting that we are putting an excellent machine into your hands; take good care of it, that's all I ask of you. But since it is a machine, mechanical difficulties can reasonably be foreseen, and it goes without saying that you can come to us with your problems, that you can count on our assistance; our disinterested assistance, gentlemen. And now, men of the Congo, take over the controls, the eyes of the whole world are upon you!

KALA LUBU: Sire! Your august Majesty's presence at the ceremonies of this memorable day is new and striking proof of your solicitude for this people that you have loved and protected. The people of the Congo have received your message of friendship with respect and fervent devotion. They will long bear in their hearts the words you have just addressed to them in this solemn hour. They will never cease to prize the friendship which the Belgian government has offered them and will unstintingly do their part to maintain a sincere collaboration between our two nations. People of the Congo, my brothers, I want you to know, to understand, that independence has not come to our country to abrogate law or tribal custom; it has come to complete them, to fulfill and harmonize them. Nor has independence come to us to undo the work of civilization. Independence comes to us under the twofold guidance of Custom and Civilization. Independence has come to reconcile the old and the new, the nation and its tribes. If we keep faith with Civilization and with Custom, God will protect the Congo.

(Uncertain applause.)

LUMUMBA: As for me, Sire, my thoughts are for those who have been forgotten. We are the people who have been dispossessed, beaten, mutilated; the people whom

the conquerors treated as inferiors, in whose faces they
spat. A people of kitchen boys, house boys, laundry
boys, in short, a people of boys, of yes-bwanas, and
anyone who wanted to prove that a man is not
necessarily a man could take us as an example.

Sire, whatever suffering, whatever humiliation
could be known, we have known it.
But comrades, they were not able to dull our taste for
life, and we resisted.
We didn't have much to fight with, but we fought,
we fought for fifty years.
And today we have won.
Today our country is in the hands of its children.
This sky, this river, these lands are ours.
Ours the lake and the forest,
Ours Karissimbi, Nyiragongo, Niamuragira,
Mikeno, Ehu, mountains sprung from the word of
fire.
People of the Congo, this is a great day.
It is the day when the nations of the world welcome
Congo our mother,
and still more Congo our child,
child of our sleepless nights, of our sufferings, of
our struggles.
Comrades and brothers in combat, it is up to us to
transform each of our wounds into a nurturing
breast,
each of our thoughts, our hopes, into a fountain of
change.
Kongo! Watch me. I raise him above my head;
I put him back on my shoulder;
Three times I spit in his face;
I set him down on the ground, and I ask you; tell me
the truth, do you know this child? And you all
answer: it's Kongo, our king.
I wish I were a toucan, that wonderful bird, to cross
the skies announcing to races and tongues that
Kongo has been born to us, our king. Long live
Kongo!
Kongo, late born, may he follow the sparrow hawk!

Kongo, late born, let him have the last word!
Comrades, everything remains to be done, or done
over, but we will do it, we will do it over. For
Kongo.
We will remake all the laws, one by one, for Kongo.
We will revise all the customs, one by one, for Kongo.
Uprooting injustice, we will rebuild the old edifice
piece by piece, from cellar to attic, for Kongo.
That which is bowed shall be raised, and that which
is raised shall be raised higher—for Kongo!
I demand the union of all.
I demand the devotion of every man. For Kongo!
Uhuru! Freedom!

(A moment of ecstasy.)

Congo! These are great days!
When this day's rags and this day's tinsel have been
burned,
Let us advance rejoicing to my unanimous step
Into the new day! Into the solstice!

(Stupor. Enter the first four Bankers.)

First Banker: Terrible, terrible! It was bound to end
this way.

Second Banker: That speech! This time we're
through. We can pack our bags.

Third Banker: *(with great dignity)* Obviously. Where
order breaks down, the banker packs his bags.

Fourth Banker: Poor Congo, drifting on uncharted
seas!

(Mokutu passes. He is preoccupied and sees no one.)

Mokutu: And I picked him for a winner. Who could

have written that speech of his? And to think I thought I could make a statesman out of him! Well, if he wants to break his neck, it's his funeral. Too bad! Too bad! Knife oversharpened cuts its sheath. *(He spits.)*

SANZA PLAYER: *(perplexed)* Let's not be too quick to judge the boss. He must have had his reasons even if we can't see them.

(Enter Lumumba.)

LUMUMBA: Well, did you like what I said? Or are you one of those people who think the sky is going to fall because a black man has the audacity to give a king a piece of his mind with the whole world listening in? No, you don't like it. I can see it in your eyes.

MOKUTU: Since you're asking me, let me tell you a little story.

LUMUMBA: I hate stories.

MOKUTU: Just to save time. When I was a boy, I went hunting with my grandfather. One day I found myself face to face with a leopard. I lost my head. I threw my javelin and wounded him. My grandfather was furious. He made me go in and retrieve the spear. That day I understood, once and for all, that you don't attack a beast unless you're sure of killing him.

LUMUMBA: *(very coldly)* You're wrong if you're against what I said. There was a taboo that needed breaking. I broke it. As for your story, if it means that you hate the Beast—colonialism—and that you're determined to hunt it down to a finish with me...everything will be all right.

MOKUTU: Did you ever doubt it, Patrice?

LUMUMBA: *(brusquely)* Good. That's enough for me. Let's make up.

(They go out. The Sanza Player comes in and sings the Lupeto song.)

SANZA PLAYER:

Nobody's better
At sniffing the wind.
They haven't the mugs
Of murdering thugs,
But noses to sniff out the wind.
They're the lupeto boys.

Those boys like to eat,
They don't care where they get it
As long as they can eat it.
They're the lupeto boys.

You ask me what's lupeto.
You haven't understood.
Lupeto's money, lucre, dough,
They're neither bad nor good.
They're the lupeto boys.

(Enter the Fifth Banker.)

FIRST BANKER: Congratulations for your shrewd advice!

FIFTH BANKER: Colleague and friend, I think you're being unfair.
Risks are the price of politics, the price
Of any action.

SECOND BANKER:
Phrases, words, hot air.
Your plan goes wrong, and you stand there and gas.

FIFTH BANKER:
Phrases, why, not at all. Chin up, my friends!

Shall we lie down like bathmats at the first
Love tap? No, listen. Follow my idea. *(He whispers in
their ears.)*
If self-determination is the style,
It can't be helped. But then, why not for all?
For you and me, it's only logical.
You catch my drift, you read between the lines?
Then self-determination for our mines!

FIRST BANKER:
    Hush, hush! Let's listen, please.
    Our colleague often gets some good ideas.

FIFTH BANKER:
    Friends, when I see this turmoil, this commotion,
    I realize there's only one solution.
    Yes, when I see this Congo, this immense
    Chaotic mass, it simply doesn't make sense
    That our Katanga, our beloved nation,
    Shouldn't cast loose. That's self-determination.

FIRST BANKER:
    Ah, now you're talking, pal. I love you. Self-
    Determined uranium? That's the ticket, eh?

FIFTH BANKER:
    And not just uranium. Diamonds, copper, cobalt.
    All Katanga. Shining, clinking, gilt-edged Katanga.

CHORUS OF BANKERS: Hurrah! Hurrah! Three cheers
    for Katanga!

Scene 7

(A nightclub. A record is playing "Franco de Mi Amor." When it stops, a woman's voice is heard over the radio.)

FIRST VOICE: This is the voice of African Moral Rearmament. Get to work, citizens. To work! And when I say "to work," it's the same as if I were saying "to arms." We are at war, citizens, at war for the future of the Congo. The mobilization of the working classes must be total, unconditional, deliberate, voluntary. The Congo has been living in prehistoric times. With independence we have acceded to the historical age, and that means the age of hard work. To work, citizens! To work!

(Another voice is heard.)

SECOND VOICE: People of the Congo, wake up. Don't let yourselves be brainwashed! Come out of your holes, your workshops, your factories. Make yourselves heard, demand your rights. Independence, yes! But don't let it be an empty word. Take it from me, citizens, it's not empty for everybody. Ask the members of parliament, ask the ministers. Who gets the cars? Who gets the women? The ministers, the members of parliament! Who gets Santa Claus? The eggheads. We demand Santa Claus for everybody! That's what we mean by independence. Hurrah for independence!

(The state is invaded by Congolese soldiers, half drunk, swinging their belts. They shout rhythmically.)

Down with the politicians! Down with Lumumba, Lumumba *pamba*, Lumumba *pamba!*...

SCENE 8

(Leopoldville, the prime minister's office.)

LUMUMBA: Get me Makessa. Where's Kangolo? Absent. Some office manager. No use looking for Sissoko. He's asleep. He never gets up in the daytime. Maybe you think things can go on like this? No, goddammit, they can't. Gentlemen, who are we? Well, I'm going to tell you who we are. We're slaves. I'm a slave, a voluntary slave. You're all slaves, or you ought to be, and by slaves I mean men condemned to work without rest. You have no right to rest. You're here to serve the Congo twenty-four hours a day. Private life is out. But at least you're free from material worries...because you won't have time for any. I know, I know. They say I ask too much, they say I'm adventurous, foolhardy and so on. Is that it? They say I'm trying to go too fast. Well, you no-good snails, let me tell you this. We've got to go fast, we've got to go too fast. Do you know how much time I have to catch up with fifty years of history? Three months, gentlemen. And you think I can afford to take it easy?

MPOLO: Mr. President, the soldiers! The soldiers are coming.

LUMUMBA: Soldiers? What in hell do they want? What are they squawking about?

MPOLO: They're yelling, "Kill Lumumba. Lumumba *pamba!*"

LUMUMBA: *(flying into a rage)* Is that all? The bastards, the traitors. Belgians, that's what they are. Lousy Flemish bastards! When I think that for fifty years they crawled for the Belgians. And the minute we settle our

African asses to give them an African government, they come around snapping at our ankles.

A MINISTER: Well, if you ask me, independence is getting off to a lovely start.

LUMUMBA: Idiot! How did you expect it to start? And how do you expect it to go on? What did you think? When I picked you as my ministers, did you think I was inviting you to a picnic? I won't try to fool you, gentlemen. There's going to be trouble, every kind of trouble before you can say Jack Sprat: mutiny, sabotage, threats, slander, blackmail, and treason. You look surprised. That's what power means: betrayal, maybe death. Yes, death and no maybe. That's the Congo. The Congo, you see, is a country where things go fast. A seed in the ground today, tomorrow a bush, no, tomorrow a forest. In any case, the things that move quickly will keep on moving quickly. Don't count on me to slow them down. Mpolo, let those loudmouthed bastards in, I'll speak to them...I'll move them. I'll turn their hearts.

(Enter the soldier's delegation.)

Come in, gentlemen. Ah, it's too bad you haven't brought your civilian friends, those union leaders, who've suddenly got so brave when it comes to holding the knife to our throats. For fifty years they've kept their mouths shut and trembled at the sight of a Belgian. And now they refuse to give a Congolese government, a government of their brothers, the few months' time it needs to get its bearings. As for you soldiers, I won't beat about the bush. Your demands are legitimate. I understand them and I intend to meet them. When you were the militia, your officers were Belgians; now that you're the National Army, you want to be commanded by Congolese. That's perfectly reasonable. And if we hesitated a moment before Africanizing the Army, it was because our good will was blocked by the ill will and the prejudices of General Massens. That shows you what to expect of the colonialists. They're obstinate, gentlemen, and they're underhanded. But we have dismissed Massens.

SOLDIERS: Down with Massens!

LUMUMBA: Massens is gone and the government will meet your demands. Each one of you is being promoted to the next higher rank: every private will be a corporal, every corporal a sergeant...

SOLDIERS: No! No! Colonels! Generals!

MOKUTU: Mr. Prime Minister, the troops demand the total and immediate Africanization of the officers' corps. The way things stand, there isn't a moment to lose.

LUMUMBA: The government is not unaware of the problem. As of the present moment I am in a position to inform you that the government is considering... no, that the government has decided to appoint a Congolese general and a Congolese colonel immediately. The general is Lundula, the colonel is our secretary of state for youth problems, Mpolo, here present.

SOLDIERS: No! We don't want Mpolo. He's not a soldier, he's a politician. We want Mokutu. To hell with Mpolo. We want Mokutu. He was in the militia for seven years. He's a soldier.

LUMUMBA: You want Mokutu? Good. I ratify your choice. It's true, Mokutu's a soldier. And Mokutu's my friend, my brother. I know that Mokutu will never betray me. Mpolo was appointed by the government. Well, I appoint Mokutu. That settles it. But the question isn't whether you're going to be officers or not, because you are officers right now. The question is what kind of officers you choose to be: parade officers? Bakshish officers? A new caste? The government wants you to be officers of the Congolese people, fired with the spirit of the Congolese people and determined to fight like tigers to safeguard our Congolese independence. What do you say?

SOLDIERS: Yes! Yes! Hurrah for Lumumba!

LUMUMBA: Congolese soldiers and officers, if the enemy attacks us, and that may be sooner than we think, it's up to you...I expect him to burn his claws like a hawk that tries to steal meat from the villagers' fire.
   Long live the Congolese Army. Long live the Congo!

SOLDIERS: Hurrah! Hurrah!

   (The Sanza Player enters and sings:)

   Pollen of fire
   Drunken springtime
   A little bird is flitting
   Forgetful of snares
   Forgetting the blowpipe.
   Birdbrain, says the trap.
   The bird has forgotten the trap,
   The trap remembers the bird.

Scene 9

(In the darkness white refugees cross the stage, carrying what few belongings they have been able to save. Suddenly red lights illumine an immense map of the Congo. On a balcony in the half-darkness two shadows: Basilio and Massens.)

First Radio Voice: Marigold calling Gardenia, Marigold calling Gardenia. Answer, Gardenia.

Second Radio Voice: Betty calling Angela. Two cars full of women and children are headed for Kitona base. You will send troops to meet them.

Third Radio Voice: Marigold calling Gardenia. Latest news from Luluabourg, Kasai province. Twelve hundred Europeans barricaded in Immokasai building besieged by Congolese troops armed with mortars and machine guns. Send troops immediately. Urgent. Out.

Fourth Radio Voice: Phoenix, do you read me, Phoenix? Dispatch received from Juba. Watsa troops in revolt. Forty Belgian officers with their families taken prisoner. They are being tortured. Urge immediate action. Out.

(Enter Basilio and Massens in uniform.)

Massens: Well, your Majesty. Now we know. They've wrecked our Congo.

Basilio: Alas!

Massens: Majesty, they're savages. Order must be restored, and I see only one way.

Basilio: I know, Massens. But unfortunately international law doesn't allow it.

MASSENS: Your Majesty, this is no time to tie our hands with juridical scruples. Human lives are at stake, European lives. That's more important than any law.

BASILIO: You're right, Massens. That's more important than any law. Very well. I give you carte blanche.

MASSENS: *(in a thundering voice)* Forward march!

(A vision of Belgian paratroopers in action. Darkness.)

LUMUMBA'S VOICE: *(shouting the Congolese war cry)* People of the Congo! Luma! Luma!

(The war tomtoms sound in the night, spreading the news of the Belgian attack.)

Scene 10

(Lumumba, Kala, and a Pilot in a plane over Elisabethville. Wind, rain, lightning.)

LUMUMBA: Damn weather! Look! Look! The wind's uprooting the trees. And the rain! The weather's as bad as the situation in the Congo, and that's something. Looks like a herd of phantom elephants stampeding through a bamboo forest. Isn't it a little early for the rainy season to be starting?

KALA: Yes, the weather's bad. Definitely...But when God is perplexed, we ignorant mortals call it fog.

LUMUMBA: Pilot, aren't we going to land soon? This trip is interminable. Where are we?

PILOT: We'll be over Elisabethville in a moment. Have patience, your Excellency. We're in the middle of a tropical hurricane. Wait. The radio operator's trying to tell me something. *(A paper is handed him. He reads it aloud.)* Isn't that nice! Msiri and Tzumbi in person in the control tower. The Katanga authorities won't let us land.

LUMUMBA: Msiri? Tzumbi? The Katanga authorities? Are we or are we not the Congo authorities? Does Katanga belong to the Congo, or doesn't it? Pilot, I order you to land. Immediately.

PILOT: It can't be done, sir. Not in this weather. They've turned out the lights on the airstrip. Look, you can see for yourself.

LUMUMBA: Traitor! Flemish dog! You disobey me? Are you in cahoots with the secessionists?

(As the plane regains altitude.)

PILOT: Where do we head for, Mr. President?

KALA: Leopoldville.

LUMUMBA: No. It's arms that we need! Arms! To Moscow! To Moscow!

SCENE 11

(At the Congolese parliament in Leopoldville. As the Senators take their places, the Sanza Player passes, singing:)

Palm wine man climbing the palm tree,
Come down, little ant,
Come down, little sparrow,
The good souls sing at the foot of the palm tree.
Up you go, palm wine man, up you go,
Sparrow drunk with freedom.

FIRST SENATOR: Honorable colleagues: The Congo has become a vast cemetery; the Belgians have been conducting themselves like the Roman legions.

SECOND SENATOR: I wish to call the attention of the government to our finances—yes, our finances. The Congolese treasury has evaporated, the north wind has blown it away. Where are we going to find money now? The Bank of the Congo has been transferred to Katanga. Are we going to sleep while Rome burns? That is the question I ask the government. I for my part intend to die in the toga of a senator.

THIRD SENATOR: Fellow senators! We haven't come here to discourage each other. But there are some things that cannot be passed over in silence. Our prime minister and our president are never here. We must have the courage to look the facts in the face. When we think they are in Leo, they are in Matadi; when they are supposed to be in Matadi, they are in Banana; in Banana the word is that they've gone off to Moanda or Boma. They fly right and left, all over the place, and always the two of them. Gentlemen, it's customary in a civilized country that when the husband goes out the wife stays home.

LUMUMBA: I for my part, gentlemen, assure you that
we don't travel enough. Ah, I wish I could multiply
and divide myself, so as to be everywhere at once. In
Matadi, in Boma, in Elisabethville, in Luluabourg, to
crush the enemy's many-headed plot. For the plot is
everywhere. Ever since the very first day of our
independence, I've seen the Belgians, men ravaged by
hatred and eaten by resentment, hatching their plot.
General Massens stirring up the militia against the
government, representing us as a gang of politicians
and unscrupulous profiteers. The Belgian ambassador,
Mynher Van den Putt, doing everything in his power
to sabotage, to undermine, to disorganize our republic,
putting pressure on all Belgian technicians and civil
servants to leave the country. From the very first day
General Massens has been setting the scene for his
raids, working up a pretext for his mercenaries to step
in. That's the Belgian plot, gentlemen. Their treaty of
friendship with us? As far as they are concerned, it's a
scrap of paper. We let them maintain staging areas on
our territory. They turn them into armed camps from
which to attack us. That's the Belgian plot. They've
shelled Kabalo, Boma, and Matadi! But the worst was
yet to come. Today, July 11, 1960, Tzumbi, our brother
Abraham Tzumbi, seconded by Msiri, incited, advised,
and financed by the Belgians, has proclaimed the
independence of Katanga, our richest province,
without consulting the population. And what is the
first act of this independent state? To conclude a treaty
of military assistance and economic cooperation with
Belgium. That's the Belgian plot. Have I made myself
clear? People of the Congo, we've got to smash that
plot. People of the Congo, we have paid dearly for our
independence. Are we going to let them throttle it
now? And you, my brother Africans, Mali, Guinea,
Ghana, we cry out to you across our borders.
(Shouting.) Africa! Do they think Africa is deaf? Or
faint-hearted? Or do they think Africa is too feeble to

deliver us? I know the colonialists are powerful. But I swear to you by Africa: All of us united, together, will subdue the monster. Brothers, already the Congo has won a great victory. We sent out an appeal to the United Nations and the United Nations has sent a favorable reply. Tomorrow Mr. Hammarskjöld, Secretary General of the United Nations, whose integrity and impartiality are recognized by all, will be with us in Leopoldville. We trust him. The United Nations will see to it that justice is done. Full justice.

Gentlemen, I have finished. In a word, our independence, our existence as a nation, our freedom, and everything that Dependa means to our people are at stake.

Brothers, I stand here before you, and through you I look every single Congolese straight in the eye. And what I have to tell him is best said by our Kikongo song:

Brother, in your hand
You hold what belongs to you.
Are you going to let another
Take it away?

You all know the answer. *Kizola ko.* I won't allow it.

DEPUTIES: *(rising and shouting) Kizola ko. Kizola ko.*

Scene 12

(Darkness, then light. In the background a group of European experts take their places around Hammarskjöld. They have just landed in Leopoldville after ferrying across the Congo from Brazzaville. The Sanza Player crosses the stage, singing.)

Father Congo
river of flowers and islands.
What swells your grey heart
and shakes it with sobs?

HAMMARSKJÖLD: *(to his experts)* Gentlemen, as we set foot for the first time on the soil of the Congo, I am sure that you all share my feeling that this is a profoundly significant moment. The Congo is not only a country, a state, an unhappy state that needs and has asked for our help and protection, it is also a proving ground for the international action that is the aim and ideal of our organization. The work that awaits you here is a great deal more than academic fact-finding. We shall be working for the future of the world.

Gentlemen, in this hour I wish not to sum up my instructions to you, but to define the spirit in which I want you to confront your task here in the Congo. And I believe that there is no better way of doing so than to cite the words of the poet:

I recognize no quarrel. I say, let us live, torch in the wind, flame in the wind,
And in us let all men be so mingled with the flame and so consumed
that in the mounting torch a greater light is born within us...
Tingling the flesh in which the itching soul keeps us still rebellious
And it is a time of high fortune when the great

adventurers of the soul
seek passage on the high road of mankind,
    questioning
the whole threshing floor of the earth, trying to
    discover
the meaning of this vast disorder, questioning the
    bed, the waters of the sky, and the tidemarks of the
    river of shadow on the earth,
perhaps even rebelling at finding no answer...

But here come our hosts. Meditate on those words, gentlemen, meditate on them and find strength in them as you go forth like a new order of chivalry upon the high road of humanity.

(The Congolese delegation enters and advances toward the Europeans.)

Gentlemen of the Congolese government, I am glad to be here in the Congo at a time when the United Nations, at your request, has undertaken to help you, by all the means at its disposal, to lay the foundations of a happy and prosperous future. Seeing me for the first time, you must wonder what sort of man I am. That is only natural. And it's a question I want to answer. I am a neutral. A good many people think there's no such animal. But there is, thank the Lord. I am a *neutral*, and I'm here to prove it. The problems confronting the Congo must be solved by conciliation and diplomacy. They cannot be solved by force and intimidation, but only in a spirit of peace and justice. And that is why neutrals can make themselves useful here in the Congo, why they can help to find a satisfactory solution to your problems. For come to think of it, what does the word "neutral" mean? It means "fair," it means "just." And when I say "just," I take the word in the most exacting sense. The just, said Meister Eckhart, "are those who have left their selves behind; who look for nothing above or below or alongside of themselves; who seek neither wealth nor glory nor comfort nor pleasure nor interest nor sanctity nor reward, but have made themselves free from all that."

In short, those who give God their due and through whom God is glorified.

That, gentlemen, is the spirit in which we have come among you. To help you to overcome your passions, to bring appeasement to your hearts. To help you to achieve justice and peace. Justice and peace. Those are my words of greeting to the Congo. Long live the Congo!

Scene 13

(As the Congolese crowd demonstrates, dancing and singing the "Independence Hot-cha-cha," the Ambassador of the Grand Occident steps forward.)

AMBASSADOR: I know my country is getting a bad reputation. They say we're trigger-happy. But is there any room for rocking-chair politics when the world is off its rocker? With people going berserk all over the world, somebody's got to make them behave. And, praise the Lord, Providence has picked us for the job...You heard what the man said. "To Moscow! To Moscow!" That's what he said. Well, I've got news for you folks. They call us the policemen of the world. Okay. But we're the fire department, too. And it's our job to check the flames of incendiary Communism. Wherever it shows its ugly head. And that includes the Congo. A word to the wise!

(The same African bar as in Act 1; the Girls and Mama Makosi moving about. Lumumba, Mokutu, and friends take seats.)

LUMUMBA: I like these places...I know it upsets the Pharisees, but...

MOKUTU: All the same, it's not going to help our reputation any. Especially abroad. They'll say we're a lot of sex-crazed apes. Yes, I know. The scenes of your youth, and all that. But things have changed. We're ministers and top brass now. You're a Mbota Mutu, a big shot, and don't forget it.

LUMUMBA: Don't make me laugh. Let the ladies' betterment societies turn up their noses. It gives me a kick. Vice was the only freedom the white men left us. And then they complain about our morals. Same as the Americans complain about Harlem...

MOKUTU: Maybe so, but you're not seriously thinking of coming here to discuss affairs of state? Hasn't the Congo got a bad enough reputation as it is?

LUMUMBA: *(ironically)* Not a bad idea. I'll think it over...but now let's talk about something serious. When the Europeans came, the Congo started to disintegrate. It began to rot, piece by piece, and to stink. The state, the family, the people. So maybe this dive with its shady mixed fauna is a faithful reflection of our Congo today. Garbage rotting in the sun. But here and there you see something fresh and new sprouting through the compost. And that's ground for encouragement. *(To Mama Makosi, who approaches.)* Well, Mama Makosi, how you doing?

MAMA MAKOSI: Hello, Patrice. Say, we're giving a big freedom ball. Can I count on you? It's going to be terrific: we've rented the Elite Bar.

MOKUTU: Don't be unreasonable, Mama Makosi. Your old friend Patrice is Prime Minister now. You can't expect...

MAMA MAKOSI: Oh, come off it. He'll always be the same Patrice for us. Wherever he goes, we'll go. And vice versa. He's not ashamed of his friends.

GIRL: Oh yes, it would be so sweet. I'm the union song leader, and you know what? We're working up a beautiful song. *(She sings.)*

When I wear my green bandana...

(Enter the Sanza Player disguised as a madman. He passes between the tables, humming.)

MOKUTU: Who's that character?

MAMA MAKOSI: He's just a crazy man. Been coming around for the last few days and we can't get rid of him.

MOKUTU: Can't you call the police?

LUMUMBA: Leave the poor man alone. He isn't bothering anybody.

SANZA PLAYER: *(declaiming)* Ah, God of the Christians! Why did you let the white men go away...?

MOKUTU: Get a load of that. He can't live without his daily ration of kicks. He's an addict.

LUMUMBA: No, Mokutu, it's worse than that...It takes

a lot of thinking to face the truth that God is dead. Our country people...

SANZA PLAYER: Oh God, why did you make black men so wicked?

MOKUTU: Good grief!

SANZA PLAYER: I came down the river, looking for the white men who left my village, and I didn't find them; the white men left our village and the black men are wicked. The black men are cursed...

LUMUMBA: See, Mokutu? It's useful to hang around these places. That's the bitter truth of our Congo. That's the disease we've got to cure our people of. Mama Makosi, I want to thank you and your bar for this lesson. And don't worry, you can count on me, I'll come to your ball, and I'll bring my Cabinet. *(They exit.)*

SANZA PLAYER: Let's throw off this mask. I've said enough. I've done enough. Even if a man has good eyes, you've got to show him certain things. But he'll see the rest for himself. And it's plain enough to see. It doesn't take a hurricane to part a chicken's tail feathers.

SCENE 2

(A meeting of the Congolese cabinet. Lumumba, Mpolo, Mokutu, Croulard [Lumumba's Belgian secretary], and others.)

LUMUMBA: Gentlemen, that is the situation. There's no time to lose. We're in the midst of a battle. On every front. The survival of the Congo is at stake.

CROULARD: I beg your pardon, Your Excellency, but Mr. Bunche, the Assistant Secretary of the United Nations, want to see you. He says it's urgent.

LUMUMBA: Who told him to come here? Who sent for him? But never mind, Croulard, as long as you've interrupted us, pass me the file on the district chiefs...And another thing, gentlemen, we've got to take up the question of visas. All sorts of people are coming in without visas. Or worse, with Belgian visas.

CROULARD: Your Excellency, Mr. Bunche is very insistent. He says...

LUMUMBA: Croulard! Will you kindly let us work? *(He rushes to the phone.)* Hello. Stanleyville? Is that you, Jean?...All right, arrange the meeting. I'll speak...I can tell you right now, there's going to be some excitement. We're going to abolish the district militias and mobilize the unemployed. Hello? Oh yes, I'd forgotten. Don't forget to order beer...by the carload...Enough for the whole population...Good-bye. *(He hangs up.)*

(Enter Isaac Kalonji.)

ISAAC: Howdy! Howdy, everybody...All that's fine and dandy, my dear Prime Minister. But when are we going into Katanga? What are we waiting for? All you've got to do is make a beeline for Bakwanga! Our partisans will rise up...Albert Kalonji has taken it on the lam...Tzumbi is saying his prayers...

MPOLO: I agree with Isaac. We need Bakwanga. That's where the diamonds are. And what's a crown without diamonds?

LUMUMBA: We need. We need. Just get me some planes. But don't worry, Isaac, I'm attending to it.

MOKUTU: Not just planes, Mr. Prime Minister... troops...no money, no troops. That's the way soldiers are, and they haven't been paid in two months.

LUMUMBA: All right, all right. We'll give you money.

MOKUTU: Thank you. But you haven't heard the last of my complaints. I won't stand for amateurishness. You made me a colonel, I'm going to be a real colonel.

LUMUMBA: What's on your mind?

MOKUTU: Well, I hear that Mpolo has been going around with a colonel's cap and a swagger stick... The government will have to choose between us. It's either him or me.

LUMUMBA: Come, come, Mokutu, there's nothing to get excited about...you were away on a tour of inspection. We thought it wise to appoint Mpolo a colonel too. In this situation two of you aren't too many. If you're not satisfied, we can appoint you general and Mpolo can be chief of staff.

(Hubbub among the ministers.)

SANZA PLAYER: That's it...A good compromise. Now everybody will be happy.

MOKUTU: I'm sorry. I'm telling you plainly. The army isn't an operetta. I'd rather resign.

LUMUMBA: All right. Mokutu remains chief of staff. As for you, Mpolo, we'll see later on. Meanwhile, take off that uniform. Well, Croulard, what about that file on the district chiefs? All those petty potentates, those police dogs who helped the Belgians to crush our people. If we want real leaders, we've got to get rid of them first. And where do you find real leaders except among the common people? Well, Croulard, how about that file?

CROULARD: I can't find it, Your Excellency...This place is such a mess. Well, here at least is a big bundle I wasn't looking for...I open it, and what do I see? Guess. A bundle of telegrams. Messages from twenty nations or more, recognizing the Republic of the Congo. And nobody's read them. Been here for two weeks. It's a mess, I tell you. A mess.

LUMUMBA: Luckily we have you, Croulard, to make a little order.

MOKUTU: *(grumbling)* And to poke his nose into a lot of things that are none of his business.

MPOLO: Comrade Prime Minister, we were speaking of Katanga just now. Maybe if we can't take Katanga for the moment, we could at least take Leopoldville. The Abako youth organizations are acting as if they owned the streets. Agitating against us under our own windows.

MOKUTU: Careful, gentlemen. A blow at the Abako is a blow at the President.

LUMUMBA: Mpolo, you're the youth minister, aren't you? Why can't you set up your own youth organization? The NCM Youth Brigade. Every time the Abako demonstrates, you stage a counter-demonstration. That'll do it. You don't need government intervention for that.

MPOLO: Okay, chief!

(Enter the Chief of Police.)

LUMUMBA: Well, well, here comes my police force. What news?

CHIEF OF POLICE: Excellency, another article by Gabriel Makoso in *Christian Conscience*. A diatribe by Monsignor Malula...and leaflets, millions of leaflets!

LUMUMBA: Never mind the leaflets. I know them by heart: Lumumba has mortgaged the Congo to the Russians, Lumumba has sold his soul to the Devil, Lumumba has received millions from the Czech Ambassador. *(Taking the newspaper.)* This is more serious. *(He glances through it.)* Oh, oh! Monsignor doesn't pull his punches. Hmm. Read it to us, Mpolo.

MPOLO: *(reading)* "And first and foremost we must denounce anticlericalism, that waste-product of the Occident, imported into the Congo by unworthy rulers. To arms against the enemies of religion wherever they may be, the Freemasons like Makessa, the self-styled atheists like the ignominious Lumumba!"

LUMUMBA: Not bad for a bishop. The ignominious Lumumba! Well, he's going to hear from the ignominious Lumumba. They want war? All right, they'll get it.
   Mr. Police Chief, do your duty. You will arrest Makoso and shut his paper down.

MOKUTU: I beg your pardon, Mr. Prime Minister. Isn't that unwise? Won't it make for unrest?

LUMUMBA: Watch your step, Mokutu...stick to your own department. You're in charge of the army. I've agreed to that. Politics is my business. And don't worry about the unrest, I'll know how to deal with it...Gentlemen, we can strike, or we can let ourselves be struck down. I have made up my mind: We will strike.

I demand that Lundula be given full powers: the army will arrest everyone, white or black, who attempts to stir up trouble. No half-measures. No hesitation. Which reminds me, the Abako is making too much noise. They've scheduled a congress in Thysville. They're talking secession. Another secession. Well, there's not going to be any congress. Their congress is cancelled. Come to think of it, they haven't a leg to stand on. The law requires two weeks' notice. They didn't give it...Agreed, gentlemen?

MPOLO: Agreed. The law is the law. No special privileges.

LUMUMBA: As for Katanga, Isaac is right. That's our main problem...the key to all our other problems... I'll see Hammarskjöld...The United Nations is here to help us...You'll get your planes, Mokutu, you'll get your planes. As Isaac says, Tzumbi had better say his prayers.

(The Sanza Player passes, singing:)

Sun and rain
Driving rain
Rising sun
The elephant
Begets a son.

SCENE 3

(Lumumba's office.)

LUMUMBA: Mr. Secretary General, I appealed to the United Nations. I was the first chief of state to put full trust in your organization. Who would have thought that my first words to you would be words not of thanks but of reproach and recrimination. Please believe that I deeply regret it. But unfortunately you have put a very personal interpretation on the resolutions of the Security Council: the Belgians are still in the Congo. And the United Nations is holding diplomatic conversations with the traitor Tzumbi.

HAMMARSKJÖLD: I am the Secretary General of the United Nations Organization. I am responsible solely to the General Assembly. I owe you no accounts. But I can tell you this much: I have no orders to massacre the people of Katanga.

LUMUMBA: You have called off the military operations that would have enabled us to enter Elisabethville without striking a blow.

HAMMARSKJÖLD: If I called them off, or postponed them, it was because Bunche's reports left no room for doubt: it would have been necessary to fight for every street, for every house in Elisabethville.

LUMUMBA: Nonsense. The population of Katanga are only waiting to throw off Tzumbi's yoke. They would have welcomed you as a liberator. But you saw fit to confer with the rebel...

HAMMARSKJÖLD: Mr. Prime Minister, I followed the dictates of my conscience. It is a point of doctrine, a point of my doctrine, that the UN must not participate in an internal conflict, constitutional or otherwise, and that its armed forces cannot be utilized in such conflicts. I am not saying there is no problem. There is. But it is a problem that I do not despair of solving. President Tzumbi has impressed me as a sensible man. I shall make every effort to reason with him and convince him. In any case, this country has suffered enough. I have no desire to add a full-scale war to its misfortunes.

LUMUMBA: I appreciate your solicitude. But tell me, what greater misfortune can there be for this country than the secession of its richest province? You speak of resistance in Katanga. Tzumbi and Msiri must have had a good laugh. They had already rented houses for themselves in Rhodesia. Your Bunche is as gullible as a child. He misjudged the situation. Unless...After all, Bunche is an American...

HAMMARSKJÖLD: That has nothing to do with it. I permit no one to cast aspersions on the honesty and impartiality of my co-workers. I am a neutral, surrounded by neutrals who put the interest of the world at large before any consideration deriving from their own personal nationality.

LUMUMBA: I leave it to history to judge that. In any event, since the UN has failed to meet its obligations, to carry out its mission, the government of the Congolese Republic will assume its responsibilities. We will reduce the secession of Katanga by force. Our troops are ready. The campaign must be concluded before the rainy season. I trust that the UN will not refuse to lend me a certain number of planes to transport our armed forces.

HAMMARSKJÖLD: Planes? I thought I had made it clear to you that the United Nations troops are by definition a peace force, not a force of aggression.

LUMUMBA: There you have it, that's the impartiality of
the UN. Every day Belgian arms and mercenaries pour
into the Congo. And you just look on.

HAMMARSKJÖLD: You are unjust. I have addressed a
strong note of protest on the subject to the Brussels
government.

LUMUMBA: A note! Yes, a note. And meanwhile the
secessionists are building up their forces. Everybody
knows it, and what do you do? You not only refuse to
take action, but you prevent us from acting. Very well!
The Congo will do without your help. We still have a
few friends in the world. We will manage without you
neutrals.

HAMMARSKJÖLD: I wish to remind you that all foreign
aid to the Congo must pass through United Nations
channels.

LUMUMBA: You don't do things by halves, Mr.
Secretary General. Very well, but permit me in turn to
remind you that it is a point of doctrine, a point of my
doctrine, that the Congo is an independent country
and that we haven't shaken off Belgian rule in order to
accept the rule of the United Nations. Good day, Mr.
Secretary General. The Russians will lend me the
planes that you refuse me. In a few days we shall be in
Elisabethville. As for you, whatever may happen, I
hope you will not one day pay too dearly for your
illusions.

HAMMARSKJÖLD: Mr. Lumumba, I learned one thing
long ago: to say *yes* to Destiny, whatever it may be. But
since we are exchanging good wishes, I hope that
whatever may befall, you will not one day have to pay
too dearly for your imprudence and impulsiveness...
Good-bye.

(The Sanza Player passes, singing:)

A magpie on a cherry tree
Preens himself and plays the peacock,
Saying "This tree belongs to me."
Oh, let me die in poverty
If riches means a magpie's tree.

Scene 4

(Darkness, then half-light. Alarming noises. Gradually, as in a nightmare, groups appear: women, witches, warriors armed with spears and blowguns. A voice rises, the Voice of Civil War.)

CIVIL WAR:
Boy, pour the palm wine.
Hot and spicy,
Thick muddy dregs.
Pour the palm wine. When I'm drunk, I ask
For my sword, my sharpened sword that hangs
On the wall with buffalo horn and *assegai.*
Pour the palm wine, boy!
When I'm drunk, I take down my bow that hangs
on the wall with my war horn and *assegai.*
Boy, by day I'll fight
and at night, I'll praise my bow,
I'll honor it with a branch of wild grape.
I'll rub it with oil at night,
At night it deserves to shine like a mirror.
Boy! My machete!
A brave man isn't made to die in his bed,
A brave man is an elephant,
A spitting serpent.
Palm wine man, pour the wine, color of enemy
  blood.
When the day returns, we'll face
The enemy eye to eye.
Boy! Pour the palm wine.
I'm drunk! On wine? On enemy blood? I don't
  know.
The spear is in my hands. Eiii!
The spear strikes and bends in the wound!
Enemy head, I'll display you in every village.

(Meeting of the Congolese Cabinet.)

LUMUMBA: Gentlemen, I've got big news for you. Our troops have taken Bakwanga. The traitor Kalonji has fled.

KALA: A victory, unfortunately, that may cost us more than a defeat.

FIRST MINISTER: I see what you mean, and I share your sentiments. We've got to admit that our army has had a heavy hand. Six thousand Balubas killed. In the church of Saint-Jean of Bakwanga forty Baluba families massacred with the most atrocious cruelty.

SECOND MINISTER: I demand that the army be recalled.

THIRD MINISTER: Our army has dishonored us in the eyes of the world.

LUMUMBA: Poor Balubas! Massacred by our soldiers in Kasai! Exterminated by Tzumbi's police in Katanga! They've been called the Jews of Africa. But a military campaign is never a battle of flowers.

KALA: We're in a pretty mess all the same. The world press is up in arms against us. Especially the Belgian papers. And Hammarskjöld is raising hell in the UN. He accuses us of genocide.

LUMUMBA: He does, does he? And where was Hammarskjöld when the Belgians were massacring our men and raping our women?
    And now we're the savages!
    So the Belgians are complaining? That's a good one. And who stirred up the Luluas against the Balubas?

Who made the Balubas think the Luluas were getting ready to murder them? Who invented chief Kalamba Mangole and started him plugging for a Lulua kingdom that would drive out the Balubas unless they submitted to the laws and customs of the Luluas? Who persuaded the Balubas and Luluas that they couldn't coexist anymore? In 1959. You remember? And what did the Belgian police do while they were cutting each other's throats? They looked on and smiled. And where was Lumumba then? In prison. And what about the Christian, civilized world press? What did it have to say then? And the world conscience? No! Do they think I'm going to let the Congo be torn limb from limb for fear of their hypocritical protests? Gentlemen, I reject your authority. *(He laughs.)* I reject your law, your morality, your whole system! Yes, my friends, let us celebrate. I want every Congolese citizen to drink a glass of beer to the capture of Bakwanga.

Tonight I'm going to make a speech on the radio to celebrate the taking of Bakwanga. Mpolo, we'll go to the Elite Bar tonight. No, to Cassian's. I know a Lulua girl. She's beautiful. Her name is Hélène Jewel. And she certainly is a jewel. Get in touch with her. I'm going to dance with her tonight. With a Lulua girl. In the eyes of the whole world.

And you, gentlemen of the press and pulpit, champions of the world conscience, I expect you to light up the dance floor with your grimaces.

SCENE 6

(Cassian's Bar. Lumumba and Hélène Jewel, dancing in a pink and green half-light.)

HÉLÈNE:
I dance things of cavernous darkness
blood's fire, keen snakes
caught in the brambles of exile.

LUMUMBA:
I dance the sprouting of man and his saliva, salt.
And alone in the depths of his aloneness man
sickens at
the taste of his flesh, insipid cassava.

HÉLÈNE:
I dance the pavonia flower that wheels around the
sun, when
every flick of the planet's lashes brightens the
smooth purple
of the living blood.

LUMUMBA:
I dance the high vessel that with its blazoned
prow governs
the panic of Desire; the pavonia bird and its
pavan.

HÉLÈNE:
I dance the joy, sown by the sun, of the
incongruous small
rain planting its dispersed copper laughter in the
briny flesh
of the sea.

LUMUMBA:
I dance the insect, more beautiful than any name,

which in the
core of the ripe fruit established its glutted
    weariness, gold and
jade and obsidian.

HÉLÈNE:

And now our dance is danced, the refrain closes its
    corolla as,
proud to have sustained the unsustainable, ablaze
    and slaked with
fire, the pavonia flower closes.

LUMUMBA:

We have danced the dance of my life! When I am
    gone, when I
am spent like the blinding blind meteor in the
    night sky,
when the Congo is no more than a season
    seasoned with blood,
be beautiful, still beautiful, keeping
of the terrible days no more
than the few drops of dew that make
the hummingbird's plumes more beautiful
for having traversed the storm.
No sadness, darling. Dance with me till dawn
and give me heart
to go on to the end of the night.

Scene 7

(A room in the President's palace. Kala is alone.)

KALA: All I hear about is blood. Blood and horror. The Luluas killing the Balubas. The Balubas exterminating the Luluas. And our army, the National Army of the Congo, massacring everybody in sight.

Oh, this war! this war!

Yes, yes, I gave my consent. But do you think it's easy to say no to that goateed devil? Anyway, it was his decision. Let him take the consequences.

He's too highhanded.

That incident with the UN soldiers, for instance. Bunche wants to see him about it, Lumumba refers him to some undersecretary. Naturally—what would you expect—Bunche ends up in my office. What could I say? Nobody tells me anything, I said. And it's true. He doesn't tell me anything...What does he take me for? A figurehead? To tell the truth, he's a strange man. I'll never get used to him. Sometimes he's so sensitive, so full of fine feeling. I remember what he said to me before leaving for New York. "President, I leave you my heart."

"I leave you my heart." There was real friendship in those words. They came from the heart...Ah, what a man!

Maybe that's what I hold against him most, his impulsiveness. Always so agitated, so excited. A ball of fire! A hammerbird, always looking for somebody to ram his head into.

Our ancestors were right, a real chief doesn't get excited. He doesn't run around in circles. He is immobile and enduring. He concentrates. He is the concentrated essence of the country. And by concentrating, he emanates a gentle persuasive light... This fellow's a hothead. He doesn't emanate, he just sets everything on fire. He's a *Kintu-Kintu!* He'd turn the whole country upside down if I let him. But I am here and I won't let him. I'm here to save the Congo and to save him from himself. Easy does it, Patrice. Go easy. Old Kala's here. He's here all right. And here to stay. They call me the old man. I'm not old. I'm slow. They say the tortoise is full of guile. Full of good sense would be more like it. I make my way slowly; slowly, *Kukutu Bvem, Kukutu Bvem.** And he's impetuous, a hothead.

I don't like hotheads even when they're right. They make me dizzy. And besides, sooner or later, they wear themselves out...But that's enough daydreaming. I've got to write this speech.

Actually I don't see why they all hound him so. But whom don't they hound? Ah, it's a bad world nowadays. They say Patrice leads me by the nose. They say i betrayed the Bakongo by accepting the presidency. They even dare to write: "Kala is Lumumba's woman." "Kala is Lumumba's wife."

That's stupid. A president is the chief. He's the king. Besides, I can dismiss him whenever I please. The constitution says so. The president makes the decisions, the ministers carry them out. Of course I don't mean to make use of my power. Patrice is intelligent, energetic, popular. Oh yes, he's popular all right. They can slander him all they like, they can't stop him from being popular. And there's strength in popularity.

And I've got to take it into consideration...But why in God's name are they all out to get him? Look what they've thought up now: Patrice is a communist. And by protecting him, I'm giving aid and comfort to the Communist International.

That's nonsense. Patrice a communist! I remember the look on his face that time, in the midst of our worst trouble with the Belgians, when I suggested a telegram to Khrushchev. Do you know what he said? "It's impossible, Mr. President. They're already saying that

---

*Onomatopoeia for the slow, deliberate movement of a turtle.

I've sold out to the communists. That would clinch it. You're a Christian, you can do it if you want to. And even so, they'll say I maneuvered you."

Hm...Maneuvered me? That would take quite a man. Quite a man. But it's true. He is quite a man. The American ambassador said to me last week: "If Lumumba went into a meeting of Congolese politicians with a tray, disguised as a waiter, he'd be prime minister by the time he left." But do they think it's so easy to fool old Kala...Do they really?...I'd better consult Bishop Malula. He's got a head on his shoulders...And I'll ask Mokutu to go with me...*(He laughs.)* I could have been a bishop myself...Why... we were at the seminary together...As a bishop I'd have had fewer worries, that's sure...But no man chooses his fate...Oh Lord, oh Lord. Oh, this presidency!...Well, how about it? Am I going to write that speech? Come along, Kala. Make a little effort. *(He starts to work.)*

(The Sanza Player enters, singing:)

Thoughts come in sudden flashes
I see the croaking frog
The chameleon on his branch
Waiting with darting tongue.

Scene 8

(Lumumba's apartment. Lumumba and his wife, Pauline.)

PAULINE: Patrice, I'm afraid. Oh God! I can feel the knives of hatred in the darkness, and everywhere I see termites, toads, spiders, the crawling vermin of envy. Patrice, I can see their filthy plots tightening around you...

LUMUMBA: What is there to be afraid of? It's true I have enemies...but the people are for me. The people are my shield. I speak to them and they understand me, they follow me. This is a revolution, Pauline, and in a revolution it's the people that count.

PAULINE: The people, yes. But the people are weak and disarmed. They're credulous. And your enemies are sly and patient, and they've got the whole world behind them.

LUMUMBA: Don't exaggerate...I have friends, too... faithful friends. We stick together...We're like a dog's hair, all in the same bed.

PAULINE: Friends, friends!...I can think of a dozen of them who owe you everything. They dance attendance, but they're only waiting for the chance to knife you. Some of them would sell you for a mess of pottage. I feel it in my bones.

LUMUMBA: Oh, you women. So cynical. Always fearing the worst.

PAULINE: And you men? And you yourself? So innocent and so trusting. You're a child, Patrice...For instance, I don't trust your Mokuto...I don't have to tell you that he was an informer for the Belgians...

LUMUMBA: I know, I know that, Pauline...But I also know what the situation was in those days. A lot of people had no other choice than to starve and let their children starve or to play the stoolpigeon. It's not pretty, no, it's not pretty. But some of the people who disgraced themselves in those days can be saved...And Mokutu is one of them...He's intelligent, shrewd... not much character, but he's grateful to me for my confidence in him...My confidence helps him to redeem himself in his own eyes...I can swear for his loyalty.

PAULINE: God protect you, Patrice. God protect you.

LUMUMBA: And besides, what can he do to me?...Stop worrying...They can't hurt me as long as Kala and I stick together, and we always will.

PAULINE: Are you so sure, Patrice? I have an idea that he's jealous of you...

PATRICE: I repeat: never have two men seen more eye to eye than Kala and I...He has his faults, but he's a patriot...He's the chief of a powerful tribe, an excellent tribe, the Bakongo! And remember the proverb: Look at the cock's beak and you'll see the whole cock.

PAULINE: All the same. So many people are trying to make trouble between you...He's secretive...sly... You just be careful. Sitting on his throne as rigid and serene as a copper god, all he seems to think of right now is holding his scepter up. But when the time comes, he's perfectly capable, if you ask me, of bringing it down on your head—without a word of warning.

LUMUMBA: And you think I'm so easy to crush? You

think I have no weapons, no friends...But we've talked enough, Pauline...I'm tired, give me my guitar. *(She gives him the guitar.)* I don't know why...I've got this sad tune running through my head...It's a Swahili song. Ever heard it, Pauline?

(The lights are slowly dimmed as he sings.)

Would you lean
Even your finger
On a rotting tree?
Life is a rotting tree.
Don't lean, don't lean
Even a finger
On the rotting tree.

LUMUMBA: *(yawning)* Ah! Dependa wears you out! *(He dozes off, then wakes with a start.)* What's this?

(In his nightmare a Bishop, Kala, and Mokutu appear stage front. Kala and Mokutu are kneeling.)

BISHOP: My children, the time has come to prove your love for the Church and to chastise the enemies of our holy religion. The Church is relying on you. In the name of the Father, the Son, and the Holy Ghost, amen.

PAULINE: Poor Patrice. Wake up. It's almost time for the news. *(She turns the radio dial, a speech by Kala Lubu is heard.)*

KALA: My dear compatriots, I have an important announcement to make: The Mayor, I beg your pardon, the Prime Minister, I mean, who was appointed by the King of Belgium in accordance with the provisional constitution, has betrayed his trust. He has taken arbitrary measures which have provoked dissension among the government and the people. He has deprived many citizens of their basic liberties. He has plunged the country into an abominable civil war. In view of all this, I have esteemed it necessary to dissolve the government. I have appointed Joseph Ileo Prime Minister and empowered him to form a new government. I have already assured myself of the total and wholehearted support of our glorious Congolese army and of its commander, Colonel Mokutu. I hope and trust that I can also count on the discipline and patriotism of the entire Congolese people. God protect the Congo!

SCENE 9

(Lumumba's office that same evening. Enter Mpolo in haste, a moment later Lumumba.)

LUMUMBA: The bastard. But he hasn't heard the last of Patrice Lumumba. President of the Republic! Who made him President of the Republic?

But maybe it's all for the best, Mpolo. The Congo of the provisional constitution, the two-headed monster born of the fornications at the Round Table, was a compromise. I accepted it only as a temporary evil. And now King Kala, on his own initiative, has shown that the time for compromise has passed.

So much the better. The time has come to get rid of King Kala. Notify the radio station. I am going to address the nation.

MPOLO: You're right. It's time for us to strike. But what about the UN? Will they be neutral?

LUMUMBA: The UN? The UN is a fiction. What exists, regardless of the color of their helmets, is men, soldiers from all over Africa. And luckily for us, the radio station is in the hands of the Ghanaians. A soldier of Nkrumah isn't going to refuse aid and comfort to Lumumba. Send for Ghana!

Scene 10

(The Radio Building.)

Lumumba: I'm glad to see you, Colonel. Ghana is a great country, dear to the hearts of all true Africans. I for my part shall never forget that it was in Ghana—thanks to Nkrumah—that the African first threw off the chains of colonialism and stood up a free man.

Ghana: Independence is one thing, disorder is another. And that is what I see in the Congo.

Lumumba: We shall overcome it, Colonel, and you will help us. I trust that Mpolo has given you my message. The people are in need of explanations and directives. I will speak on the radio tonight.

Ghana: So I have heard, Mr. Lumumba. Unfortunately, Monsieur Cordelier, the United Nations delegate in Leopoldville, has given strict orders: all political activity in the Congo is suspended until further notice, and no member of any political faction is to be given access to the radio.

Lumumba: So now Cordelier is giving orders in the Congo! But let it pass...In any case, his orders don't apply to me. I shall address the country not as President of the National Congo Movement but as Prime Minister.

Ghana: Mr. Lumumba, we have a proverb in our country: "The state is an egg. Squeeze it too tight and it will break; not tight enough, and it will fall and smash." I don't know whether you have squeezed too tight or not tight enough, but the fact is that there is no longer a Congolese state.

LUMUMBA: Am I to understand that you, on your own responsibility, deny me the use of my country's radio?

GHANA: I am only a soldier, sir. I carry out orders.

LUMUMBA: Oh, oh! Perhaps you didn't realize, colonel, that your president is my friend? That Ghana, more than an ally, is our brother country? That the government in Accra has promised me its total and unconditional support? Your cowardice and insolence leaves me aghast. And I warn you that I shall not fail to inform your president, my friend, Kwame Nkrumah.

GHANA: Sir, here in the Congo I am not in the service of Ghana, but of the United Nations. I am a soldier, sir, not a politician. As for my relations with Nkrumah, the two of us will straighten that out when the time comes, without your help. You have enough to do in the Congo.

LUMUMBA: I understand. You call yourself a soldier. No, I'll tell you what you are. You're just one more traitor.
   Nkrumah wrote me: "Brother, you must keep as cool as a cucumber." He's right. Treason is worse than toad venom, worse than the scaly pangolin coiled around its branch. To keep calm in the presence of an African traitor I'd need to have water in my veins like a Ghanaian cucumber, not Congolese blood.

GHANA: (drawing his revolver) Everybody knows that a man who sets foot in this lousy country has to be prepared for anything. But there's one thing I'll never put up with, less in this filthy Congo than anywhere else, and that's the insolence of a half-baked communist.

LUMUMBA: Fire! Go ahead and fire! You see that I'm as

cool as a cucumber.

GHANA: *(returning his pistol to its holster)* Come to think of it, no...The Congolese will attend to it themselves.

(Exit Ghana, enter the Sanza Player and Mokutu with a detachment of paratroopers.)

SANZA PLAYER: Fellow Africans, that's the tragedy. A hunter catches sight of a crowned stork in the tree top. Luckily the tortoise has seen the hunter. The stork is saved, you will say. And indeed, the tortoise tells the big leaf, who's supposed to tell the creeper, who's supposed to tell the bird. Oh no! It's everybody for himself. Result: the hunter kills the bird, takes the big leaf to wrap the bird in, and cuts the creeper to tie up the leaf...And oh yes, I forgot. He even walks off with the tortoise. Africans, my brothers! When will you understand?

Scene 11

(Lumumba's home, occupied by Mokutu's para-troopers.)

LUMUMBA: Thank you for coming. I'm glad you recognize that I am entitled to an explanation.

MOKUTU: There's nothing to explain. Civil war, foreign war, anarchy. Patrice, I'm afraid you're a luxury the Congo can't afford.

LUMUMBA: Can you be sincere? Do you really think you're saving the Congo? Doesn't it occur to you that by wrecking our constitutional government before we've even had time to set it up, you are endangering the very life of your country?

MOKUTU: You'd have made things easier for us by stepping down of your own accord. But that's too much to expect of a politician. I have no other course than to dismiss you. But the old man is mistaken. I'm dismissing him too...I've decided to neutralize the government.

LUMUMBA: When I hear big words like that, I can't help smelling a rat. Exactly what are you driving at?

MOKUTU: It's perfectly simple. The President fires the Prime Minister. The Prime Minister strikes back and fires the President. I'm firing both of you. We're sick of politicians.

LUMUMBA: In other words, you've decided to seize power. Well, after all, you won't be the first colonel to stage a coup d'état. But watch your step, Mokutu. The day when every disocntented officer feels entitled to make a grab for power, there won't be much left of our country. A gang of thieves is no substitute for a state.

MOKUTU: Don't you dare to impugn my honesty. I am a soldier and always will be. I have appointed a committee of specialists to run the government until order is restored. Meanwhile I'm calling off the civil war. I have ordered the army to suspend operations against Kasai. There's plenty of work to do right here in Leopoldville.

LUMUMBA: Mokutu, I won't remind you of our friendship, of the struggles we've been through together, but...

MOKUTU: No, there's no point in talking about the past. Sure. I helped you to get out of prison. I was with you at the Round Table conference in Brussels. I campaigned for you day and night. Five years of friendship. But I refuse to let friendship interfere with my duty as a citizen and a Congolese patriot. This is the parting of the ways. It's my duty to neutralize you.

LUMUMBA: You're right, this is no time for personal sentiment. But have you ever stopped to think about Africa? Look here. No need of a wall map, it's engraved in the palm of my hand.

Here's Northern Rhodesia; its heart is the Copper Belt. A silent country, except for a foreman's curses now and then, the bark of a police dog, the burbling of a Colt—they've gunned down a black man, who drops without a word. Look here, next door. Southern Rhodesia. Millions of Negroes robbed, dispossessed, herded into the so-called townships.

And here's Angola. What's its main article of export? Not sugar, not coffee, but slaves. Yes, colonel, slaves. Two hundred thousand men a year sent to the mines of South Africa in exchange for good money to help replenish Papa Salazar's empty treasury.

And dangling from it like a rag, this little island, this rock, San Tomé, devouring niggers by the thousand, by the million. Africa's penal colony. *(He sings.)*

> They took our boy away,
> Sent him to San Tomé
> 'Cause he had no card,
> Aié
> He never came back 'cause death
> Took him away,
> Aié
> They sent him to San Tomé.

Funny you never heard that song. I'll teach it to you, Mokutu, if you give me time. Well, further down there's South Africa, the racist slave camp, with its tanks and planes, it Bible, its laws, its courts, its press, its hatred, its lies—its hard, cruel heart. That's our Africa, Mokutu. Prostrate, bound, trampled, a target for white men's guns. But there's hope, you'll say. They suffer, but they hope. And it's true. Because deep down in their dungeon, like a diver deep under the sea, they see a spot of light on the surface, a spot of light, growing, growing. Why shouldn't they hope? There's been Ghana, Guinea, Senegal, Mali...Dahomey, Cameroun. Not so long ago, Togoland. And now the Congo. And imprisoned Africa says to itself: "Tomorrow will be my turn. Tomorrow isn't so far off." And they clench their fists and breathe a little freer. The air of tomorrow, the good salt air of freedom.

Mokutu, do you know what you're doing? You're blacking out the little patch of light over the prisoner's cell. The great rainbow bird is wheeling over the cells of a hundred and fifty million men; at both ends of the horizon the double serpent is rearing up, bearing promise of life, a hope of life and sky. But with one stroke of your stupid club you strike it down, and the scaly coils of malignant darkness come down on the whole continent.

MOKUTU: I won't follow you in your apocalypse. I'm
not responsible for Africa but for the Congo. And in
the Congo I mean to restore order. Order, do you
understand? Order.

*(The Soldiers have come in silently and occupy the
whole stage.)*

ACT 3
SCENE 1

(Camp Hardy in Thysville. A prison cell. Mpolo, Okito, and Lumumba on narrow cots. Morning. Lumumba tossing and moaning in his sleep.)

LUMUMBA: Oh! Oh!

OKITO: He's got one of his nightmares again.

MPOLO: Poor Patrice. He's struggling like a fly caught in syrup.

LUMUMBA: *(waking up and rubbing his eyes)* There's no way out! What a dream! Big ferocious birds were attacking me from all directions, I was thrashing around like a madman trying to defend myself. It was awful.

OKITO: The proverb says: We eat with the sun, not with the moon. I don't like dreams.

LUMUMBA: I do, even when they're terrible. There's wisdom in them. We forget it too soon when we wake up.

MPOLO: I know. I know. Our ancestors! You can have them. Right now they're kind of stingy with their favors.

OKITO: Yes, they've forgotten us in the bitter savannah.

LUMUMBA: Courage, friends. The people were taken by surprise, but they're pulling themselves together now. You know the legend. We'll sacrifice Lumumba, the gods will be appeased and smile on the Congo. Sure. Things will pick up...The Belgians will disarm,

Tzumbi will return to the fold, the UN will pour in aid by the shipload, and so on. But friends, it doesn't work. Things are going from bad to worse. Waste, disorder, anarchy, corruption, humiliation. You'll see, it won't be long before they come begging us to take the reins again.

MPOLO: Unless to eliminate that possibility they decide to do away with us first. Something tells me they're not going to stop halfway. We never do in the Congo.

OKITO: The Congo, the Congo! The international bankers, you mean. They're touchy. At the slightest poke they go out of their minds. The buffalo, that's what it is, the buffalo.

MPOLO: When the buffalo shits, the whole world stinks.

LUMUMBA: All that is true; our life is at the mercy of the first killer on the payroll. Black or white, it's all the same. If he's black, a white man has sent him. Yes, they can destroy us, but they can't defeat us. It's too late. We've got the jump on them. History will leave them behind.

MPOLO: You certainly are a prophet, Patrice. You march ahead and proclaim the future. That's your strength and your weakness.

LUMUMBA: Part praise, part blame, I accept that verdict, Mpolo. Especially if it can infect you with my unshakable faith in the future.

MPOLO: Yes, part praise and part blame. Sometimes I wonder if we weren't trying to go too fast.

LUMUMBA: I regret nothing, Mpolo. Does an architect

project half a house? No, he plans the whole house at once. When the sky was black and there was no horizon in sight, wasn't it necessary to show the way with one magic stroke?

And let's not underestimate our strength. It's enormous. We've just got to know how to use it. Look, here are two letters I've just received, that escaped the vigilance of Mokutu's thugs. One's from Van Laert, the other's from Luis. Isn't it marvelous? Luis, a Spaniard! Why should he be interested in the Congo? After all, those people have their own problems. And Van Laert. A Belgian. My friend, my brother in Brussels. I bet you he's thinking of me right now, this very minute, same as I'm thinking of him. Those people are with us. They're with us because they know that the battle we're fighting isn't for ourselves, or even for Africa, but for all mankind. And Africa. Yes, I know, it's divided, it seems to be weak, but it won't fail us. Wasn't it here in Africa, from the solemn encounter of muck, sun, and water, that man was born? What is man but a certain way of dispelling the mists of life, by standing erect and holding the head high? All right, Mpolo, I'll talk to the soldiers, they're Congolese, I'll break their hearts. *(To the jailers and soldiers.)* Well, comrade jailers, how about a glass of beer? But I'm sorry, all I've got is Polar.

JAILER: Don't let that worry you, boss. Primus or Polar, it's all the same to us. We won't argue about the brand, we're too damn thirsty.

LUMUMBA: Drink, friends. And how's the country getting along?

JAILER: The country? Nothing's changed. People are beginning to wonder if Dependa isn't a swarm of grasshoppers come to ruin us.

LUMUMBA: Let's not blame Dependa for what her

enemies do. But never mind. How about the army? Have the men been paid?

JAILER: Nobody's been paid for two months.

LUMUMBA: Hmm. Maybe it's because there's no money left in the till. And what about Mokutu? And Kala? And the UN? What have they been doing?

SOLDIER: That's what I'd like to know. If the treasury's empty, where's the money? Just tell me that. You ought to know, you were a minister. But hell, you're like all the rest of them, a nigger egghead.

LUMUMBA: Take it easy, friend. Take it easy. You want to know where the money is. I'll tell you. It's in Katanga. Yes, sir, in Katanga. In Tzumbi's treasury. And I'll tell you something else. It's because I tried to get it back that I'm here!

SOLDIER: That's the truth. That's what I've been telling the boys. Some believe me, some don't. Anyway, it's a mess. You say it's the Katanga police that get the money?

LUMUMBA: Sure, the police. And Tzumbi. And Msiri. And the Belgians. But come along, men, why all these gloomy thoughts? Let's have another round.

(*The Soldiers pour themselves beer. Glasses are passed around.*)

LUMUMBA: Soldiers, I see that a lot of you are Batetelas. Glad to know it. I'm a Mutetela myself. We're the tribe that put up the last fight against the Belgians sixty years ago. We saved the honor of the whole Congo. And I'm doing my duty as a Mutetela by fighting the last battle maybe, to prevent our country from falling into the clutches of a new colonialism.

Soldiers of other tribes, I trust you no less; I know the army as a whole is loyal to me as its legitimate commander. The army had nothing to do with Mokutu's treachery. His tools were his handpicked praetorians, his paratroopers. He puts them up at the Hotel Memling and stuffs them like geese. Where does he get the money? I'll tell you. Partly from the Americans. But mostly out of the funds the UN gave him to pay you with. You fellows aren't staying at the Memling. I know the life you lead. You do all the dirty work. No hope of promotion, no pay. Your ribs stick out so the top brass and their bodyguards can roll in fat. When I appointed the first black officers, how could I imagine that quicker than lava spurts from a volcano, a new caste would be born, the caste of colonels and new masters, and that those voracious, insatiable dogs would monopolize all the benefits of Congolese freedom?

SOLDIER: To hell with Mokutu. We're letting you out. Go on home. Maybe you'll help us fill our bellies.

SECOND SOLDIER: Hurray for Lumumba! When he talks, he says something.

SOLDIERS: Down with Mokutu! Down with Mokutu!

SOLDIER: If I catch him, I'll cut his gizzard out.

LUMUMBA: I respect your opinions and I don't want to influence you. But I want you all to know that the situation is critical. Two months after independence the kid is walking into the gullet of a wild beast. If I, Lumumba, brace myself and hold on for dear life, it's to save the Congo from the claws of the beast. Will you help me?

SOLDIERS: *(shouting)* We're with you. You're our chief. Down with Mokutu!

> *(The Soldiers open the gates of the prison and carry Lumumba out in triumph.)*

SCENE 2

(African bar. Men and women. Same atmosphere as in Act I, Scene 2. A woman sings.)

WOMAN:
Who's seen my husband?
Nobody's seen him.
A bamboo splinter
Has pierced my heart.

(Suddenly the door opens. Enter Lumumba, Mpolo, and Okito.)

MAMA MAKOSI: Patrice! You here?

LUMUMBA: See for yourself.

MAMA MAKOSI: I knew they couldn't hold you.

LUMUMBA: It's a good thing to have faith. A lot of people wouldn't have given two cents for Lumumba's hide. Yes, here I am. Free. Freed by our Congolese soldiers. Go get my wife and children. This is my headquarters from now on.

MAMA MAKOSI: You're right. They betrayed you, the whole lot of them. Kala. Mokutu. Your buddy Mokutu. I never did like him. He looks like a sneaky little girl. Here you're safe, the house is yours, and the people will protect you.

LUMUMBA: You'll have to forgive me. My presence is likely to upset your routine around here.

MAMA MAKOSI: Never mind about that. Just tell us what those scoundrels did to you.

WOMEN: Yes, yes, tell us about it.

(The Sanza Player sings.)

Nut, nut
One cocoanut, just one,
Its oil is enough
To fill the bowl.

LUMUMBA: Thank you, friend. You've given me the courage and strength to defy the whole world. But what do you want me to tell you? The details? What's the good of details? I've better things to tell you. I'll tell you about Africa. Yes, Africa! The eyes, the back, the flanks! Africa is like a man who wakes up in the morning and sees that he's being attacked on all sides.
    Attacked by hawks and vultures. He hasn't hid from one before the next is on him with its dripping beak. Makes me think of our Mukongo dance of the twelve masks: we had riches, beauty, assurance, potent medicines, and then came the Spirit of Jealousy and Evil with its powerful fetishes, sullying the cheeks of our virgins, felling our warriors, bringing corruption and dissension. A hideous nightmare! In the end, thank God, the Spirit of Evil was defeated, and we brought back Prosperity. Do you hear me, all of you? We'll bring back Prosperity, and we'll keep her. Prosperity's coming back to the Congo, friends. Let's drink to her! But let's not be selfish. I'm going to pass on the good news to our foreign friends, to the whole world. Call in the gentlemen of the press.

MAN: Yes, the press. Let them come. But we want them to know that you're our king! Our legitimate king! Put on the leopard skin.

CROWD: Yes! Yes! The leopard skin!

LUMUMBA: Friends, don't make me do that. One day in the bush I met my animal soul: it had the form of a bird. My sign is a bird, that's better than a leopard. To enter the new day, the bronze wings of the ibis.

MAN: You're right. The chiefs and kings have all betrayed us. You're better than they are. You are our inspired guide, our Messiah. Glory be, Simon Kibangu is back again.

CROWD: *(singing)*
We are the orphan children.
Dark is the night, hard is the way.
Almighty God, who's going to help us?
Father Congo, who's going to give us a hand?

(The Man holds out to Lumumba a kind of stole which Lumumba waves away.)

LUMUMBA: And what do I do but give you a hand? With all my strength. Beyond my strength. But I won't wear a stole any more than a leopard skin. It may come as a disappointment to you, but I'm not Simon Kibangu. He wanted to give you back your strength, our Congo *ngolo,* and for that he deserves to be remembered. He wanted to go see God all alone, all alone, as your ambassador, to demand your rights, and for that you have every reason to glorify him. The white men confiscated God for their own benefit, and Simon Kibangu tried to win him back. But they robbed us of more than God, they robbed Africa of herself. Africa is hungry for its own being. And that's why I don't want to be a Messiah or a prophet. My only weapon is my tongue; I speak, I awaken, I'm not a redresser of wrongs. I don't perform miracles, I'm a redresser of life. I speak, I give Africa back to herself. I speak, and I give Africa to the world.

(Uncertainty in the crowd. Enter Pauline Lumumba. She and Lumumba embrace.)

PAULINE: Oh God, how happy I am! I was so worried. Those people are brutes. They're capable of anything. But here you are! Saved! But you're not safe here in Leo. We're going away. To Stanleyville. I've arranged everything. In Stanleyville the whole population's behind you.

LUMUMBA: Stanleyville? All I've been doing is fighting secession, and you want me to organize a new secession? No, I won't desert, I won't run away. And there's nothing to be afraid of here. My enemies have learned their lesson. They know the Congo can't get along without me.

PAULINE: You've always been stubborn and intractable. A regular mule. Does that man even give me a thought? Patrice, I'm talking to you. And you look up above me.

LUMUMBA: Above, below, I don't know. Both, I guess. Above I see Africa, and below, mingled with the muffled drum of my blood, the Congo.

PAULINE: Admit, Patrice, that I never turned you aside from your duty, but Africa's not your wife. You have other responsibilities besides the weal and woe of Africa. Do you remember the day we were married, Patrice? My father poured the palm wine, you took a sip, you held out the glass for me, I took a sip, and so we drank together till the glass was empty. I haven't got the name of a country or a river, I've got the name of a woman: Pauline. That's all I have to say. Except one question: Do you want the people to see me with my head shaved, following a funeral procession? And the children? Do you want them to be orphans?

LUMUMBA: It can't be helped. In my heart I've always called you Pauline Congo, and your double name has helped me doubly to control my weakness. And I'm prepared to defy the whole world if I know I can count on you. If I die, I leave the children a legacy of a great struggle. And you will help them, guide them, arm them. But let's not be pessimistic. I'm going to live through this struggle and win. Forgive me, Pauline. Go to Brazzaville, try to see Luis. Tell him what's been happening. And now I have to speak to the press.

PAULINE: *(exits slowly, singing)*
Alas, alas, who's seen my husband?
Nobody's seen my husband.
A bamboo splinter
Has pierced my heart.

(Enter the gentlemen of the press.)

LUMUMBA: Make yourselves as comfortable as you can, gentlemen. Excuse the surroundings. They don't mean a thing. No, as a matter of fact, they mean a great deal. They mean that I put my trust in the people. It's a humble place, but here at least the heart of the Congo beats in its own way, more freely than in any government palace. I've called you here to tell you, and for you to tell the world, that the Congo is taking up where it left off. I was deposed by a childish coup d'état, but now I'm back in the saddle. My government is the only legal government of the Congo. It intends to make itself respected, to restore and reinforce the unity of the Congo. We do not seek revenge. The era of hatred is ended. Now it is time to build the Republic in peace and dignity. Gentlemen, I am counting on you to inform world public opinion of our peaceful intentions. My government will do everything in its power to maintain friendly relations with all foreign countries. In return, I expect every foreign government to recognize that the Congo is an independent country and intends to preserve its full independence and sovereignty.

REPORTER: Mr. Lumumba, that sounds like a prime minister's speech of investiture. But aren't you being unrealistic? Are you aware of the present political situation? Are you aware of your own situation?

LUMUMBA: Thank you for your concern. Let me set your mind at rest. I am the Prime Minister of the Republic of the Congo. I have the support of the people, and the Parliament has given me an overwhelming vote of confidence. I therefore have every legitimate right to speak in the name of the Congo. Gentlemen of the press, it is your noble mission to inform your readers. I call upon you to do so with scrupulous honesty.

(Women rush in, in a panic.)

MAMA MAKOSI: Patrice, the paratroopers! They've surrounded the house.

MPOLO: Don't worry about them, Patrice, our boys are ready. The people are with us. Mokutu's thugs will get more than they bargained for.

LUMUMBA: No, Mpolo. There has been enough bloodshed.

MPOLO: But we can't just sit here with our hands folded.

LUMUMBA: I'm not a religious man, but I am convinced of this: that justice cannot be won by violence.

MPOLO: In this situation nonviolence is suicide.

LUMUMBA: Exactly, Mpolo. If I have to die, I want to die like Gandhi. All right, show those people in. I grant them an audience.

(Enter Kala, Mokutu, and a group of Paratroopers.)

MOKUTU: *(To the Paratroopers)* Get rid of all these people. *(To the newspapermen.)* Excuse me, gentlemen, the show is over. Now we have work to do. I'll see you again in due time. Good-bye.

(The newspapermen, girls, and customers are removed.)

KALA: *(to Lumumba)* I come to you with an offer. It may seem surprising. But not if you bear in mind that for me the welfare of my country outweighs all other considerations. I hope I find you in the same frame of mind.

LUMUMBA: I have never served any other interests than those of the Congo. Say your piece.

KALA: Our government cannot function without an executive.

LUMUMBA: I'm glad to hear you say that. I am the prime minister. I have not been overthrown by the Parliament. Consequently there is no government crisis. If there seems to be, it is only because certain people have acted illegally.

KALA: You don't seem to understand. No one can turn back the clock. Try to be realistic for once. Ileo is the man of the situation. He is level-headed, reassuring. The country is in flames. Let him put out the fire. Once that's done, we shall see...I'm only asking you to have a little patience. Just a little patience. The banana ripens slowly.

LUMUMBA: I hate time. I detest your *slowly*. And why do you always want to reassure people? Give me a man who upsets them, who tells them what the bad shepherds are doing to us.

KALA: I am offering you a place in the Cabinet. Choose any portfolio you wish. Vice-president, minister of state, minister of anything you like. Do you or do you not accept?

LUMUMBA: *(airily)* Say, that reminds me, how's Youlou getting along? Yes, Fulbert Youlou. I hear he's sent away to Paris for a new soutane. Pure nylon.

KALA: *(shocked)* This is no time for jokes. I expect a serious answer.

LUMUMBA: It's not a bad idea, come to think of it. Gives his wives less washing to do. But don't get hot and bothered. I'll give you your serious answer. Mr. President, I will not be your Quisling.

KALA: What's that?

LUMUMBA: I will not, by my presence, lend support to a policy that I disavow. And still less will I sponsor a government of corrupt traitors.

KALA: Do you know what I came here for? To save your life. To give you a chance to save your skin. Don't tempt fate.

LUMUMBA: Do you know what you're asking of me?

KALA: Asking? Are you so sure that you're in a position to give?

LUMUMBA: If I weren't, you wouldn't have honored me with your visit. You came here to ask me for the seal of legitimacy. Very well, in the name of the Congo, I refuse it.

MOKUTU: Mr. President, there's no use arguing. You're talking to a lunatic. Never mind. I'll take him down a peg.

KALA: You asked for it, Patrice. Good-bye. He's all yours, Mokutu.

MOKUTU: All right, Mr. Lumumba, it's your funeral, you ordered it. Soldiers. This man is your prisoner.

Scene 3

(Elisabethville, the seat of the Katanga government. The dominant characteristics of the Katangese leaders are hypocrisy and ecclesiastical unctuousness, except for Msiri, who is a savage. Zimbwé and Travélé are slightly drunk. During the whole scene whiskey and champagne are poured generously.)

Mokutu: It is not a pleasant mission that has brought me here. You have violated your agreement with the Leopoldville government which I represent. You stated your conditions. They were reasonable and we subscribed to them. We have carried out our side of the bargain. And you? Katanga has not only maintained its secession but given the whole world to understand...

Tzumbi: Come, come...An agreement. That's a big word. There has been no agreement...in the strict sense. Just friendly conversations among good friends...

Zimbwé: Tut, tut. Words. Let's not talk about words. Agreement, treaty, conversation. What difference does it make? The main thing, in my opinion, is to distinguish between the spirit and the letter. For the letter kills...

Travélé: You took the words out of my mouth. And the spirit saves. *(He laughs idiotically.)*

Tzumbi: Zimbwé and Travélé are right. The spirit of our conversations was that the elimination of Lumumba was the *sine qua non*...

Mokutu: Good Lord, man. Haven't we eliminated him?

MSIRI: Don't be childish. Do we have to spell it out for you? A single blow isn't fatal to a snake like Lumumba. Lumumba is still a menace to the Congo.

TZUMBI: Forgive our good friend Msiri, he may be uncouth but he has a heart of gold. And plenty of wisdom. It's true that we don't care much for Leopoldville. The UN, your populace, your soldiery ...Too much noise and agitation. And I don't want to be unkind, but you people in the government lead the life of Reilly...Oh well, that's none of my business. The point is we think Lumumba would be better off in Katanga.

MOKUTU: He's a troublesome prisoner. I'd be only too glad to get rid of him. But sending him to Katanga would raise certain delicate problems—both domestic and international. The people are devoted to Lumumba. And you know how world opinion feels about democratic forms, what a fetish they make of democracy.

ZIMBWÉ: Tut, tut. Democracy. That's a big word with you Leopoldville people. Well, my dear colleague, we're democrats too, here in Katanga, but in our opinion, democracy means only one thing: democracy is what serves the interests of the people. And this transfer, I am sure we all agree, will serve the interests of this country's people.

TRAVÉLÉ: *(laughing)* Just as I said. It's the spirit that saves. The spirit.

MSIRI: You spoke just now of an internal problem. There's no internal problem. The people! The people! Bah! The people obey the man with the biggest stick. If you know how to command, the rabble will crawl. That's the only question. Do you know how to command? Will you ever learn to be chiefs?

MOKUTU: All right, all right, Msiri, don't get excited, we'll try. In any case I will submit your proposal to the government. Good-bye.

TZUMBI: Au revoir. You mean au revoir. Because this time we can call it an agreement. We are bound by an agreement. Remember that. And don't forget to tell Kala that this time we'll let Lumumba land. *(He laughs.)*

ZIMBWÉ: Land. Hee-hee. I get it.

TRAVÉLÉ: *(laughing)* It's the spirit that saves...and the letter that kills...And when I say kill, I mean kill. Your health, Mokutu!

(As the light fades, the Sanza Player passes, singing.)

Oh little sparrow hawk, oh! oh!
Oh little sparrow hawk, spread your wings.
The sun's drinking blood, oh oh!
Little sparrow hawk, little sparrow hawk,
What blood is the sun drinking?

Scene 4

(United Nations Headquarters in New York.)

HAMMARSKJÖLD: Have you heard the news? I've received a cable. They've taken Lumumba to Katanga; there's good reason to fear for his life...it's dreadful.

MATTHEW CORDELIER: Yes, in view of the customs of that delightful country, the Lumumba question seems to be settled once and for all.

HAMMARSKJÖLD: It doesn't seem to trouble you very much.

CORDELIER: Since Mr. Lumumba is not a personal friend of mine, I can only take a professional view of the matter. You will admit that it simplifies the political situation of the Congo.

HAMMARSKJÖLD: Tell the truth, Cordelier. You hated him. Why not admit it? And you people call yourselves neutrals. I should have kept my eyes open. You never stopped plotting against him.

CORDELIER: The UN is an organization, no, an organism that doesn't take kindly to the foreign body known as sentimentality.

HAMMARSKJÖLD: I have a strong case against you. You kept him out of the radio station, you prevented him from defending himself when his enemies had every opportunity to spread their insidious propaganda. On pretext of reserving the Leopoldville air field for United Nations planes, you cut him off from the outside world while Belgian planes were landing in Katanga around the clock...In short, we pinned down his arms while his enemies struck him. Nice work!

CORDELIER: Your sympathies are carrying you away. You sound like the Soviet delegate.

HAMMARSKJÖLD: The worst part of it is that Zorine is right, thanks to you. You deceived me. The whole lot of you. And to think that I lent my name to your odious acts.

CORDELIER: Mr. Secretary General, let me defend myself.

HAMMARSKJÖLD: No, you can't expect me to say what Lord Jim said to Doramin: "I take it all on myself." No, I won't be silent. I've been silent long enough. Tell me, Cordelier, what do you think of Jesus Christ?

CORDELIER: That's an odd question. I'm a Christian ...a Methodist, and you know it.

HAMMARSKJÖLD: What do I care if you're a Methodist and a Christian? Anybody can beat his breast and say "I'm a Christian"...What I'm asking you is not what Matthew Cordelier thinks of Christ—who cares?—but what side you, Matthew Cordelier, would have been on one thousand nine hundred and sixty-one years ago when in Judaea, under the Roman occupation, one of your contemporaries, a certain Jesus, was arrested and put to death. And now get out of here, you murderer of Christ!

Scene 5

(A training camp in Katanga. A white mercenary, in front of him a dummy representing a Negro. He cleans his revolver and sings.)

MERCENARY:
In the south, in the tropics,
in the desert, in the jungle,
in the marshes of the deltas

rain, mosquitoes, fever
weather-beaten skin
knight of new day
my heart swells in my heart
for liberty and justice.

(He stands up, goes into position, and fires at the dummy). Swine, baboon, savage, magician, ungrateful bastard! Nun raper. Bing! Bing! Bing! *(He fires.)* Ah, the devils! They won't die. Look at him with his big white eyes and his big red face. Bing, bing, bing! Take that! *(He fires.)* I've seen them. Even when they're dead, they keep coming at you. We had to kill them ten times. They say their magicians promise to turn our bullets into water. Bing! Bing! Bing! *(He fires, the dummy topples over.)* I don't guess that one turned into water. *(He laughs.)* But Christ, I'm wringing wet! Oof! It's hot. Christ, am I thirsty! Stinking country! *(He wipes his forehead and pours himself a drink. He sings.)*

I had some trouble with my folks,
They didn't like my kind of jokes,
The fights, the debts, the broads, the junk,
I wasn't cut out for a monk.
My girl was cute, my girl had curves,
But she was getting on my nerves.
I hugged her tight, I packed my trunk,
And lit out for the Congo.

(It grows dark. When the light goes on again, the white mercenary is still holding his smoking revolver, but on the ground the dummy has been replaced by two corpses, Okito and Mpolo. Enter Msiri and a mercenary, pushing Lumumba. Suddenly Msiri flings himself on Lumumba and strikes him in the face.)

MSIRI: D'you see the way your buddies spat out the bullets? Ha ha ha. Well, that leaves just you and me. *(The Mercenary tries to interfere. Msiri snatches his bayonet.)* No, I've got a personal account to settle with our friend here. *(To Lumumba.)* I'm told you think you're invulnerable. Is that a fact? Will you answer when you're spoken to?

LUMUMBA: It's Msiri all right. I was expecting this meeting. It had to be. We are the two opposing forces. You're the invention of the past. And I an inventor of the future.

MSIRI: They tell me you Kasai people have powerful magic. Ocelot skin or some such thing. This is the time to show what it's worth.

LUMUMBA: My magic is an invulnerable idea. As invincible as a people's hope, as the fire that spreads from bush to bush, as the pollen in the wind, as a root in the blind earth.

MSIRI: *(prodding him with the bayonet)* How about this? Or this? I suppose you don't feel it? Cutting into your hide...cutting, cutting...closer and closer to the heart!

LUMUMBA: Careful. My heart has a hard pit, a flint that will break your blade. It's the honor of Africa.

MSIRI: *(sneering)* Africa! Africa doesn't give a hoot in hell. Africa can't do a thing for you. Msiri is right here. And Msiri is man enough to drink your blood and eat your heart.

LUMUMBA: All night I heard wailing and laughing, sighing and scolding...that was the hyena!

MSIRI: You arrogant son-of-a-bitch! Can't you see death looking you in the eye? You're living your death and you don't even notice it.

LUMUMBA: I'm dying my life, and that's good enough for me.

MSIRI: Look! *(He thrusts in the blade.)* All right, prophet, what do you see now?

LUMUMBA:
   I will be field, I will be pasture,
   I will be with the Wagenia fisherman
   I will be with the Kivu drover
   I will be on the mountain, I will be in the ravine.

MSIRI: Let's get this over with. *(He presses the bayonet.)*

LUMUMBA: Oh, the dew over Africa. Comrades, I see the flaming tree, I see Pygmies with axes busy around the precarious trunk, but the head grows, the head grows, and it calls out to the tumbling sky in the first foam of dawn.

MSIRI: Bastard! *(Lumumba falls.) (To the Mercenary.)* Dog, finish him off.

   (A shot. The mercenary gives Lumumba the coup de grâce. Darkness. When the light goes on, a group of

statuelike figures is seen in the background: the Bankers, Kala, Tzumbi, Mokutu. Slightly to one side, Hammarskjöld. Pauline Lumumba enters.)

PAULINE:
A cage, four clouds. Lycaon, Lycaon
    of the flashing eyes!
The alphabet of fear
Mumbled as the buzzards fly overhead.
Close to the ground treason nibbles its shadow.
Higher, a hovering batlike flight of premonitions.
Below, on the black-white that torpor
Pours unceasingly, shipwreck
Repeats with gentle beckonings its invitation
To the most beautiful marriage of disaster and the
    stars.

(Giggling slightly, the Sanza Player steps forward, dressed like a Congolese sorcerer; straw skirt, bells on his wrists and ankles. He crosses the stage chanting.)

SANZA PLAYER:
Hey you, the great god Nzambi,
What a big fool you are!
You eat our ribs, you eat our asses,
Hey, Nzambi, what a big fool you are!
You eat our hearts and livers!
Hey, Nzambi. You eat too much.

(About to leave the stage, he turns back, faces the audience and twirls his mpiya, *a bundle of cock plumes, an instrument of divination.)*

Sing, women! Men, give me song!
In the sand of falsehood I scratch.
Spur, I scratch! Down to the truth I scratch.
        Scratching spur!

I am the *nganga,*
        The cock of divination.

HAMMARSKJÖLD: Congo!
   Through the matrix of original sin
   The logic of things past penetrates
   To the black hearth of our selves,
   The terrible inner fire that gives forth evil.
   Oh, that the just should become unjust;
   That sincerity should become a machine to crush
      sincerity!
   Oh God, why did they choose me
   To preside over their diabolical alchemy!
   But Thy will be done! Thy will, not mine.
   I await the order. I hear the order.
   It's only the first step that's hard.

   (He takes a step.)

It's only the first step that counts.

   (He goes out.)

A BANKER: For my part, I see no ground for political speculation. A mere episode of folklore, as it were, an outcropping of that Bantu mentality which periodically, even in the best of them, bursts through the frail varnish of civilization.

   In any case, and this is my main point, you've seen for yourselves that we had nothing to do with it. Nothing whatever. *(He goes out with great dignity.)*

TZUMBI: *(stepping forward)* You'll see. You'll see. I'll be blamed for the whole business. I tell you in all sincerity: this crime is part of a plot against my person. *(He goes out.)*

KALA: See for yourself: nobody obeys me in the Congo.

I told them to prune the tree, not to pull it up by the roots. *(He goes out.)*

MOKUTU: I had no personal animosity toward him. Everyone knew that, that's why the politicians of this country were so careful not to inform me of the plot against him. Oh yes, I know. I found it necessary to put a temporary stop to his career, to neutralize him, as I put it. And that will be held against me. But God himself has an eraser on his pencil. I fully expected that what political expediency had made me do, political expediency would make me undo. But crime foiled my plans.

(Darkness, then light. A sign indicates: July, 1966. A public square in Kinshasa, Independence Day.)

WOMAN: Hurrah for Mokutu. Mokutu uhuru!

MAMA MAKOSI: Uhuru Lumumba!

WOMAN: Careful, citizen. Uhuru Mokutu is what you've got to say.

MAMA MAKOSI: I say what I think. Uhuru Lumumba.

THE WOMAN: In any case, down with colonialism! Boo! Boo! Here come the coffins!

MAMA MAKOSI: The coffins? What coffins?

SANZA PLAYER: Death butts into everything in the Congo!

WOMAN: Why not? Death is life. The first coffin is for the Belgian Congo; the second is for daddy's Congo; the third is for tribal conflict. It's wonderful! Hurrah for Mokutu!

A Voice: Hush! Hush. The General is going to speak!

A Voice: Shut up. We want to listen.

Mokutu: *(in a leopard skin, haranguing the crowd)*
Patrice, martyr, athlete, hero—I turn to you for the
strength to carry on my task. *(Sensation. Mokutu
pauses for a moment with head bowed.)*

Congolese,
It is my wish that from this day on
The finest of our boulevards should bear his name;
That the place where he was struck down become
   the shrine of our nation;
and that a statue erected at the gate of what was
   formerly Leopoldville
signify to the world
that the piety, of a nation will never cease
to make reparation for our crime,
the crime of which we are all guilty.
Congolese, may this day be the beginning of a new
   era for the Congo!

*(As the curtain slowly falls, the Sanza Player steps
forward and sings:)*

The sorgho grows
The bird rises from the ground
Why shouldn't man
Have a right to change?

If a man is hungry
Do you deny him food?
So why say no to a country
That's thirsting for hope.

But just a minute! Let's not go off half-cocked.
A beginning is only a beginning
And if we're going to do this thing
Let's not do it by halves.

If you're going to grow
Then grow straight
And if you're going to rise from the ground
Then you must learn to soar.

Everyone's got a nose.
It grows, it shows, it blows.
Now that you're standing on feet of your own
Getting stronger and fatter
You'd better keep it clean.
This is the end of my chatter.

Jean-Pol Fargeau

BURN
RIVER
BURN

Translated from the French by
Jill Mac Dougall

Rouge pour le plaisir,
Vert pour guérir.

For

Sony Labou Tansi, Salif Keïta, Titine, Sike, Issa de
Douala, Laïssa-Ann, Solo, Jacqueline Lemoine,
Sawa-Joy, Bass, Lina, Issa de Dakar, Rita, Annie,
François, Elie, Lottin, Alex, Jacques, Jacob
Yakouba, Tom, Bokar, Raymond, Alain, Roger,
Aïcha, Claude Njike, Dick Tiger, Oumar, Thérèse,
Emmanuel de Banyo, Ina Césaire, Gilbert, Bassek,
Norbert, Moussa, Seidou, Nsame, Naomi, Jean-
Vasty, Mamadou Djoume, Lucas, John Bocovo,
Francisco, Maurice, Ngobo, Philippe Laburthe-
Tolra, and Claire, Isaach de Bankolé, and to the
memory of Zanzibar.

This English translation of **Burn River Burn** was given its first public reading at Ubu Repertory Theater as part of Ubu's International Festival "Homage to the Revolution" on April 22, 1989, with the following cast:

Doctor Winslow	**John Braden**
Doctor Barrere	**Michael Littman**
An albino	**Ron Gold**
Totensarg	**Rusty Laushman**
Pourthalès	**Ron Gold**
Tifauge	**Robert Blumenfeld**
Isaac	**Ron Brice**
Blanche	**Ellen Liberty**
Captain	**Michael Littman**
Broker	**Rusty Laushman**
Babe	**Steve Koherr**
Aloïse	**Ellen Liberty**
Poppée	**Joy Hooks**
Saltine	**Ron Gold**
Domingue	**Lee Dobson**
Aline	**Roberta Hairston**
Jean	**Spencer Barros**
Ben	**Vince Lacey**
Chamousset	**John Braden**
Pioche	**Ron Gold**
Keith	**James Fisk**
Loulouze	**Renée Flemmings**
Nanni	**Roberta Hairston**
Athénaïs	**Jay Hooks**
Waguanu	**Vince Lacey**
Desrosiers	**James Fisk**
Égalité	**Lee Dobson**

Directed by **Achim Nowak**

JEAN-POL FARGEAU was born in Marseilles in 1950. From 1974 to 1980, he was actively involved, both as playwright and actor, with Dépense, a group he co-founded with the composer Philippe Gorge and the director Alain Fourneau. He wrote four plays for the group: *Sur l'ascension des hautes montagnes, Une Cocaine allemande, Chansons dans la nuit,* and *L'Affaire Crusoe.* His next play, *L'Hotel de l'homme sauvage,* was given a staged reading at the Jardin d'hiver in Paris in 1982 and produced in 1985 at the Théâtre National de Chaillot under the direction of Stuart Seide. Another play, *Voyager,* was produced the same year at the Théâtre des Saints Anges in Marseilles under the direction of Alain Fourneau. In 1985 and 1986, Fargeau traveled to Cameroon and co-wrote the screenplay of *Chocolat* with Claire Denis, the director of the film. *Chocolat* was France's official selection at the 1988 Cannes Festival and opened to excellent reviews in Europe and the United States. In 1987 Robert Gironès directed Fargeau's *Ici-Bas* in the old slaughterhouses in Poitiers, and a year later Fargeau's *Goethe-Wilheim Meister* was premiered in Marseilles, at the Théâtre du Gymnase. *Brûle, Rivière, Brûle (Burn River Burn)* was written in 1988, thanks to a research grant from the French Ministry of Foreign Affairs that allowed Fargeau to travel to Cameroon, Senegal, Guiana, and the Caribbean. The play was cast in Africa and Martinique the following year, during a trip he made with the director Gironès that also included readings, workshops, and meetings with African artists to discuss slavery and the French Revolution. Jill Mac Dougall's English translation of the play was given a staged reading in the spring of 1989 as part of Ubu Repertory Theater's 1989 festival "Homage to the Revolution," an official program of the American Commemoration of the Bicentennial of the French Revolution. The play was premiered at the 1989 Avignon Festival and subsequently toured France. Most recently, Fargeau wrote the screenplay for Claire Denis' film *S'en fout la mort,* starring Jean-Claude Brialy and Isaac de Bankolé, and a new play, *Beaucoup love,* which will be produced in 1991-92 under the direction of Alain Milianti. Fargeau's plays are published in France by Les Editions Théâtrales and Actes-Sud/Papiers.

JILL MAC DOUGALL was directly involved in theater research and production in France, Zaire, the Ivory Coast, and Quebec for over twenty years. Since 1979, she has been translating works of French-speaking writers such as Marc Sauvageon, Anne Legault, and Lise Vaillancourt. Her translations of Diur N'Tumb's *Lost Voices* and Bernard Zadi Zaourou's *The Eye* are included in Ubu Repertory Theater's anthology *Afrique,* and her translations of Abla Farhoud's *The Girls from the Five and Ten* and Fatima Gallaire-Bourega's *You Have Come Back* were published in Ubu's anthology *Plays by Women.* Mac Dougall is also a scholar and critic who specializes in cross-cultural performance.

CHARACTERS

DOCTOR WINSLOW, *60*
DOCTOR BARRERE, *50*
AN ALBINO, *around 30*
TOTENSARG, *Pourthalès' associate, 40*
POURTHALES, *a prosperous merchant, 55*
TIFAUGE, *a plantation owner, 35*
ISAAC, *a black servant, 25*
BLANCHE, *Pourthalès' wife, 25*
CAPTAIN, *of a slave ship, 45*
BROKER, *40*
BABE, *Tifauge's son, 10*
ALOISE, *Tifauge's wife, 30*
POPPEE, *a rich Creole[1] woman, 40*
SALTINE, *an idle white man, 35*
DOMINGUE, *black overseer of the Tifauge
    plantation, 40*
ALINE, *a slave, 16*
JEAN, *a slave, 20*
BEN, *a young slave, 10*
CHAMOUSSET, *physician of the plantation, 55*
PIOCHE, *steward of the plantation, 25*
KEITH, *a subject of the British crown, employed
    in a sugar company, 35*
LOULOUZE, *a servant in the Big House, 25*
NANNI, *Babe's nurse, 65*
ATHENAIS, *a field slave, 30*
WAGUANU, *leader of the maroons,[2] 25*
DESROSIERS, *commissioner of the new
    French Republic, 30*
ÉGALITÉ, *a black Jacobin, 30*
REPUBLICAN SOLDIERS

1794

(An eighteenth-century laboratory with retorts, jars, stuffed animals, bones, forceps, and scalpels. On the dissecting table lies the cadaver of a black man. Two physicians wearing wigs bustle around the table. An albino is seen in a cage.)

DOCTOR WINSLOW: In a white man afflicted with jaundice, bile, as it spreads through the body, will color the skin yellow and apparently, if the bile were black, it would color the skin black. But as soon as the discharge stops, the epidermis takes on its natural white color. We must thus assume that bile flows perpetually in Negroes.

DOCTOR BARRERE: It is a proven fact that Negroes are only to be found in climates that bring together conditions producing excessive and relentless heat. This heat is so conducive to not only the reproduction but the conservation of Negroes found in our islands, where the heat is strong but nothing compared to Senegal, that their new-born, susceptible to the island air, must be kept in a closed, heated room for the first nine days. If this precaution is not respected and they are exposed to the air at birth, they are seized with convulsions of the jaw, and unable to feed, they expire.

DOCTOR WINSLOW: It is thus the excessive heat of these parts of the globe that produces this color, more precisely this tint that penetrates the Negro body, because their blood is blacker than that of white men. The stifling heat is unknown in mountainous regions; it does not exist in more elevated parts of the globe, which explains why, even beneath the Equator, the inhabitants of Peru, or the inhabitants of the African interior, are not black.

DOCTOR BARRERE: Everything we've discussed here concerning the origins of the Negro's color appears irrefutable. But here is a living aberration that defies the rules. This white Negro is the offspring of father and mother who were brought from the African Gold Coast and who were extremely black. The subject was born on the Dominican Island, which proves that albinos are to be found at not only ten degrees from the Equator but up to sixteen or perhaps twenty degrees north, as they are said to exist in Santo Domingo and Cuba.

DOCTOR WINSLOW: Can he talk?

DOCTOR BARRERE: Like a book. Speak, animal, say whatever comes to mind.

ALBINO: Me good. Me no eat people. Me baptise'. Me pray to God. Me....

DOCTOR BARRERE: Perfect. That's enough.

DOCTOR WINSLOW: What an extraordinary specimen!

DOCTOR BARRERE: Some travelers claim that Negro females carry their young on their backs while they work and it is for this reason that Negroes have big bellies and flat noses. The mother, bending and rising, bumps the nose with her back and the child, in an effort to avoid the shocks, pushes his stomach forward and leans back as far as possible. They all have black, wooly hair, and this quality differentiates them from other humans, because their features are not, in fact, any farther from those of Europeans than the Tartar face might be from the French face. I would say that most Negroes are snub-nosed because their parents flatten their noses and also press their lips so that they will become thicker. Those who have not been subjected to such practices have noses as pronounced, lips as thin, features as fine as the European. However, this is only true of the Senegalese specimen, who is the most attractive and well-built of all Negroes.

ALBINO: *Yé pété toute mô dents, pou empêché mô mangé kane, mê y gain longtemps dîló pa kâ coulé di mô zié.*[3] [They broke all my teeth so I couldn't eat sugar cane, but my tears dried up long ago.]

(Bordeaux. The mansion of Pourthalès, a wealthy merchant.)

TOTENSARG: Our last expedition in Mozambica proved a total fiasco. Out of five hundred Negroes, only two hundred were brought to port alive and in marketable condition. Of the survivors, only one hundred and ten are truly select, India-quality specimens. In the future, it might be wiser to operate on the Angolan coast, where the merchandise is more expensive but less fragile. I must add that our people are experiencing great difficulties in trading such a miserable lot.

POURTHALÈS: Totensarg, have you got the inventory of our "Bordeaux City" cargo?

TOTENSARG: Yes, here: three hundred fourteen casks of sugar, one hundred and two bales of cotton, three hundred sixty-seven barrels plus ten sacks of coffee.... Mere trifles! And, I forgot, only one container of indigo.

POURTHALÈS: Gentlemen, we are on the brink of ruin.

(The servant Isaac enters.)

All this paperwork is making me thirsty.

TIFAUGE: Getting back to our business, is that your final word?

POURTHALÈS: Impossible, Tifauge, I cannot lend you a cent. Creditors, money lenders, stockholders are constantly harassing me. And your debt is considerable.

TIFAUGE: So you're throwing me to the dogs?

POURTHALÈS: Is it my fault that you waste your fortune in Paris? Cut off relationships with that radical

Massiac group, those seditious scoundrels who are bringing our colonies to bankruptcy; their opposition to the Assembly's policies is leading to insurrection. Obey the law, you gentlemen planters; learn to compromise with the mulattos and you'll see, your Negroes will return to the job and our money to the bank.

TOTENSARG: There are strange rumors running about. The last I heard was that savage hordes were ransacking plantations and burning crops. There is plundering, and sometimes killing, blind execution. At the other end, Marquis, your friends are plotting, beating the country, raising armies. That they fire on revolting slaves is one thing, but that they fire on regular troops ...! To top it all, they are molesting compatriots who are allied with colored people.

TIFAUGE: Should I, to please you, sell my sister to one of these bastards?

POURTHALÈS: Who's talking of sleeping with them? Trading, dear citizen, merely trading.

TOTENSARG: *Lieber, lieber* Pourthalès. Your words are like honey. I have only one master on this earth and I am prepared to sell my soul to the devil if it would increase my profits.

TIFAUGE: This is garbage.

POURTHALÈS: Do you hear this, Totensarg? This ungrateful soul?

TOTENSARG: Hee-hee!

TIFAUGE: Today you're strutting about like peacocks, but wait a bit. Tomorrow your *sans-culottes*[4] will rebel, throwing aside their own accomplices, scavengers like you who profit from the confusion, who move in the shadows, who feed off the Revolution.

TOTENSARG: I have here in my pocket a perfectly legitimate certificate of honest citizenry.

TIFAUGE: Bought from vulgar thieves and cutthroats, bought with the money you're extorting from me. Be careful. If an official committee were to investigate your schemes, they might slit your throats.

POURTHALÈS: I have been seen on the Champ-de-Mars, surrounded by my battalion, celebrating the Supreme Being.[5] Can you say as much? And he tries to moralize, this ex-aristocrat who knifes us in the back, who robs the state and my company, who plots against the Republic! What about this latest fraud you've conducted? What you sold as molasses was a paltry burlesque, full of filth. We had to melt the sugar to extract the stones that had formed. Learn, dear friend, that through your fault Signor Nogueyra of Lisbon managed to strip me of thirty percent of the profits.

TIFAUGE: You have no heart.

POURTHALÈS: Why the devil would I bother with such a cumbersome organ?

(In the bedroom.)

BLANCHE: Stay a little longer, he's working.

ISAAC: He will kill us both.

BLANCHE: Please.

ISAAC: Mistress, I am getting dressed.

BLANCHE: Lord, but you're beautiful.

ISAAC: Having lost one's head, as you have, you can
fall in love with anything. *(He picks up a book.) Topo
kalati, topo! O si mapula. Bobē! Ma songa mongo ma
kaki eyem'a ngo ndē o ja mbukē ke senge o eyang. O
sine mba mulema! O tondi nde bukate ewus'a bakala!*[6]
[Speak, book, speak! You won't. Evil! Your teeth lock
in the tongue and you remain silent as a rock in the
field. You break my heart! You only like the magic of
the white people!]

BLANCHE: What are you saying? Don't you trust me?

ISAAC: I would like to know the formula that makes
your bibles speak. When you move your lips, they
answer you as they answered my masters, from before,
over there.

BLANCHE: Say: I love you.

ISAAC: Your hips of ivory....

BLANCHE: I will keep you, always.

(In the boudoir.)

POURTHALÈS: I have sold Isaac. He leaves on the first ship for the islands.

BLANCHE: What has he done?

POURTHALÈS: He's a Negro, that's enough. Do you love me, adorable wife?

BLANCHE: You bought me from my father.

POURTHALÈS: Are you ill? A stay in our Blaye lands would do you a world of good. You leave tomorrow.

E la nave va.

IsAAC: I am home, alone with my sister; my mother is
    digging the earth with the women and my father is
    hunting with the men. In the yard, I hear wings
    beating, as if the hyena had come to bleed the chickens.
    I call Ajali, our slave, but there is no answer. I tell
    Matubi, "Stay here." I take the stick and I go outside.
    There is no animal, only the puppy who's barking at a
    shadow. I feel hands on my mouth and a rope that
    burns my wrists. I struggle; it's a stranger; he is hitting
    me on the head. His brother is speaking my language;
    he spits in my ear, "If you scream, I will strangle you."
    These bandits drag me to the woods, far from the
    village. I cry, I beg for mercy; they laugh at me with
    insults in strange words. We walk, we walk in the
    bush. They are very clever; they avoid fires and paths,
    they listen to the bush, they smell the wind that bends
    the grasses, they know the scent of man and they flee
    from that. One day we spy warriors and they shut me
    in a bag. When I refuse to eat, they stuff food down my
    throat. I don't like them with their filed teeth and
    carved cheeks. They say they will make me beautiful
    and file my teeth too and I don't want this. I see the
    sun rising; I think of my father and my mother and
    Matubi and I want to die. Later we cross the
    mountains; we cross the forests and the savannah. We
    stop near a big river. Others speak like them; I am
    learning some of their words; their huts are made of
    straw mats. Now there are many of us; they have tied
    us together by the neck with a wooden yoke they call
    "mayombe." They hit us with sticks. At last, after days
    and days, we come to an enormous river they call the
    ocean. For the first time, I see horrible creatures who
    have but one toe and floating yellow hair and their
    skin is white and red. They wear strange clothes and
    sometimes they put their hair on top of their hair.
    Their only country is a hollowed thing. They have

many kingdoms far away and they have no wives and they rule with thunder. The black people who brought me are their friends; they call them white or French and they drink together, a water that makes them lose their memory, and they say that their god is more powerful than the ancestors and that his name is Moses or David. I am sure they are going to eat me but the black men say: "They are taking you to work in their fields."

(The West Indies. A penlike enclosure in the savannah. Under a palm tree, armed sailors are guarding a group of captives. A broker is rubbing one of the younger male captives with palm oil and lemon juice. The captain, in shirt-sleeves, is using roots to polish a woman's teeth. One of the sailors is shaving the head of an old man.)

CAPTAIN: Don't forget to pull out those white hairs. He's at least ten years too old. I'm in a hurry to start the sale. Then it's money and women for us!

BROKER: With all the drugs and the fresh crab I give them... The open air will do the rest.

CAPTAIN: May I be hanged if we don't fool the toughest customers. Those dupes won't have seen such a pretty lot for a long time.

BROKER: We'll even sell the cripples the first day.

CAPTAIN: Hey, you. Play a little on the bullwhip; they're all rusty, I want them to shake a bit. Make it lively or our customers will leave without opening their purse.

(One of the sailors begins cracking the whip. Some captives jump; others sprint to the cadence of the whip. Without uttering a sound, they beat on calabashes, clay pots, and kettles.)

(The marketplace, baking in the sun. Sweat, dust, variegated crowd. Peddlers move among the strollers, offering the latest gazettes, perfumes, drinks, and tobacco. Black servants in livery hold immense parasols over the delicate, powdered heads of their masters. Elegant ladies wade through the muck and the trash, hunting for gewgaws among the merchant stands. Musty odors of oil frying and musk-scented bodies waft through the air. Firecrackers explode under women's skirts. "Bien grillé! Dokonon! Y pa che, manzel! Dize milet! Pom' cannelle!" ["Roasted nuts! Dokonon! Dizé milet![7] Cinnamon apples!"] Near a tall stockade fence, buyers jostle each other and try to peer through the cracks between the boards to get a look at the merchandise. A soldier pushes them away wearily. The brokers, their wigs askew, are rubbing their hands. The captain, standing on a rum cask, is showing off. An attractive young mulatto woman is pouring brim-full cups of punch.

BROKER: They're ripe, Captain.

CAPTAIN: Come here, you beautiful wench. Ah, what an ass she has!

BROKER: A goldmine!

BABE: *(perched on Isaac's shoulders)* Higher, come on, I can't see anything.

ALOÏSE: Get down, Babe, you're going to break your neck.

BABE: Father, you promised. I want my own.

TIFAUGE: Come, my dear. Entertainment is so rare.

ALOÏSE: But all these people....

POPPÉE: These bodies, this smell! The spectacle is getting me all excited. Impale me, adorable monster.

SALTINE: Divine, you reek of crime.

POPPÉE: I don't want to come until the bartering is in full swing.

CAPTAIN: Ladies and gentlemen, fellow citizens.... I am Dam Joulin, captain of the seven seas, at your service. It is my privilege and pleasure to offer you an exceptional lot of Negroes freshly arrived and in perfect health. Solid teeth. Iron muscles. No trace of yaws or pox. I give you my word as a *sans-culotte.*

VOICE IN THE CROWD: Hey, Danton, get on with it. Open the holy fucking gates, will you?

> *(The captain fires in the air and the doors to the stockade are slammed open. In a brief flash the captives are seen, naked and petrified. The crowd rushes in. There is wild confusion as they swarm over the "merchandise," running in every direction. One grabs a man; another is seen dragging a woman by the hair. There is bickering over possession of the sister or the brother; an adolescent is pushed toward the brokers; a child is wrenched from its mother. In the clouds of dust that have been kicked up during the scramble, only silhouettes rushing about can be seen. Pandemonium and an enormous racket. "How much for this one?" "Three thousand." "You must be joking!" "Take it or leave it." "That one's mine." "No, she's mine; I saw her first." "Four thousand for this gentleman." "Who is next?" "Get your hands off him, you jack-ass, I just purchased him. Thief!")*

(Midday in the fields. Men and women, covered with dirt and sweat, numbed by incessant, repetitive work, are tilling the powdery soil in a uniform rhythm. Domingue is lying on a mat in the meager shadow of a palm roof. He is dozing, his head resting in Ben's lap. The boy brushes away the fat flies that buzz around the man's face. There is not the slightest breeze. The only sounds are the heavy breathing of the field workers and the monotonous scratching of their hoes in the parched earth. This goes on without respite for an apparently interminable period.

Furtively, a woman moves away from the group and steals into the shelter. Ever so carefully, she picks up one of the gourds. Domingue grabs her by the ankle as she turns to leave. The water spills on the ground.)

DOMINGUE: *To ka pren mô pou oune tèbè?* [Do you take me for a moron?]

ALINE: *Nou swèfe.* [We're thirsty.]

BEN: It's time for a rest.

DOMINGUE: *(He slaps the boy.)* Shut up, you little shit. Hey, *manzel* Aline, seems your mouth is as dry as cotton. Why don't you do me a favor and lap up the water you spilt. Come on, lap it up, drink to your heart's content. I don't want a drop left.

(The hoes have stopped moving. One of the men steps forward.)

JEAN: Leave her alone or I'll crack your skull open.

DOMINGUE: You jackass, you must really be stupid. Come on, you want fifty lashes? Just try me.

(The two men struggle. Domingue is winning. Aline runs away.)

Little shit, go fetch her back. And, you mad devil, you're going to be sorry you were ever born. The rest of you, move your butts, get back to work.

(The slaves begin to sing. Domingue shivers.)

(The Big House. Dinnertime, sticky heat. Loulouze is operating the ceiling fan. The servants are gathered around Aloïse.)

ALOÏSE: My dear children, thank the Lord for all the blessings that He grants you through His infinite mercy. Blessed are those who follow his commandments, who observe decency, sobriety, and obedience. Your mistress wishes you to be good husbands, adoring wives, affectionate parents. As long as you listen to me, you will never lack anything. Go now and may God keep you.

SERVANTS: Amen.

ALOÏSE: You may serve dinner now, Isaac.

CHAMOUSSET: It's about time.

TIFAUGE: This Congo fellow is stubborn. I'm going to make an example of him. Domingue, take care of it.

DOMINGUE: And the girl, Master?

TIFAUGE: Thirty lashes. Tell them to give you something to eat in the kitchen.

DOMINGUE: Thank you, Excellence.

(Ben is sitting under the table. He catches pieces of food that Babe hands to him.)

TIFAUGE: So, Pioche, how are we doing?

PIOCHE: Sir, I've finished the inventory of the buildings, the livestock, the tools, and machines. The mill must be renovated; the cogs and the frames are rotted through. Lastly, the Negroes....With all due respect, Marquis, if I could suggest....

TIFAUGE: Yes?

PIOCHE: Couldn't the rations of the field workers be increased?

CHAMOUSSET: A philanthropist in the islands! Zac, bring on the wine!

TIFAUGE: Gentleman Steward, here is a piece of advice: you came from the gutter; be careful we don't send you back.

KEITH: You know, Pioche, in England abolitionists are prolific but they're not getting anywhere. Slavery is a necessary evil. We haven't found anything to replace it yet.

BABE: Doctor Pierre, it's awful. My pony is limping.

CHAMOUSSET: You're too hard on that animal.

ALOÏSE: Dear Chamousset, I beg you. Babe is making himself ill over this.

CHAMOUSSET: I'll look at that leg later. It will be a change from my dysentery cases, anyway.

ALOÏSE: *(sighing)* This is what I get from being so good to them. The yams are half-raw and the meat is burned.

KEITH: Our spys say Republican soldiers landed on the northern island three days ago.

TIFAUGE: Damn it.

KEITH: His Majesty's government is very concerned with your problems. If you can convince your friends and neighbors to fight the Jacobin trash, together we can throw them back into the ocean. His Majesty's vessel carries arms and gunpowder and soldiers who are ready to fight for your cause.

ALOÏSE: Louis, must the weaker sex show you the way? I am at your side.

KEITH: We are in a state of emergency, Marquis.

TIFAUGE: Very well, Mister Keith, I will speak to my peers.

KEITH: Fine, a wise decision, my friend. You will sign a contract with my company. Your sugar and coffee will sell for more in London. Let's shake hands on that. We'll make these regicides pay for their crimes.

(In the bush, just before dawn.)

LOULOUZE: Spirits of the bamboo trees, dead children who whisper, oh, cover my tracks, mend the broken branches. Right the fallen grasses, closing on my steps.

DOMINGUE: Psst. Psst.

LOULOUZE: Who is it? ... Legba, the master of the crossroads? It's you. Were you following me?

DOMINGUE: Where were you?

LOULOUZE: *Lague mo, mo lasse.* [Leave me alone, I'm tired.]

DOMINGUE: You were in the hills again, with the maroons, weren't you? Your lover is one of them, isn't he? What are you hoping for? Those fugitives can't do a thing for you. One day Master will be rid of them. You need a man like me. How many times did he take you tonight? I can do better. Come back to my cabin.

LOULOUZE: Groveling dog, I'd as soon die. *Aille tété râte!* [Go fuck yourself!]

DOMINGUE: You've been running, the sweat is pouring down your breasts.

LOULOUZE: You'll never have me! *(She spits on the ground.)*

(Someplace in the woods.)

BABE: Ben! Where are you? Come back here. Ben!

BEN: I'm right here.

BABE: Don't do anything stupid.

BEN: There, I've got one! *(He emerges from the bushes holding an iguana by the tail.)* Look. It's a big one.

BABE: It's moving.

BEN: We're going to eat it.

BABE: I don't want to, that's disgusting. Throw it away, that's an order!

BEN: I'm hungry.

BABE: You're worse than an animal.

(Night, in front of Chamousset's cabin. He is preparing an infusion with roots. A slave is lying on the ground with his foot bandaged. Athénaïs is dressing Aline's lacerated back.)

PIOCHE: How can they treat people with such brutality? They are forced to work, live on starvation rations, and they beat them bloody.

CHAMOUSSET: *(to Athénaïs)* Make her drink this potion. She has to sleep. And pour us another, my sweet little whore.

PIOCHE: Doctor, you're drunk.

CHAMOUSSET: How do you like them, Pioche? Look at my little blossom, isn't she wonderful? She works from morning till night; she cooks, launders, and caresses on top of that. And never a cross word, never a tear. It's quite peaceful. Just between us, sonny, I think she likes you. Here, I'll lend her to you. You'll wind up doing it behind my back anyway. But, I get to look, right? She's a jewel. I couldn't do without her. To tell you the truth, white women don't interest me anymore. Finished, zero, pffitt.... Don't look so disgusted. You'll come around, too.

PIOCHE: You are raving, it's nauseating. Go back to France.

CHAMOUSSET: I will die in this place, do you hear me, greenhorn? I will die here. Maybe you don't like women, my sweet? Is that it? Speak up, there's something for every taste, yours for the taking. Athénaïs, baby, he's saying nasty things to Daddy. Come, my beauty, come here. She's hiding my rum, the bitch. Bloody whore, give me my rotgut.

PIOCHE: Filthy old goat.

CHAMOUSSET: I'm going to cut the nose off that bitch. Damn! *(He collapses on the ground.)*

ATHÉNAÏS: *Pô diab!* [Poor devil!] He has been drinking since this morning. Come on, get up, *papa ménage* [house daddy], you are heavy. Come on, we are going home, *tit fie* [little girl] is tired, please.

PIOCHE: You're all scarred. Did he do this to you?

ATHÉNAÏS: Monsieur Pierre is good to me. He is dying.

PIOCHE: But he's nothing but a brute!

ATHÉNAÏS: Monsieur Lucas, your head is so full of things.

PIOCHE: Let me help you, I'll carry him.

(In a ravine, the camp of the maroons. It is night.)

WAGUANU: You who were born feet first, who are powerful-powerful, heal me. I have a lump in my chest that is rising to my throat, that keeps me from eating, it's like a live devilfish. And after three days, I throw up. This white man! My hand is shaking with rage. Manmam Mambo, I am going mad.

NANNI: Take this liquid, drink it slow-slow, it opens the mind. The *loas* speak, *rapadou.*[8] I see them, they are leaving from Guinea; they come in long canoes to the Creoles. Do you have the presents?

WAGUANU: I brought pumpkins and potatoes and corn and cassava. Help us.

NANNI: Mmm-mmm, *pitit caye,*[9] offer a rooster as well. *(She begins to sing.) Ezili kâlikâ elu/ A la loa ki rèd/ Ezili u mâdé kochô/ M'apé ba u li/ Ezili mâdé kabrit dé pié/ Koté pum prâ pu ba-li/ Ezili kanlkan elou/* Ah, what a difficult *loa/ Ezili,* you are asking for a pig now/ I will give you this/ *Ezili,* you are asking for a goat with two feet/ Where can I find such an animal for you?

WAGUANU: *Abobo.*[10]

(The yard of the Big House at noon. Jean, lying flat on his stomach, is stretched between four posts. His back, buttocks, and thighs are streaked with dark brown wounds.)

DOMINGUE: Untie him.

(Isaac cuts the ropes. Domingue pulls Jean up by his ears. The doctor examines him perfunctorily.)

CHAMOUSSET: The eye is still bright; he'll hold up.

DOMINGUE: Take this shovel and dig.

(Later. Jean kneels over the trench he has dug.)

DOMINGUE: Lie down in the hole.

JEAN: *Bon t'chê, coumandé! Fai croix, mwen pé ké rifaï.* [Pity, commander! I swear, I'll never do it again.]

DOMINGUE: I have heard enough from him.

(Isaac buries Jean alive.)

(The Big House in the middle of the night. Babe's room.)

BABE: A falling star!

NANNI: That's a werewolf crossing the sky. I know. That woman has tasted human flesh. Perched on top of the *mapu* tree, waiting for her prey. Her eyes are shining. We must cut down the tree where she nests.

BABE: You're telling lies.

NANNI: Her bed is empty each night. Go, see for yourself. Turkey wings grow on her; her armpits and her mouth spit out fire. When night falls, she rubs her ankles and her neck with leaves.

BEN: I'm not scared.

NANNI: Her skin is kept fresh and cool in a jar.

BABE: You're crazy.

NANNI: You don't love your old nurse anymore?

(The secret camp of the maroons at night. Loulouze is bent over Waguanu, who is sleeping.)

LOULOUZE: If I knew how to write, I would write you a letter, but I don't, so I dance for you. Can you see me? I offer you each of my gestures. At night, after a long, long day, I'm next to you by the fire. I watch you eat and I adore the little twig that's trapped in your hair. I would like to be that crumb of cassava that's stuck to your chest, there near the nipple, or that scar that runs across your shoulder. I love you because you're my color. You are mine, pretty nigger; your breath drugs me like the smell of rum that floats over the freshly cut sugar cane. When, by chance, our toes brush each other, among the dogs that are lapping up some abandoned gourd, you send my blood boiling. It's a burning rush of lava that carries away the mountain-side. My soul is starving for your muscles stiff with fatigue. I love the rage you hold inside you and that hollows out your cheeks, the torn shirt that falls on your hard belly. You are a palm tree straight in the sky, you are God; and when your tongue twines around mine, I forget all the worries. I also love your brutal laugh that breaks out like a storm; it wrinkles your eyes shut and opens your mouth so I can see your perfect teeth ready to bite the stars. And oh how I love your look, your stubborn brow that says, "I am the one who will burn the master's house." You are the revolt, my brother.

(A squad of Republican soldiers in the bush.)

DESROSIERS: Let's halt a while, men. Show me the map.

ÉGALITÉ: This is where the plantation is.

DESROSIERS: At this pace we won't get there before dawn.

ÉGALITÉ: The maroons are in these ravines. We'll have to cut a path through with our sabers.

DESROSIERS: I want them to join us. I need every man I can get to carry out our mission. What do you call this fruit?

ÉGALITÉ: *Parepu.*

DESROSIERS: I'll never get used to this heat.

ÉGALITÉ: You don't like my country?

DESROSIERS: How would I know? Let's move on.

(At dusk, in front of Domingue's cabin. He is smoking. Aline is cooking manioc patties.)

DOMINGUE: Hurry up, *badjio,* I'm hungry. Did you see my new fancy pants? Nice, heh? Pure silk. Am I handsome? The master is pleased, I'll get a third pig. He promised me his gold watch for Christmas. Can you feel my little cock?

(He caresses her. The familiar sounds of the night are soon drowned out by a din. It grows louder. Domingue pushes the girl toward the cabin. Out of the shadows jumps a group of men armed with sticks, sugar-cane knives, and stones. They surround the couple. Waguanu is at the head of the group.)

WAGUANU: Out of the way, little sister. I have come to destroy the terrors of the night.

DOMINGUE: Jes'....

(Waguanu slashes Domingue's shoulder with his knife. The circle closes around the overseer; the blows begin to fall.)

(The Big House late at night. Loulouze is at her station, operating the fan. Isaac is pouring punch and liqueurs. With the exception of Aloïse, the masters have been drinking all evening.)

SALTINE: A toast, Mister Keith. To business!

KEITH: To the King! And to the queens that I serve. And to the knave that I am.

CHAMOUSSET: By God, I like this redcoat.

ALOÏSE: Have you ever been to Otahiti, Mister Keith?

KEITH: Alas, Madame, my commerce has never led me to that part of the globe.

CHAMOUSSET: Land ahoy, ca'pn. *(His speech is increasingly slurred.)* Ho-hish. Haul down the great sail. Deck-boy to the foremasht.

POPPÉE: What a time we had, my friends! I thought we'd never get here. Mosquitoes simply devoured my arms and legs. How can one survive in this desert, in this gloomy savannah dotted with smelly little hamlets? Tifauge, I am bored.

SALTINE: What would you say to a hunt, lovely Poppée? I think I know where we can find some maroons; their leader used to be a coach driver.

POPPÉE: Nothing daunts me, darling; there is no extremity to which I wouldn't stoop. And I am an excellent shot, as everyone knows. Or...why don't we have a picnic! A pickanninic!

TIFAUGE: We were walking among smoking ruins. Behind us a raging fire consumed the earth and ignited the sky. Everywhere people were running, haggard, covered with soot, or screaming with pain over the charred body of a loved one. Burnt palm trees fell sputtering into the filthy waters of the port. A living torch crossed our path; it was a priest. You were carrying Babe in your arms. The poor child's skull was exposed and blackened by a terrible burn; one last lock of scorched hair hung on his neck. You were rocking him, humming a well-known tune. I asked a Negress who was squatting in the middle of the fire if there was still a cemetery where we could bury our son. The woman started insulting me and throwing stones. When I turned around, you had disappeared. I wandered around like an idiot in the devastated cotton fields. Then a rain of ash fell over everything.... A rather disturbing dream I had there.

POPPÉE: A game of cards, gentlemen? Faro? Big stakes, I feel inspired tonight.

ALOÏSE: You will have to excuse me. *Adieu. (She leaves.)*

SALTINE: Your Loulouze is an appetizing wench, Tifauge.

TIFAUGE: She's yours as you please. Isaac, more punch!

POPPÉE: Punt, Mister Keith.

CHAMOUSSET: Oh la, the boat is rocking. To your bunk, sailor.

(Outside, in the dark. The doctor bumps into a bloody mass. Pioche, strung up by his feet, is swinging at the end of a rope.)

CHAMOUSSET: Athénaïs! Is that you, my little chickadee? What the devil...? Hey, rabbit, are you deaf or what? He's sweating like a pig. Come down from your perch, musn't sleep. I'm cold. It's cold here.

(Dawn. The masters are entrenched in the Big House. Slaves and maroons stand outside. Domingue's head is mounted on a spike. Desrosiers and his escort step over dead bodies.)

TIFAUGE: I will destroy you all.

DESROSIERS: He had made one fine mess, your Waguanu.

ÉGALITÉ: Surrender, Tifauge, you haven't got a chance.

WAGUANU: We must kill all the others.

DESROSIERS: Citizens, peace. Listen to me, you who have lived under the yoke of despots, I am the bearer of great news. The world has turned. The Convention just signed the death warrant of slavery. The slave traders and the man-eaters are no longer. Some have perished, choking on their own rage. Others have fled to royalist territories. They were but the pawns of kings, for only kings love to live among chattels. They are the ones who put you in chains on the African coast and sold you to the white men. And it's again the tyrants of Europe that wish to perpetuate this infamous trade. The Republic is now adopting you as her children. From today on, all men, regardless of their color, are French citizens and are free to enjoy the rights set out in our Constitution. Across the ocean, servants, workers, peasants, jouneymen reach out their hands to you. All have the same hate for aristocrats and money. I, Numa Desrosiers, Commissioner of the new French Republic, am here to post and enforce this Declaration of Justice all over the country, in the mountains, the forests, the towns, the military posts.

TIFAUGE: Assassins! You can rape our women, burn

our homes, desecrate our churches, but this land is ours! Slave, do you think a vulgar piece of paper is going to whiten your face and give you a soul? Has base lead ever been turned to gold? God won't allow it. In Paris sons of butchers launch sublime decrees. Bravo! Constitution, the Rights of Man! Words, just words! Born of the monstrous coupling of a rotten bourgeois and a whore philosopher.

(Loulouze marches up to Tifauge and slaps him right and left; then, calmly, she returns to her place with the others.)

BEN: Blood!

DESROSIERS: Friends, I admire your passion in demanding his skin. But are we barbarians, wild beasts, torturers? I have in my baggage a machine that is legal and fit to wash away the scars of your branding. The blade of this machine is so sharp it can cut a banana tree with one blow. Free Men, is this not a wonderful day?

WAGUANU: You speak well, Commissioner, but I have an animal that's eating me inside. I want to tear it out immediately.

ÉGALITÉ: *Nègue, vini bô mô. Mô savé tô ka craîne ce blangue ya, ça bougu'-a a oune blangue, mê à oune frer'. Mô connaïte li, nou goumin cont' ce prussien ya. Missié gain courage, i sincère, li gain oune seule parol'. En France i ka lutté pou ça qui con' tô ka souffri di l'injustice di lan mizé. L'ouvri ça bi caisse ya, tô ka trouvé bagaz pou fai ce colon ya tende tô pou fai l'ouvri zié colon ya, mêm ça ki pi sourdo. A noû couri déyié yé, a nou fouté derhô, cé salop'ia ki pa lé baille nou roune faveur. Baille mô lan main pou sîmin grain la Raison a sou yè!*

[Brother, let's embrace. I understood your mistrust of the white man and this man is white but he is my brother. I know him; we fought the same enemy together; he is courageous and sincere and he will keep his promise. In France, he fights for people who have been subjected to injustice and misery, just as you do. In those crates you will find convincing arguments, enough to persuade the most arrogant of planters. Let us chase these cruel conspirators who cling to their privileges. Help us to sow the good seed of Reason.]

(Waguanu and Égalité fall into each others' arms. Ben climbs onto Desrosier's shoulders, waving the Commissioner's sword and his tricolor hat. There is an atmosphere of fête and fraternity.)

DESROSIERS: Égalité, I'm requisitioning this house. Lock up these ex-aristocrats. Then let's eat. I haven't had a thing since yesterday.

(A slave cabin.)

BABE: I'm thirsty. Take off the irons, please.

BEN: Stop whining, they'll hear us. How do you think I got in here?

BABE: What's that horrible thing?

BEN: You've never seen a rat head? I copied the big machine in the yard. You tie the rat here and then hop! Cut clean off.

BABE: *Coté mo papa que me maman?* [What have they done to my father and mother?]

BEN: *Tô guiole.* [Shut up.]

BABE: You're my friend. I'm not ashamed to sleep beside you.... You'll be my partner, we'll share everything.

BEN: Too bad, it's over. I'm going to tear out your nerves one by one and your skin, too, just for a start. Then, maybe we can talk.

(Desrosiers' quarters in the Big House.)

TIFAUGE: Have you ever seen the plains when the glistening leaves are dripping with dew? There are days when the sun and the rain embrace above the tree-ferns, just before dusk. And the golden light that inflames the feathery dells as they roll out to the sea? And the icy fog of the ravines that cuts through to the bone? Did your father build a house or clear away acres to plant sugar cane here where nothing grows? Is it your Babe who played with hummingbirds in the yard? Your heart is a triangular piece of metal; it drops brutally from a wooden frame stained with blood. Drums, Nigger carmagnoles![11] All I see around me is laziness, empty talk, deserted fields, abandoned mills. The shops are closed, the warehouses are empty, and the ships rot in port. Who will fill the stomachs here? Who will put the sugar in the cups of Marseilles and Tourcoing? You can't manage without us.

DESROSIERS: Have you finished your homilies?

TIFAUGE: Spare my wife and son.

DESROSIERS: *(He points to Ben.)* This boy never even knew his mother. Take him away.

(Tifauge exits, escorted by a soldier.)

Who told you to shine my boots, son? Here, I'll do it.

BEN: When you leave soon, take me with you. I want to write books.

DESROSIERS: I would love to have your hair and your ebony body. I don't know why.

(The yard of the Big House. The whites, guarded by two sentries, are grouped under a mango tree. Ben and Isaac are squatting on the ground and playing a game of tic-tac. A man is beating a drum for Aline and Athénaïs, who are dancing.)

NANNI: I have spent nights and nights sitting up with you or sleeping at the foot of your bed. I have told so many stories I can't begin to count them on my fingers. Even if my eyes were ripped out, I could see you're sad simply by touching your cheek. Nanni do this, Nanni do that. The master wants the servant, he rolls her in the prickly grasses. And all those little white babies glued to my breasts with their serpent mouths. But I am worn out, Mistress. I loved a man once; his name was Dizout. They took him away from me; one day your father sold him to the neighbor. I cried and you said, "Quick, Nanni, brush my hair." Often when it was dark, I ran to meet him; he would take me there, under the moon. I would run back before morning so I wouldn't get whipped. Dizout only thought about himself; he demanded everything but he gave nothing in return. I thought a little honey might drop from his lips but all I ever tasted at that fountain was vinegar. White or black, men are men; they wound like acacia branches. When I speak to God, he doesn't listen. Why would he bother with a withered, old bean from Angola? Today, freed from chains, I am worth nothing; I have to learn to say no. It is a hard word to learn.

ALOÏSE: When I must put my head on the guillotine, I don't want them to touch me. You will take the scissors and cut a circle in my blouse, down to the shoulders. And you're the one who will cut the locks that fall on my neck.

(Evening, after dinner. The blacks are gathered around the hearth. Loulouze is imitating her mistress, Aloïse. Aline is strutting about like Poppée, and Isaac is impersonating the defunct Chamousset. They try to outdo each other. There is broad parody, laughter, and shouting. Desrosiers stands to the side, sipping wine and looking on in silence. Égalité and Waguanu begin singing and clapping their hands. Nanni goes to Desrosiers.)

NANNI: Come, I'll teach you how to dance.

(The Big House turned upside-down. Babe's room, guarded by sentries.)

POPPÉE: Everyone has a price.

SALTINE: That's all I have.

POPPÉE: Nanni, take this purse and get us out of here.

NANNI: There are soldiers everywhere.

POPPÉE: I'll throw in this necklace.

NANNI: Waguanu called me a half-breed dog. Tonight I'll take you to the creek.

POPPÉE: Don't forget, you have a lot to gain. We'll go to Saint Kitts; I'll set you up there. You're not like the others.

NANNI: Drink, Madame.

(The nurse moves away. The couple swallows the hemlock Nanni has prepared.)

SALTINE: As soon as we're safe....

POPPÉE: Kiss me.

SALTINE: Safe....

(They lie down.)

(In the Big House. Desrosiers is composing a letter. Égalité pours hot water into a basin, where the French officer soaks his feet.)

DESROSIERS: My skin is covered v^{..} h rashes as if I had been burned with a hot iron. M. feet and even the palms of my hands are full of cracks and sores. It's this damned climate.

ÉGALITÉ: What do you plan to do?

DESROSIERS: We've hit the bottom. The territory is idle and famine will set in soon. Perhaps ... a purge.... The Negroes must take up the hoe again.

ÉGALITÉ: The sound of the whip still echoes in their ears.

DESROSIERS: I have prepared a speech.

ÉGALITÉ: Citizen, what you call by the sweet name of "public good" is nothing but the sinister interests of the merchants and the state. We flaunt our philosophy and our freedom, but today we are as much slaves of our prejudices and our emissaries as we were ten centuries ago. Let me refresh your memory. No people may be subjected by right to another people; there should be no laws except those that the said people establish themselves. It is absurd; it is nonsensical that a country be governed by a legislature that is thousands of miles away. The idiotic error committed by the inhabitants of these colonies was to accept sending deputies to the National Assembly. But this is the exclusive work of the white colonialists who have decided for all. In fact, everyone has the right, the duty to throw off the yoke of the central government, to choose another ruler or to constitute their own Republic. And why not? Since the supremacy that the government pretends to hold over them was merely usurped, founded on despotic principles, and only exists by the right of might. I would go further than this. Supposing that the inhabitants of these colonies declared independence, how would we dare find fault in the fact that they followed the example of the English colonies? What twisted logic would allow us to condemn that which we have applauded elsewhere? The white man has no excuse for having proclaimed himself the tyrannic master of the blacks. The laws of nature precede those of society and man's rights cannot be prescribed. To throw off the shameful injustice to which the black man has been subjected, he is authorized to use every means, even murder, even if he were forced to massacre down to the last oppressor.

DESROSIERS: The good of the Republic....

ÉGALITÉ: Your Republic is a whore mistress. She has cheated us. Her capitalist's dream of establishing colonies wihtout slaves. And if that's your dream, patriot, I spit on it.

(Loulouze enters. Desrosiers is vomiting.)

DESROSIERS: What do you want?

LOULOUZE: I am just looking at you. I have made some coffee.

DESROSIERS: I haven't drunk coffee for ages; it has a taste of blood.

LOULOUZE: So, you have heard the mango fall from the tree?

DESROSIERS: Citizen, I have work to do.

LOULOUZE: When do you find the time to make love?

(Someplace under a palm tree.)

ISAAC: So, I am on the path with my uncle Peme.
Night is falling; we are looking for my mother, who
was taken by Those-Who-Disinter-the-Dead. The little
bit of a man who warned us is walking ahead. He says
that once he was as big as a giant and that with his
charms he could transform himself into whatever he
wished. Sometimes he was a monkey, then a mosquito,
then a baobab tree, then a crocodile-man; he changed
as he wished, so there was no way of knowing whom
one was dealing with. All this happened, he says, "at a
time when I was living on the mountainside, at the
edge of the inhabited lands, where there are neither
trees nor water. Since then a magician has stolen my
potions and my power and I am worthless." I think he
is boasting, and that he is not as queer as he pretends,
and that he is a bigger bragger and liar than a hundred
griots put together. After five days in the woods, this
man, who calls himself Mpum, tells us that his second
wife, Sisim, is waiting for him near the stream with
palm wine and that he is going to fetch some because
he is very thirsty. Mpum, since that is his name, leaves
us there in the middle of the forest, ordering us not to
budge because my mother might appear at any
minute. I am hungry but my uncle's arrows and his
spear remain in their quiver because there is no game
in the bush, no birds in the trees. We strain to listen
but there is not the slightest call, not even the rustling
of leaves. My mother still does not appear. My uncle
Peme says that Mpum, the pygmy, if that is his name,
has played a trick on us and that it is time to go back to
the village. We retrace our tracks, which is easy for a
hunter like my uncle. We walk three days and three
nights and another day. On the fourth night the drum
speaks. At a bend in the path my uncle says: "Don't
look behind you, someone is following us. It's an old
woman whose breasts sag like empty goatskins." I

cannot stop myself from turning around. I see a young virgin covered with pearls and jangling bracelets; she has only a clump of grass hiding her sex. Her voice is very gentle; she begs me to come to her; she says she has not eaten for a month. I want to go to her. My uncle says that if I take one step toward this creature, he will knock me out. "That is one of the living-dead," he repeats. "She will drag you to the Valley-from-Where-None-Return." After that my mother is waiting by the river; we tell her about our journey. She is crying. She tells us that nine days before a giant had told her we were lost forever in the bush. She presses her lips to mine and breathes life into my mouth.

BABE: And then?

ISAAC: That is all.

BEN: Fill up my lungs, Isaac, give me your warmth.

(Maternally, Isaac brings his lips to each boy's mouth.)

(The courtyard behind the Big House. The soldiers are eating. Alone, Desrosiers is lost in his thoughts.)

ATHÉNAÏS: Eat, Commissioner.

DESROSIERS: I'm not hungry.

ATHÉNAÏS: You are sick.

(Tifauge comes crashing in, spilling calabashes and basins in his wake. Above his bared chest, a large, red, crescent-shaped wound crosses under his chin. With a gasp, he dies in the arms of Desrosiers. Égalité appears, covered with blood. He throws off his clothes.)

ÉGALITÉ: You have poured into my soul, drop by drop, poisons more dreadful than those of Dahomey. Your philters have clouded my judgment, have made me a stranger to myself. I have decided to cure myself. I am going another way.

(Égalité stands naked, his uniform trailing in the dust. Athénaïs hands him a piece of cloth, which he ties around his waist.)

DESROSIERS: Like water through my fingers.

(In the ruins of Chamousset's cabin. Keith is tied up. Waguanu is trying on his Republican outfit.)

KEITH: They have made a monkey out of a jaguar. All that's missing is the Phrygian bonnet.

WAGUANU: Fucking trouble-maker.

KEITH: Revolt, throw off their tutelage. We the English would like nothing better than to buy your products. Think about it.

1989

(A large Mediterranean port. An azure sky swept clean by the wind. On the jetty, strewn with empty soda cans, Babe and Ben are skateboarding. The boys perform intricate figures and jumps. Their paths cross and mingle like twin rivers. "Move your feet. Bouge. *It's always the same. Drumbeat. Yeah. Turn the sound up.* Monte le volume. *It's a survival system." Below, the sea lazily licks the large stone blocks spotted with tar. The hot haze masks the white islands on the horizon. Farther away, invisible, is Africa. The blaster spits out:)*

Sitting in the morning sun
I'll be seated when the evening comes
Watching the ships roll in
Then I'm watching all away again
Yeah, I'm sitting on the dock of the bay
Watching the tide roll away, ooh
I'm just sitting on the dock of the bay
Wasting time
I left my home in Georgia
Headed for the Frisco bay
I've had nothing to live for
Looks like nothing's gonna come my way
So I just come sitting on the dock of the bay
Watching the tide roll away, ooh
I'm sitting on the dock of the bay
Wasting time
Look like nothing's gonna change
Everything still remains the same
I can do but ten people tell me to do
So I guess I remain the same
Yes, I'm sitting here resting my bones
And this loneliness won't leave me alone
Yes, two thousand miles I roam
Just to make this dock my home!

[OTIS REDDING, "Dock of the Bay," 1968]

∿

Notes

TRANSLATOR'S NOTE: The major portion of this play was written in contemporary "standard French" that I have translated according to the oral poetics I perceived in the text. The passages in other languages (French West Indian Creoles or Jula) are transcribed from the original text and translated into contemporary "standard English" in the flow of the dialogue. Both Fargeau as the author and I as the translator felt it was necessary to transcribe these passages in the original, since the drama is historically and geographically grounded in the French Antilles.

[1]*Creole* means "of mixed origin" and may thus refer to a person of European or African descent born in the Antilles, or to the language spoken on the islands. Poppée is evidently of European descent.

[2]Maroons are fugitive slaves who, in this case, banded together and organized a revolt.

[3]This passage is in Caribbean Creole.

[4]The *sans-culottes* ("without breeches" worn by the upper classes) were extremist radicals of the French Revolution.

[5]*L'Être Suprême* is a reification of the spirit of the French Revolution that was heralded in grandiose public celebrations during the revolutionary period in France.

[6]This passage is in Jula, a West African trade language.

[7]Caribbean delicacies: *Dokonon* is a treat made with coconut and sugar; *dizé milet* is a cake.

[8]A *loa* is a "divine horse," a god of African origin that crosses the Atlantic to appear in the voodoo trance ceremonies of the southern Americas. *Rapadou* is raw sugar.

[9]*Pitit caye* is an onomatopoeia. The song that follows is in Haitian Creole.

[10]*Abobo* is the closing to a traditional West African prayer.

[11]The *carmagnole* is a costume and a dance, both popular during the revolutionary period.

Wendy Kesselman

OLYMPE AND THE EXECU-TIONER

**A play commissioned by
Ubu Repertory Theater for its 1989
festival "Homage to the Revolution"**

Author's note: This published version of *Olympe and
the Executioner* is a work in progress. The author
plans to make revisions.

To Brian

Olympe and the Executioner was premiered in a studio presentation at Ubu Repertory Theater as part of Ubu's International Festival "Homage to the Revolution" on May 30, 1989, with the following cast:

Celeste	**Haley Fox**
Executioner	**Madison Arnold**
Nounou	**Anne Pitoniak**
Olympe	**Katherine Borowitz**
Pierrot	**Roger Bart**
Executioner's Wife	**Brenda Currin**
Grandmother	**Anne Pitoniak**
Philippe	**Joseph Fuqua**
First Market Woman	**Nancy Kerr**
Second Market Woman	**Maggie Wood**
Georges	**Kirk Jackson**
Le Franc De Pompignan	**Robert Langdon Lloyd**
Michel	**David Jaffe**
Ange	**Timothy Britten Parker**
Stage Directions and Parrot	**Paul Graffy**

Directed by **Gitta Honegger**
Lyrics and Music by **Wendy Kesselman**
Set by **Kari Nordstrom**
Lighting Consultant: **Mark London**

WENDY KESSELMAN'S plays, *My Sister in This House, The Juniper Tree, Maggie Magalita, I Love You, I Love You Not, Becca, The Griffin and the Minor Canon,* and *Merry-Go-Round,* have been widely produced in this country and abroad. Kesselman received the Susan Smith Blackburn Prize and the First Annual Playbill Award, and she is a four-time winner of the ASCAP Popular Award in Musical Theatre. She has received a Guggenheim, a McKnight, and two NEA fellowships and is a member of the Dramatists Guild. Kesselman is presently at work on an adaptation of Dickens' *A Tale of Two Cities,* which was commissioned by Stage One in Louisville, Kentucky. She has published nine children's books and a novel. *Olympe and the Executioner* was commissioned by Ubu Repertory Theater for its 1989 festival "Homage to the Revolution," an official program of the American Commemoration of the Bicentennial of the French Revolution. A studio presentation of the play was made at Ubu during that festival. It was subsequently given readings at the McCarter Theater in Princeton and by the Drama League in New York and was a finalist for the 1990 Susan Smith Blackburn Prize; it is also a finalist for the Drama League Playwrights Award Competition.

CHARACTERS

OLYMPE*
NOUNOU
PIERROT, *a street singer*
EXECUTIONER, *Monsieur de Paris*
EXECUTIONER'A WIFE
CELESTE, *the Executioner's daughter*
GRANDMOTHER, *the Executioner's mother*
MICHEL
ANGE, *Monsieur de Dijon*
LE FRANC DE POMPIGNAN
PHILIPPE
GEORGES
MARKET WOMEN

PLACE

France.

TIME

Before and during the Revolution of 1789.

Olympe de Gourges was a playwright, pamphleteer and advocate for women's rights during the French Revolution.

*Pronounced Olamp

> *(Paris. A bare stage. Celeste, the Executioner's daughter, runs in, barefoot, a huge loaf of bread in her arms. She is dressed in black.)*

CELESTE: *(looking out)* Papa. Papa!

> *(There is silence.)*

Papa.

> *(Silence still. She throws the bread on the floor. The Executioner comes in, also dressed in black.)*

I won't go anymore. Don't make me. *(holding out her thin arms)* Look. Look what they did. Just like yesterday. Big ones this time.

> *(The Executioner watches her, silent.)*

Don't you believe me? *(She pulls back her sleeve. Beneath it her shoulder is bleeding. She lifts her skirt. A deep gash runs along her leg.)* Don't you care?

> *(The Executioner moves to pick up the loaf of bread from the floor.)*

No. All you care about is that. All you wait for is that. Go ahead. Pick it up. Eat it.

> *(The Executioner picks up the bread, slowly turns it over.)*

It's all right. Don't worry. I protected it for you.

> *(Carefully, the Executioner dusts off the bread, covers it with a black cloth. Celeste lunges forward, snatches the cloth away.)*

Don't cover it in black. It's not dead! *(She flips over the loaf of bread.)* Like this! The way it's supposed to be. The way it is at the baker's—upside down, waiting for me. A special loaf for a special girl. The one loaf no one looks upon. The one loaf no one's hands will touch. No matter how hungry they are. No matter if they're starving. *(She pauses.)* The door jangles when I come in. They cram together in the back—afraid to touch me, afraid to be near. They know who it is— Celeste, the executioner's daughter, come to pick up his loaf of daily bread.

(The Executioner looks away.)

Bread marked for us, Papa. Bread for our family. No one dares to look at me. I don't have to pay. I grab the loaf and run—down back alleys, past swinging carcasses, through streams of butcher's blood. Rats snap at my ankles. I lose my shoes. But no matter how fast I run, they always catch me. And I feel the first stone. *(looking at him)* I don't want to eat it, Papa. Please. Don't ask me. I'm not going again. No matter what you do.

(The Executioner moves closer, takes out a large knife. He picks up the bread and slowly begins slicing it. He cuts off two slices, looks up, holds out one slice to his daughter. She stands still, the black cloth in her hands, watching him.)

Scene 2

(Montauban. Light comes up on Nounou, an old peasant, looking for Olympe. On a table lies an enormous loaf of bread.)

NOUNOU: A big thick loaf, crusty on the outside, spongy on the inside—right out of the oven, all hot, Marie Gouze—just the way you like it. *(She continues to look for Olympe.)* Little savage! Out climbing the hills again—ripping your dress, losing your shoes—when you should be home in bed. Next thing I know you'll be up in the hayloft with the boys, pulling down your pants. Out in the mud with the pigs, showing them your breasts. Wild in the middle of the night. Just like your mother!

(Olympe appears, barefoot, her dress torn, her hair wild.)

OLYMPE: Leave my mother out of this, you old witch!

NOUNOU: *(grabbing her, trying to drag her in)* Calling me a witch now she is. The one who raised her. Suckled her from a baby.

OLYMPE: *(trying to get out of her grasp)* I'm not coming in if you say one word against her.

NOUNOU: *(clutching Olympe's mass of hair)* Look at that rat's nest! What am I going to do with that? *(taking out a huge pair of scissors)* Might as well cut off the whole thing.

OLYMPE: *(slipping out of her grasp)* Not my hair. Don't you touch my hair! *(watching her from a corner)* Old witch.

NOUNOU: Oh witch, witch. Let's see that precious hair.

(Pulling Olympe toward her, she attacks the knotted hair with a thick broken comb.) Such curls! The curls of a princess! Every night I fix them for you and the next night you're back like a lost wild cat again.

(Suddenly Olympe covers her with kisses.)

Don't kiss me to death. You don't kiss witches.

(Olympe gives her another kiss.)

You've been up there again, haven't you? No matter how many times I tell you, you just keep going. *(grabbing her by the neck)* He'll break your heart. Like he broke your mother's. *(watching her face)* I bet you didn't even get a glimpse of him. *(Olympe winces.)* I knew it! You're like bitter wine to him. A bitter taste.

OLYMPE: But he's my—

NOUNOU: *(overlapping)* He looked after you for a week once. That's all you'll ever get from him.

OLYMPE: *(throwing her arms around Nounou)* Why? Why didn't he keep me?

NOUNOU: And your mother? What would she have done? Your mother's married to a very nice man.

OLYMPE: *(pulling away)* A butcher.

NOUNOU: Better a butcher than that fancy aristocrat on top of his goddamned hill. Who does he think he is— Monsieur Le Franc de Pompignan—the King? Now he's married some rich bitch who'd like to see you carved up on a plate. *(warningly)* Keep away from him! *(holding the wriggling Olympe still)* Slippery as an eel between my fingers. Already that stringbean Pierrot trails after you, when he's not drifting all around France.

OLYMPE: He's a singer. He writes his own songs and travels from town to town. *(sly)* He's written one about me.

NOUNOU: Let me take his songs and travel up to the North. *(stroking Olympe's luxuriant hair)* You're too pretty for your own good, Marie Gouze. Someone so pretty has nowhere to go in Montauban. They'll spoil it for you. They spoiled it for your mother. You'll love someone. And you'll be destroyed.

OLYMPE: I don't love anyone, Nounou. Only you.

NOUNOU: Ah, but you will, my pretty one. *(drawing her close)* With that hair, those eyes, that wild look of yours. They won't be able to get enough. You'll kill men one day. Devour them like you devour everything else around here. One day you'll be wild for the whole world. And the world will be wild for you.

> *(Olympe slips away, grabs a great hunk of the bread and begins eating it voraciously.)*

Sprouting up faster than a turnip. Those feet—you'll never grow into them! You're spreading, my lamb. Spreading! *(Snatching the loaf away from Olympe, as she reaches for it again.)* Glutton! Before I know it you'll eat through the rabbit hutches, the hen houses, the cow stalls—all the way to Paris! It's no good having such an appetite, my girl. And such curiosity to match. *(leaning her head against Olympe's)* Once a mother said to her daughter—"Here's a nice hot loaf, crusty on the outside, spongy on the inside, and a bottle of wine to take to your grandmother's." In the middle of the forest, the girl ran into a big bzou, a wolf who said—"Where are you going, little girl, little girl?" *(pulling Olympe's hair)* "To my grandmother's —with a loaf of hot bread and a bottle of wine." "Ah...and which path are you taking?" asks the bzou, the big wolf. "The path of thorns or the path of stones?"

OLYMPE: The path of thorns.

NOUNOU: Ah well, then I shall take the path of stones.

(Light comes up on Pierrot, a street singer.)

PIERROT: *(sings)*
OLYMPE DE GOUGES
THE BUTCHER'S DAUGHTER
WHOSE FATHER DROVE ANIMALS TO THE SLAUGHTER
WAS WILDER THAN ALL OF THEM
BUT NOBODY CAUGHT HER
OLYMPE DE GOUGES
THE BUTCHER'S DAUGHTER.

OLYMPE DE GOUGES
THE BUTCHER'S DAUGHTER
BATHED NAKED IN ICY MOUNTAIN WATER
AND EVERYONE WANTED HER
AH, EVERYONE SOUGHT HER
BUT NO ONE CAUGHT
THE BUTCHER'S DAUGHTER.

OLYMPE DE GOUGES
THOUGH NO ONE TAUGHT HER
FOUND OUT SHE WAS SOMEBODY ELSE'S DAUGHTER
HER REAL FATHER SHUNNED HER
REJECTED AND FOUGHT HER
AND TOLD HER TO STAY
A BUTCHER'S DAUGHTER.*

SCENE 3

(Paris. The Executioner and his Wife are in bed.)

EXECUTIONER: *(moving about in the darkness)* I can't sleep.

WIFE: *(pulling the covers over to her side)* You've been sleeping all night.

EXECUTIONER: I've been trying.

WIFE: You've been sleeping. I've seen you.

EXECUTIONER: I know myself.

(The Wife is silent.)

I'm up.

(Silence again.)

Don't you care?

(Still silence.)

I said, don't you—

WIFE: *(interrupting)* Of course I care. I'm your wife, aren't I?

EXECUTIONER: It's the third night in a row.

WIFE: You've been busy.

EXECUTIONER: No more than usual.

WIFE: You sleep like a stone. Just wrap yourself around me.

(They move around in the bed.)

Close your eyes.

EXECUTIONER: They keep opening.

WIFE: Turn over on your side. Try not to think of anything.

EXECUTIONER: I don't think. I see. *(He pauses.)* You know what I see? *(Giving her a little push, as she begins to drift off.)* Do you know what I—

WIFE: *(waking)* Look. It's four o'clock in the morning. Who has to get up any minute—you or me? The next one isn't scheduled till the twenty-fifth. Am I right?

EXECUTIONER: Right. Absolutely. You're always right.

WIFE: You can stay in bed all day. I, on the other hand, have things to do. I can't lounge around like some people. *(pausing)* Are you listening to me?

EXECUTIONER: Of course I'm listening. Keep talking. It puts me to sleep. *(abruptly sitting up)* Wait.

WIFE: What?

EXECUTIONER: I hear her.

WIFE: Nonsense.

EXECUTIONER: She's up. Definitely.

WIFE: I don't know how you hear these things.

EXECUTIONER: I know her breathing.

(He listens. Light comes up on Celeste, the Executioner's daughter.)

When she was little she always woke up the night before. Now she wakes up even when there is no execution.

WIFE: When she was little she never woke up.

EXECUTIONER: I'm worried about her. *(quiet)* She won't go for the bread. She refuses to go for the bread.

WIFE: She has to go.

EXECUTIONER: Someone has to. It can't be me. With me they won't stop at a few stones. *(looking away)* She's too intense. If she keeps going like this, she'll never find a husband. Never get married.

WIFE: What are you so worried about? She's still a child. An innocent child. Why think about marriage now? There'll always be someone. Our family covers all of France.

(There is a cry from the other room. In her bed, Celeste turns violently from side to side. Quiet.)

Listen. She's having another nightmare.

(In the other room, Celeste moans again.)

CELESTE: Papa.

EXECUTIONER: *(after a pause)* I'll go.

WIFE: Why is it always you she wants? You she needs?

(The Executioner is silent.)

All right. All right. Go to her.

(He doesn't move.)

Go.

(He looks at her.)

Please.

(Light comes up on Nounou.)

NOUNOU: So the wolf took the path of stones and arrived first at the house. He killed the grandmother, poured her blood into a bottle, and sliced her flesh onto a platter. Then he got into her bedclothes and waited in her bed.

SCENE 4

(Light comes up on Olympe and Pierrot, the street singer.)

OLYMPE: Leave me alone. Stop following me. You're always two steps behind.

PIERROT: That's because you're so beautiful, *ma belle.*

OLYMPE: I'm not. Go away.

PIERROT: More beautiful than anyone in Montauban. Than anyone in the country. Perhaps more beautiful than anyone in France. *(beating his drum)* Come up in the hayloft with me. I'll teach you how to play.

OLYMPE: Play?

PIERROT: The drum, Marie Gouze. Your mother used to play. There's a picture of her in the museum. You look just like her.

(Olympe smiles.)

Once you learn you can play anywhere. Go anywhere. They always want someone to play.

OLYMPE: Thank you very much, but I'm not interested in playing. *(She turns away.)*

PIERROT: Not even in the big chateau on top of the hill, Marie Gouze? Wouldn't you like to play there?

(Olympe whirls around, glares at him.)

Oh, I know where you go. I follow you. Remember? I'm always two steps behind. *(Stepping forward as she steps back.)* In the dark, when no one's around, you climb the stones till your feet bleed, get over the wall, swim the moat. At the gate you plead with them, beg them to let you in. But no one lets you pass, do they, Marie Gouze? No one even deigns to talk to you.

OLYMPE: They did once. He did.

PIERROT: Monsieur Le Franc de Pompignan?

OLYMPE: He took care of me.

PIERROT: He never cared for anyone in his life.

OLYMPE: For my mother.

PIERROT: Years ago. He abandoned her too.

OLYMPE: He was in love with her. He still is.

PIERROT: Mmm.

OLYMPE: He writes plays. Verses.

PIERROT: Aah.

OLYMPE: *(smiling)* He read me something once. Something that rhymed—before I fell asleep. A long time ago in a cloud-blue room. I was his princess then.

   (Pierrot is silent.)

   (soft) I have a book. By someone named Rousseau. I stole it. *(watching him)* I can't read it. But I'm going to learn how. I'm going to teach myself.

   (Pierrot smiles.)

   You know something? *(coming closer)* I can't even write my own name. I can't even sign it. This is how I have to sign. *(She draws a large X in the air.)*

PIERROT: That's nothing to be ashamed of. So does half of France.

OLYMPE: He tried to teach me. But I couldn't learn fast enough. You get that from your peasant stock, he said. That slowness.

PIERROT: You're not slow, Marie Gouze.

OLYMPE: I can't even speak the language properly. Not the way he speaks. Pure and proper French.

PIERROT: Neither can I. Neither can anyone. The whole country speaks in dialect.

OLYMPE: Not Paris.

PIERROT: Ah, so it's Paris now, is it? Paris where you want to go. *(Moving nearer. Half whispering.)* Doesn't he have a mansion there too?

OLYMPE: *(leaping away)* I hate you, Pierrot. I hate you forever.

PIERROT: Don't talk like that, Marie Gouze. I'm leaving tomorrow. I may never come back.

OLYMPE: Oh, you'll come back. You always come back.

PIERROT: You never know. *(He tries to embrace her.)* One kiss before I go.

OLYMPE: *(grabbing his drum and pulling back)* One step and I'll smash this over your head! *(Raising the drum above her head, as Pierrot moves toward her again.)* I mean it.

PIERROT: *(laughing)* All right, all right. I see you do.

(He bows gallantly and reaches out his hand for the drum. She thrusts it into his arms and runs off. Pierrot laughs again.)

See you in Paris, *ma belle*—if not before.

OLYMPE: *(reappearing for an instant)* I'll see you drowned in the Tarn first—you and that damned drum of yours!

PIERROT: *(watching her go, sings)*
OLYMPE DE GOUGES
THOUGH WE BESOUGHT HER
WALKED LIKE AN ANIMAL TO THE
SLAUGHTER
WE TRIED HARD TO WARN HER
BUT NOBODY CAUGHT HER
AND SO WE LOST
THE BUTCHER'S DAUGHTER.

(Light comes up on Nounou and Olympe.)

NOUNOU: *(tapping Olympe's forehead twice)* Knock, knock. *(smiling)* "Come in, my dear." *(pulling Olympe closer)* "Hello, grandmother. I've brought you some bread and milk." "Have something yourself, my dear. There's meat and bread in the pantry." *(She pauses.)* And as the girl ate, a little cat whispered, "Slut! To eat the flesh and drink the blood of your own grandmother." *(Pausing again as Olympe looks up.)* Then the wolf, the big bzou, says, "Undress and get into bed with me."

(Light comes up on the Executioner's Wife.)

WIFE: *(calling into the other room)* What is it? What's going on?

(Light comes up on the white bed of Celeste, the Executioner's Daughter. The Executioner is sitting on his daughter's bed, holding her head back. There is blood spattered on the sheets and pillowcase, blood on Celeste's white nightgown. Light comes up on Olympe, pulling herself up the thick vines of the chateau wall. A single window is illuminated.)

EXECUTIONER: She's having another nosebleed.

WIFE: Again? God—it's the same every night.

(Olympe peers in the window. Le Franc de Pompignan sits at his desk, his head bent, writing with a long feather pen. Olympe watches him a few moments, bends even closer and, with a rapid movement, grabs the pen from his hand. Le Franc looks up, startled, directly into the eyes of Olympe. Abruptly, he stands up.)

EXECUTIONER: It's soaked right through the pillow. She's upset. Frightened.

WIFE: I know she's upset. *(to herself)* I have to clean it up.

EXECUTIONER: Don't worry. I'll take care of it.

(Quickly, Olympe slides down the chateau wall.)

NOUNOU: *(pulling Olympe toward her)* "Where shall I put my apron?" asks the girl. "Throw it on the fire— you won't need it anymore." "My bodice?" "Throw it there too." "My skirt? My petticoat? My stockings?" "Throw it all in. You won't need any of it anymore."

WIFE: Well, hurry up. I'm not waiting forever.

EXECUTIONER: I'll just stay till she's asleep.

WIFE: She's got to get up soon anyway, you know.

(The Executioner looks up.)

She's got to go for the bread.

NOUNOU: When the girl got in bed, she said, "Oh grandmother! How hairy you are!" "It's to keep me warmer, my dear." "Oh grandmother—what long nails you have!" "To scratch myself better, my dear." "And what big nostrils you have!" "To take snuff better, my dear." *(She pauses.)* "Oh grandmother. What big teeth you have." *(another pause)* "It's for eating you better, my dear." *(looking at Olympe)* And he ate her.

(The morning light comes up on Celeste, her head thrown back on the bloodstained pillow of her bed.)

SCENE 5

(Light comes up on Pierrot and Olympe. Pierrot has his drum slung around his neck, a pack on his back.)

PIERROT: So they're marrying you off, Marie Gouze, I hear. Just so you stay out of trouble. To someone whose name is Pierre—like mine. Why don't they marry you off to me?

OLYMPE: Because he runs a restaurant—conveniently close to home. We're going to supply the meat.

(Pierrot laughs.)

I can't stand watching him eat. All those ruthless little bites. *(turning away)* I'll never get to Paris now.

PIERROT: You will if you come with me. We'll go everywhere—every city, every little town—and tell them what's happening.

OLYMPE: Happening, Pierrot?

PIERROT: In the next city. In the next town. In Montauban. Montpelier. Arles. Chartres. Orléans. Marseilles. Chateauroux. Clermont-Ferrand. Rennes. Rouen. Le Havre. Paris. *(pausing)* Versailles.

OLYMPE: Versailles! Where the King lives.

PIERROT: Things are happening, Marie Gouze. All over France. A great hope has risen. A hope for change. *(Moving closer as she stares at him.)* Don't you want change, Marie Gouze? To be able to read, able to write, able to be all you want to be. All you can be. We have that hope now. We shall never give it up. It must be spoken for. Fought for. From now on to decide for ourselves whoever we want to be. *(He beats the drum.)* Come with me and we'll sing all about it.

OLYMPE: How can I, Pierrot? I have no voice. You can sing. You can tell them. I have nothing to say.

PIERROT: More than you know, Marie Gouze. What's keeping you here? *(watching her)* Monsieur Le Franc de Pompignan? You'll never get anywhere near. You think he cares for the likes of you and me? Look around you. All of France has nothing to eat. Do you think he even notices? France is dying, Marie Gouze. Just look.

(Olympe is still.)

One day you'll look. One day you'll see. *(laughing)* But if you don't come now, by the time I get back you'll have a dozen kids, a restaurant next door and your father's butcher shop right down the street. You'll rot here forever in Montauban—with one eye on that castle on the hill.

(Olympe is silent, staring at the ground.)

I'm only teasing, Marie Gouze. You know how I am. But much as I'd like to, I can't force you to come. You're not ready. When you are, no wall will stop you. You'll climb them all and see Paris on the other side. *(He grins at her.)* If you want to, you'll get there.

(She looks up at him and smiles.)

Scene 6

(The sound of a cello. Light comes up on the Executioner playing his cello, while his daughter, Celeste, dances around the room.)

EXECUTIONER: You're happy today, Celeste. I like to see you happy.

CELESTE: I'm always happy when you play. *(She whirls around him.)* It takes me to a different world. It soothes me.

(She drifts off. The Executioner smiles after her.)

EXECUTIONER: Me too. Especially after a hard day's work.

(He looks up, afraid Celeste has heard him. But she is dancing dreamily, lost in a world of her own. The Executioner goes back to his playing. After a few moments, the Grandmother comes in. She walks rigidly, carefully, almost as if she were on stilts. She glances up for a moment, folds her hands, then rigidly walks out again. Celeste stops dancing immediately.)

CELESTE: Grandmother!

(There is no response.)

She's angry. She doesn't like it when I dance.

EXECUTIONER: Nonsense. She loves everything about you.

CELESTE: *(laughing)* About you, you mean.

EXECUTIONER: *(putting down his bow, chuckling)*

Well, she is my mother. Of all the boys, I was always her favorite. The one who did exactly what she wanted.

CELESTE: I wish I could do what she wanted.

EXECUTIONER: You do.

CELESTE: No. She wants me to be still. Silent. Knitting or something.

(The Executioner laughs, picks up his bow and taps her on the head with it.)

EXECUTIONER: Go back to your dancing. She'll forget all about it.

CELESTE: You know she won't. She won't say anything, but—*(confidentially)* I feel nervous around her sometimes.

EXECUTIONER: How about me? How do you think I feel?

(Celeste laughs, is suddenly quiet.)

CELESTE: She... She doesn't approve of me.

EXECUTIONER: Of course she approves of you. She always wanted a girl in the family. There have been so few girls.

CELESTE: I thought she only liked boys.

EXECUTIONER: She always said a girl would bring a bit of life into the household. Someone we could all take care of, dote on, love. Someone we could cherish. *(He pauses.)* Someone who wore white dresses, flowered hats. Someone who sang. *(smiling)* And danced.

(looking at her) Someone like you.

CELESTE: Like me? Me? But I'm none of those things.

EXECUTIONER: *(looking at her dark clothes, her pale face)* Like you. Yes. Exactly. Exactly like you.

Scene 7

(Night. The sound of drifting summer music. A midsummer country dance, held on a hillside. Wine flows, dresses swirl, music plays. Beneath glowing lanterns, couples move together and apart. Laughter, gaiety, whispers. Abruptly all the lanterns are extinguished. Shrieks. Consternation. Candles are lit. Flickering briefly, they go out. Total darkness. Someone giggles. Sudden laughter.)

A MAN'S VOICE: Where's the wine? I can't find the wine.

A WOMAN'S VOICE: In you hand, dumbell. You're holding the bottle. Come on, let's have a swallow.

MAN'S VOICE: Dance with me. Just because the lights go out, it's no reason to stop dancing.

WOMAN'S VOICE: Dance with you? I can't even see you.

ANOTHER WOMAN'S VOICE: It's starting to rain.

ANOTHER MAN'S VOICE: So what's a little rain—think you'll drown? *(A pause)* Hey. That's not rain.

SECOND WOMAN'S VOICE: What do you mean? It's raining buckets. *(She shrieks.)* Ouch! What was that?

SECOND MAN'S VOICE: A hailstone, my dear. I said it wasn't rain.

SECOND WOMAN: Hail! Are you mad? It's the middle of July. *(shrieking again)* Ow! There goes another one.

FIRST MAN: Come on, love. Put your arms around me. Dance.

SECOND WOMAN: Stones big as artichokes. I've never seen anything like it.

FIRST WOMAN: Dance? I'm getting killed out here. Come on—let's go in.

SECOND WOMAN: It's pitch black. Can you see?

FIRST WOMAN: Not a thing.

(They stumble off in the dark. Giggles. Groans. Then silence.)

OLYMPE: I'll dance with you if you want. I don't mind the dark.

FIRST MAN: Who's that?

SECOND MAN: Marie Gouze, isn't it? Marie Gouze, the beauty. I'd know that voice anywhere.

OLYMPE: Olympe. Olympe now.

SECOND MAN: So I've heard. Olympe after your mother. But with a fancy last name too.

OLYMPE: De Gouges.

FIRST MAN: Get a torch—quick! So we can see the beauty.

SECOND MAN: *(laughing)* De Gouges? From Gouze to de Gouges? Turning into an aristocrat, are you—after your famous—

THIRD MAN: *(breaking in)* I've got one! Right here.

FIRST MAN: Well, light it, man. For God's sake—get it lit!

THIRD MAN: I'm trying.

FIRST MAN: Hurry, man. Before she disappears.

THIRD MAN: I can't. Damn! Everything's too damned wet!

FIRST MAN: Where are you, my beauty?

OLYMPE: *(her voice silky)* Here. Right here. Just reach out your hand.

(There is the sound of the First Man falling.)

FIRST MAN: Ow! Where?

OLYMPE: Before you. Behind you. Wherever you want me to be. Turn around—you'll feel me.

ALL THREE MEN: *(bumping into each other)* Where? Where?

FIRST MAN: I'd like to feel you, my beauty.

SECOND MAN: So would I. Olympe de Gouges.

THIRD MAN: That wasn't the name her husband gave her. What happened to him?

SECOND MAN: Drowned in the flood we had last spring. Floated right down the River Tarn—unlucky bastard.

THIRD MAN: Lucky for us. The whole town's hungry for her. *(low)* I used to watch her bathe in that river.

SECOND MAN: *(hoarsely)* We all watched. God, those hips. Those thighs. That pearly skin. Dance with me, Olympe.

FIRST MAN: What about me? She promised me first.

THIRD MAN: How can we? There's no music anymore.

OLYMPE: *(invitingly)* There's the hail. We can dance to the hail. *(beginning to dance, her feet moving in the darkness)* Come on, I'll dance with all of you. It's my last night before I go away.

THIRD MAN: Where are you going, my beauty, my fair Olympe?

OLYMPE: Paris.

FIRST MAN: Who's taking you to Paris? Marrying somebody new?

OLYMPE: *(laughing)* And give up my freedom a second time? Never. But I'm going. I'll get there somehow.

SECOND MAN: How, Marie Gouze? In Paris, for a beauty like you, it's either marriage or—

FIRST MAN: *(breaking in)* And if that's what you want we've got all you need right down here! *(He chuckles deeply.)*

OLYMPE: I told you. I'm going! Tonight's my last night in Montauban.

FIRST MAN: Well, come on then—dance!

SECOND MAN: Dance!

(The First and Second Man start dancing with Olympe.)

THIRD MAN: Hey, wait! I got the torch lit. It's lit now. At last! Look.

(For just a moment, the torch flares up, revealing

Olympe's glowing shoulders, her breasts, her hair all around her. The Men swoop down on her, as Olympe puts both hands on the torch, quickly extinguishing it. The sound of the hail grows even louder, the sky darkens even more.)

FIRST MAN: God, this darkness. If we're not careful, we'll fall right into the Tarn. I don't even know where it is.

(There is silence.)

OLYMPE: I do. It's where you used to watch me bathe. *(soft)* You can watch me bathe again. *(softer)* You can bathe with me. Come. I'll cradle you in my long wet hair.

THIRD MAN: In your wet arms, Olympe.

FIRST MAN: In your wet breasts.

SECOND MAN: Cradle us deep in your long wet legs.

OLYMPE: All right then. Follow me. Touch me.

Silence. Then a sharp intake of breath from all three men.)

THIRD MAN: Ah. That flesh. At last I've got my hands on it.

FIRST MAN: Those round arms. Those feet. This belly.

SECOND MAN: These breasts. These amazing breasts.

THIRD MAN: That wild mane. Right between my fingers.

FIRST MAN: For years I've felt you in my dreams at night.

SECOND MAN: For centuries, Olympe de Gouges.

OLYMPE: Come on! I'll take you to the River Tarn. Hurry! It's right down there. Listen. You can hear it.

(The three men rush after her. There is a tremendous crack of lightning, illuminating their bodies.)

THIRD MAN: Wait! Watch out for that tree! The hail's coming down like rocks. Like boulders.

SECOND MAN: It's battering down the tiles. The cows will all be killed.

FIRST MAN: And our crops? Our wheat? This year's been bad enough already. It'll destroy everything. What's God doing to us? It's an omen, I tell you.

SECOND MAN: A call to arms!

(Another flash of lightning illuminates them fully, standing on top of the hill.)

OLYMPE: Look! Ah, look. The lights have gone out as far as you can see. Over the whole countryside. Over all of France. In the middle of summer. In the middle of July! *(reaching out her arms)* There's darkness over the face of the earth.

(The sound of the hailstorm continues to build as light comes up immediately on Pierrot, standing on a Paris street corner.)

PIERROT: *(sings)* THE KING HAS GONE OUT
HUNTING AGAIN
IN GOLDEN SUNLIGHT
WITH ALL OF HIS MEN
THE LAST SHOT RANG ON THE LAST STROKE

OF TEN
IN HIS RED VELVET DIARY
HE WROTE SIMPLY, "RIEN."

BAD HUNTING
POOR HUNTING
NO HUNTING TODAY.

"RIEN, RIEN," OH NOTHING AT ALL
ON THE VERY SAME DAY
OF THE BASTILLE'S GREAT FALL
JULY FOURTEENTH SEVENTEEN EIGHTY-
NINE
OUR DEAR LITTLE FATHER
JUST SAT DOWN TO DINE.

AND HE HAD A GOOD BREAKFAST
AH THAT I WILL SAY
A BREAKFAST HE DOTES ON DAY AFTER DAY
TWELVE CHOPS, A CHICKEN, A GREAT HEAP
OF HAM
NINE EGGS AND EIGHT MUFFINS
AND PLENTY OF JAM.

BAD HUNTING
POOR HUNTING
NO HUNTING TODAY.

THE KING HAS GONE OUT HUNTING AGAIN
WHILE OUR CHILDREN LIE STARVING
EVERY SIX OUT OF TEN
THEY CRY AND THEY WHIMPER
BUT THEY'LL EAT GOD KNOWS WHEN
AS LONG AS THEIR KING KEEPS HUNTING
AGAIN.

AND THE DATE OF THE DIARY
WAS JULY FOURTEENTH
JULY FOURTEENTH, SEVENTEEN EIGHTY-
NINE
A DAY TRIUMPHANT
A DAY FOR ALL TIME

BUT THE KING SIMPLY SCRIBBLED
AH, NOTHING
OH, NOTHING
NO, NOTHING WAS MINE.*

*Copyright © 1990, "Bad Hunting." Lyrics and music by
Wendy Kesselman.

(Paris. Olympe, elaborately dressed, her hair done up in an elaborate coiffure, is at her dressing table. Philippe stands before her, immaculately dressed, unable to take his eyes off her.)

OLYMPE: Ah. So you're early. I thought I said not to come till midnight.

(Philippe steps back.)

You musn't arrive too early, you know. The ball doesn't start till one.

(Philippe watches her, spellbound.)

Are you listening to me? Last night we started dancing at three. *(yawning)* I'm barely awake.

(She holds out her hand. Philippe takes it, grazes it lightly with his lips. She watches him in the mirror.)

Ah well, now that you're here, you might as well stay. You can help me. That is—if you want to.

(She bends toward him, her face close to his. Laughing, as Philippe stares at her.)

You know how to help a woman, don't you? A woman in distress.

(He looks at her questioningly.)

Yes, you see, I am in distress—though I may not look it. And do you know why? Because I've left the most difficult thing for last. *(pouting)* I always have such trouble with it. *(She looks at him.)* Have you guessed my little mystery? Oh come now, don't make such a face. It's my powder, dear Philippe. The powder for my hair. *(her hand lightly stroking her elaborate coiffure)* Very simple really. *(smiling at him)* I want you to powder me. *(soft)* Would you like that?

(He hesitates, unsure of what to do.)

Don't be shy. It'll be easy. I can tell—you have a delicate touch. Come. Bring your mask. It's right behind you.

(Philippe brings the long pointed paper mask with two huge holes cut out for Olympe's eyes. He stands still, holding it.)

Well, don't just stand there. Put it on me. *(tenderly)* Fool.

(Carefully, he places the mask over her face. She holds the mask delicately with one hand.)

The powder is right in front of you. Next to the mirror. Go ahead.

(Philippe takes the powder and begins spraying it delicately, all over the extraordinary masses of Olympe's hair.)

Careful. Don't get it on anything else.

(He moves around her, spraying, occasionally lifting a strand of hair, a descending curl, careful not to get the powder on her neck, her dress, her high lifted breasts.)

That's right. That's good. You're even better than my hairdresser. *(smiling)* My hair likes to be powdered. See how it responds.

PHILIPPE: It responds beautifully.

OLYMPE: Ah.

PHILIPPE: You have beautiful hair. Very beautiful hair. *(He sprays on a few final touches, then steps back.)*

OLYMPE: Is it ready? Have you finished? *(a pause)* Shall I do you?

PHILIPPE: Me? *(looking in the mirror)* I thought I was done.

OLYMPE: You need to be retouched. *(She pauses.)* There's another mask. Why don't you put it on?

(He hesitates for a moment, then reaches for the mask and holds it up to his face. Olympe begins retouching the powder on Philippe's wig.)

PHILIPPE: Mmm. That feels nice. Sweet.

(Olympe laughs and continues powdering, moving all around him, backing away, then coming closer, occasionally brushing up against him.)

OLYMPE: *(spraying on the final touch)* There. It's done. Finished. Take a look.

(For moments they stare at themselves, then turn and face each other. They bow. They curtsey. Holding their great pointed masks, they whirl around. The masks bump into each other. They laugh. Groping, they take hold of each other's hands and primly, properly, begin to dance a minuet. Back and forth they go, back and forth, their masks frequently bumping into each other, their feet perfectly in step. Occasionally, they stifle a laugh. Suddenly Olympe steps back, lets her mask fall to the ground. She pulls several long, slender ivory hairpins from her enormous coiffure. Her powdered hair falls around her. She is splendid.)

Well, what do you think?

PHILIPPE: *(transfixed)* Magnificent. You're magnificent.

OLYMPE: Well then. You've done everything else so well—*(She moves to the mirror, picks up a powder puff and holds it out to him, touching his long, pointed mask.)* Now you may do the rest.

PHILIPPE: The rest? *(He pauses.)* Where do I start?

OLYMPE: *(smiling)* At the bottom, silly. Always start at the bottom and work your way up to the top.

(He steps forward and takes the powder puff from her hand. She sits down. He kneels at her feet. Slowly, he takes off her slender white satin pumps. Gently, softly, he begins powdering her feet.)

Slow. Go slow. We have plenty of time.

(As he continues, delicately powdering her feet, her ankles, her calves, her knees, she bends further and further toward him, revealing her naked breasts. He pulls back, overwhelmed, spilling the powder on her breasts.)

Ah. Now look what you've done. I told you to be careful. *(looking down at him)* You must take it off.

(Uncertain, he reaches his hand out toward her breasts.)

No. Not like that. *(She takes his hand, pulls it to her mouth and licks it gently.)* Like this.

(He moves forward. She reaches out her hand and pulls off his mask. He moves close, closer, and licks

the powder off her breasts. She leans back. He undoes the bodice of her dress. She reaches out and pulls off his wig. His long, loose hair tumbles down, mingling with her white powdered curls. He grabs a handful of powder and, opening her dress even further, rubs it all over her body. Pulling off his jacket, his vest, his shirt, she smooths the silky powder on his arms, his neck, his chest. Their clothing is flung everywhere. They are naked, laughing, their bodies totally dusted in white. The thick white powder fills the room.)

SCENE 9

(A breadline. Four o'clock in the morning. Two women stand huddled in the cold.)

FIRST WOMAN: *(stamping her feet)* Freezing tonight. Colder than ever.

SECOND WOMAN: Don't worry. It'll get colder with the dawn. *(looking around)* The line's even longer than yesterday.

FIRST WOMAN: Getting longer every day.

SECOND WOMAN: And every day we get here earlier. Four o'clock in the morning for a lousy loaf of bread. Pretty soon we'll be here at midnight.

FIRST WOMAN: I left him sleeping like a log again. You'd think he'd come out for it once in his life. But we're the ones for the bread.

SECOND WOMAN: Oh, we're the ones for the bread all right. That's one privilege they'll never take away.

FIRST WOMAN: And what does our dear little King do? Nothing. He should remember to feed his starving children now and then.

SECOND WOMAN: Ah, don't blame the little father. He's thinking things over.

FIRST WOMAN: Like what? His next ball? His next banquet? His next necklace for Antoinette Deficit? Or maybe just his next dinner. All those creams in all those cream sauces—while we're stuck with a loaf of filthy bread we can't even choke down our throats. A little late, isn't it—to be thinking things over?

SECOND WOMAN: God knows what they put in the stuff.

FIRST WOMAN: Unmentionables.

SECOND WOMAN: They say they don't even make it out of flour anymore.

(Light comes up on Olympe and Philippe walking arm in arm, wearing elaborate powdered wigs.)

FIRST WOMAN: Garbage. Garbage mixed with straw. That's what our bread is made of. Rotten grain mixed into the dough. Warehouses stuffed with slowly rotting grain. And the price keeps rising, rising.

(Olympe hesitates, looks in the direction of the breadline. Unaware, Philippe walks on, then turns back, his hand held out for her. But she stands still, watching, listening, no longer aware of him.)

But our flour, my dear—shall I tell you what they're doing with that?

(Olympe stands frozen, as if hypnotized, as the Second Woman lays a restraining hand on the First Woman's arm.)

A thousand sacks of flour a day! Do you hear? A thousand sacks a day. Used to powder their picture-perfect precious wigs. *(pointing to Olympe's massive wig)* That's what they're doing with our flour, don't you know? They're fucking putting it on their fucking hair! *(quiet)* I'll tell you what I'd like to do with that hair. *(taking a step toward Olympe)* When you have a baby starving.

SECOND WOMAN: Or two.

FIRST WOMAN: Your   whole   family.

> *(She steps out of the breadline. Philippe walks back,
> stands in front of Olympe, his eyes on the First
> Woman, his hand just touching the hilt of his
> sword. The Second Woman yanks the First Woman
> back into the breadline. Calmly, Philippe holds out
> his arm for Olympe. She doesn't move. He lifts her
> arm, places it on his own and tries to steer her
> away.)*

OLYMPE: *(under her breath. Soft)* Wait.

> *(Philippe drags her away. But she is still listening,
> craning her neck in the direction of the breadline.)*

SECOND WOMAN: My youngest's been sick for over a
week now—vomiting day in and day out. I don't know
what to do with her.

FIRST WOMAN: *(raising her voice in the direction
Olympe has gone)* What do you expect? *(pointing)*
Look at those loaves—dark, crumbling, stinking sour.
(raising her fist) What do they want to do—kill us?

> *(From down the street, Celeste, the Executioner's
> Daughter, appears. She is dressed in black and walks
> slowly, her eyes lowered. The women see her, freeze.
> Celeste approaches the breadline cautiously. The
> women stare at her. Celeste, anxious, stops, takes a
> step, stops again, then continues toward them.
> When she is almost upon them, the women look at
> each other, then quickly separate to let her pass.)*

Scene 10

(The Executioner's home in Paris. The Executioner is sharpening his sword. His Wife is sitting at the table, writing. The Grandmother is sitting rigidly opposite the Wife.)

WIFE: I can't believe this. What did you—do it on purpose?

(The Executioner looks at her sharply. The Grandmother glares at her.)

Wasn't the blade sharp enough?

EXECUTIONER: *(sticking the point of the sword in the floor)* I'm telling you—it slipped. Right out of my hand. It's slipped before. It'll slip again. Nothing's perfect.

WIFE: Incredible. You think we can afford a fine like this?

EXECUTIONER: *(looking at the Grandmother. Quiet)* I told you I was sorry, didn't I?

WIFE: Don't be sorry for me. What about the poor man? How many times did it take?

EXECUTIONER: Eleven.

WIFE: Eleven? Are you joking?

EXECUTIONER: The blade kept getting stuck.

WIFE: God, that's revolting. How did you manage?

EXECUTIONER: It worked out. On the eleventh blow. *(pausing)* The crowd was ready to kill me. They started with stones. But someone had an axe. The police tore them off just in time.

(Light comes up on Olympe, sitting on a park bench, dressed in white. She is writing in a notebook with a feather pen. From the opposite direction, Celeste appears in her thin black dress. She runs past Olympe, her head lowered, clutching a loaf of bread. A stone flies in, barely missing her. She drops the bread, falls to the ground. Olympe stands up, picks up the bread, holds it out to Celeste. Celeste leaps to her feet, takes the bread from Olympe, turns to go, stops. For just a moment, she turns back, gazes at Olympe. Then, clutching the loaf of bread, she runs on. Olympe remains standing, immobile, her hands still outstretched in the direction of the fleeing girl.)

WIFE: You never know these days. Careful. You've got to be careful.

EXECUTIONER: I'm more than careful. *(raising the sword)* This blade could slice a hair of your head in two. I sharpen it. I know. It has weight—the sword. Power. *(pausing)* But something always gets stuck, goes awry. The collar, the hair, the nape of the neck.

(There is silence.)

WIFE: I feel sorry for the poor man.

EXECUTIONER: He was in agony. Begging me to get it over with. Pleading with me to die.

WIFE: Who would think they'd want to die?

EXECUTIONER: Oh, but they do. Anything's better than that terrible waiting. And this was no common criminal to get the rack, the rope. This was a nobleman. So he got the sword.

GRANDMOTHER: *(leaning forward)* Who was it?

(There is the sound of running feet.)

EXECUTIONER: Shh. Not now. *(Quiet)* We'll talk about it later.

> *(Celeste comes in, a loaf of bread in her arms. She is out of breath, disheveled, her hair drenched in sweat. A trickle of blood runs down her forehead. Her grandmother stands up. Her mother takes a step forward. Celeste stands still, staring at them. Then she lays the bread on the table and runs to her father. For a moment he holds her close, then takes several large fresh leaves, crushes them between his fingers and applies them to her wound.)*

Scene 11

(*An elegantly furnished Paris apartment. Olympe and Le Franc de Pompignan stand facing each other.*)

LE FRANC DE POMPIGNAN: Who let you in? (*moving past her toward the door*) I told them never to—

OLYMPE: (*stepping in front of him*) You know me then? Monsieur Le Franc de Pompignan?

LE FRANC DE POMPIGNAN: (*after a pause*) You've changed, of course. From the scruffy ragamuffin constantly being booted out the chateau gate in Montauban.

OLYMPE: (*smiling*) Yes. I've changed.

LE FRANC DE POMPIGNAN: You've become—how shall I put it? A lady. (*He smiles just slightly.*) Of sorts.

(*Olympe is silent.*)

Well. Now that you're here, I suppose I can't boot you out again.

(*Olympe smiles. Le Franc's face remains inpenetrable.*)

What can I do for you? (*silence*) How may I help you? Presuming, of course, that you need help. (*He pauses.*) I mean...you do want something of me.

OLYMPE: I—I sent you my manuscript. My play.

LE FRANC DE POMPIGNAN: (*after a moment, his hand just grazing an unbound manuscript on the table before him*) Yes. I have it right here.

OLYMPE: Have you read it?

LE FRANC DE POMPIGNAN: *(smiling slightly)* Well, shall we say, I began. I tried. *(pausing, as she stares at him)* If I may ask again, how may I be of assistance? What exactly do you want? Do you need money? Have you any—

OLYMPE: *(overlapping)* To write. I want to write.

LE FRANC DE POMPIGNAN: Ah. To write. Yes. Of course. *(a pause)* Well, you have written—*(his finger lightly tapping her play)* This.

OLYMPE: In the right way. To be able to say what I really feel. *(She pauses.)* I see things. Every day. Every hour. Everywhere I go. Women. Children. Beggars. Not only in Paris. At home in Montauban. People I reach out my hand to. People I can touch. People in poverty. Despair. A girl running, clutching a loaf of bread. A stone flying after her. Don't you see them, Monsieur Le Marquis? Don't you feel them too?

LE FRANC DE POMPIGNAN: Suppose I do. What then?

OLYMPE: I want to write about them. Tell their story.

(Le Franc laughs.)

LE FRANC DE POMPIGNAN: Well go ahead, my dear. By all means. It really doesn't concern me.

OLYMPE: *(coming closer)* Please. Show me. Teach me how. I want to—I need to learn.

LE FRANC DE POMPIGNAN: Show you what exactly?

OLYMPE: It's easy for you. I know that. You write poetry. Plays.

Le Franc de Pompignan: Nothing is easy. For anyone. How long did it take you to write—*(He lifts a corner of her manuscript.)* this? For example.

Olympe: Forty-eight hours.

Le Franc de Pompignan: Forty-eight hours! Indeed. *(He chuckles.)* Well, we can't all have what we want in this life, my dear. I can't help you to write. No one can. You simply haven't got it in you. *(flipping through the pages of the unbound manuscript)* You can't even write French, my dear child. You can hardly even speak it. How do you expect to write a full-length play? You can't spell. You have no grammar. You write in a barely legible hand. There are mistakes on every page, in every sentence—from beginning to end! Please do me the honor of making this the last time you send me anything you have written. There's not a line in here that's memorable. *(Looking down at the play. Quiet)* This is...at best...embarrassing.

Olympe: *(soft)* You could have helped me. Sent me to school. *(softer yet)* You could have taught me.

Le Franc de Pompignan: Let's not be absurd.

Olympe: You could teach me now.

Le Franc de Pompignan: Forty-eight hours! Amazing! *(He laughs aloud.)* Only someone with genius could possibly—

Olympe: *(interrupting)* I have genius.

Le Franc de Pompignan: Ah! You have genius. *(slapping her play)* That's hilarious. And where, may I ask, does your genius come from?

Olympe: You.

(Le Franc steps back.)

I get it from you. You're—

LE FRANC DE POMPIGNAN: *(tossing the unbound pages of her play in the air)* That's a lie! Just village talk. Forget it.

OLYMPE: I can't.

LE FRANC DE POMPIGNAN: You must! Stay in your place. Be who you are. Don't think you can be anyone but who you are. A butcher's daughter from Montauban! You'll never be anything else. *(quiet)* You should have stayed in Montauban. *(He pauses.)* But you're here now. You found your way to the capital. You have beauty, just like your mother. Even as a child. You have admirers—what more do you want? Live the galant life, Olympe. Stay out of the theatre. And out of politics too. It's no place for a woman these days. *(He looks at her.)* I can give you no better help than that.

(Olympe is silent, looking down.)

And now, if I may suggest... My wife, fortunately, is away today, but if she were ever to know—if she were ever even to guess—*(He pauses.)* Your very name—*(He stops.)*

OLYMPE: *(after a moment)* I may not come again?

LE FRANC DE POMPIGNAN: From now on this house must be closed to you.

(He steps forward, lightly grazes her hand with his lips. Olympe bends down, picks up the scattered pages of her play. She stands still, hesitating.)

OLYMPE: I just wanted to say—I didn't mean—I never thought—In no way have I ever wanted to embarrass you. *(a pause)* Monsieur Le Marquis.

(He is silent.)

Never. An embarrassment. That's the last thing I want to be. For you. *(looking down at the play in her hand)* I only thought—I only hoped you might—*(She looks up. Le Franc's face remains impenetrable.)* No.

(Still silence)

Well then. *(She looks at him, curtseys slightly. She smiles. His face does not change. She turns to go, stops, turns back.)* You were right. There is something I came here for. Something I didn't know myself.

LE FRANC DE POMPIGNAN: *(wary)* What is that?

OLYMPE: A word. One word.

LE FRANC DE POMPIGNAN: Ah. *(A pause)* Which one?

(Olympe is silent.)

Hurry. I have an appointment.

OLYMPE: *(stepping forward)* You know the one.

(Le Franc moves back.)

I'm too intense, aren't I? Just like I was outside the chateau gate in Montauban.

LE FRANC DE POMPIGNAN: My appointment. Please.

OLYMPE: My word.

(They stand silent, facing each other.)

Do you think I can't hear it humming in your head? It hums in mine. It never stops. It's who I am. What you made me. The one word that says I belong to you.

LE FRANC DE POMPIGNAN: *(turning away)* You never belonged to me.

(Olympe grabs hold of his jacket.)

OLYMPE: Please. Tell me. Why I'm not a human being with thoughts and feelings the same as you. Why I'm worthless. Why I have no rights of my own. You have to say it. You must!

LE FRANC DE POMPIGNAN: I don't have to say anything! Don't try to manipulate me. *(trying to shake her off)* Get off, I tell you! What do you want from me? Money? Land? My name perhaps? You'll never get it. As a girl—a girl child—a—*(snorting)* You don't even exist. You're not entitled to anything!

OLYMPE: I don't want anything. Only the word that belongs to me. The word you were about to say. I won't leave until you do.

LE FRANC DE POMPIGNAN: *(pulling her across the floor with him)* You'll leave. I'll make you leave.

OLYMPE: *(clinging to him)* You'll have to boot me out, Monsieur Le Franc de Pompignan—just like in Montauban. Only we're in Paris now and everyone will see, everyone will know.

LE FRANC DE POMPIGNAN: You wouldn't dare, little girl child! Little—*(He stops. Soft)* Bastard. *(A pause)* All right. You want me to say it? I'll say it. I'll say it for you. *(almost spitting out the word)* Bastard! Bastard!

Little girl baby who should never have been born. Good only to be thrown away. Out of my sight. Out of my life! *(dragging her to the door)* Little bitch. Little bastard bitch. *(Almost kicking her away from him. Exhausted)* There. Satisfied? Are you satisfied now?

(Olympe picks herself up, stands very tall, very straight, holding the pages of her script to her breast.)

OLYMPE: *(In tears. Smiling)* Yes.

Scene 12

(Celeste stands before a white enamel basin of water. She is holding a white cloth. Carefully, she unbuttons the top buttons of her thin black dress, pulls it down over her shoulders. She dips the cloth in the water and washes blood off her neck, her chest. For a moment she stands still, holding the bloodstained cloth in her hands. She drops it into the basin, watching it float in the water. Slowly, she lifts her hand and puts it inside her opened dress. She closes her eyes.)

SCENE 13

(Olympe lies in bed, her magnificent long hair covering her white shift. Beside her lies Georges. The morning light shines on the rumpled sheets. A parrot sits on a swing.)

OLYMPE: *(her arms around Georges)* Shhh. Don't move. Stay like that. Just like that. *(She pauses.)* I don't want you to move.

GEORGES: I won't.

OLYMPE: And don't talk. It's better when you're still.

(He is still.)

That's right. Like that. Absolutely like that. Perfect. *(after a long moment)* Now. Talk. Go ahead. Say something.

GEORGES: *(softly)* What shall I say?

OLYMPE: Anything you like. Come. Tell me in my ear.

GEORGES: But what would you like?

OLYMPE: *(smiling)* Use you imagination, Georges. Don't all Parisians have great imaginations?

(Georges moves even closer and whispers something in her ear.)

Oh, come now. You can do better than that.

(He whispers something else.)

Or that. Come on, Georges. Talk to me. I want you to talk to me.

PARROT: *(leaning forward)* Talk to me. Me! Me!

GEORGES: *(looking up)* Olympe? Was that you? *(a pause)* It didn't sound like you.

OLYMPE: *(laughing)* No, Georges. It wasn't me.

GEORGES: Well then, who—

OLYMPE: *(overlapping)* Come on. Try again.

(Again, Georges whispers in her ear.)

That's more like it.

(Holding her close, Georges presses her head back and continues whispering, faster now.)

Oh, I like that. I like that very much.

(One hand clutching her cascading hair, Georges moves his other hand down her body, whispering urgently all the while. Olympe's ear is pressed to his mouth.)

You surprise me, Georges. Go on. More. I want to know more.

PARROT: *(moaning sensuously)* More. More. Tell me more, Georges.

(Georges leaps up, clutching the sheets around him.)

GEORGES: Olympe. There's someone in this room.

(Olympe laughs.)

I'm telling you. I heard someone. Keep down.

OLYMPE: I know you did. I know.

GEORGES: *(tense)* Well, who is it, for God's sake?

PARROT: *(squawking)* For God's sake, more! *(passionate, low)* I want to know more.

OLYMPE: *(trying to stifle her laughter)* Be still now, Jean-Jacques. That's enough.

GEORGES: *(looking at the parrot)* Jean-Jacques?

OLYMPE: Rousseau.

PARROT: Rousseau! Rousseau!

GEORGES: I didn't know you read Rousseau.

OLYMPE: *(proudly)* All his books. Every one. He's the reason I learned how to read.

GEORGES: I've never even seen you open a book.

OLYMPE: You've never noticed, Georges.

GEORGES: What goes on in that beautiful little head these days? A parrot named Rousseau—why not?

PARROT: Why not? Why not? *(intense)* I'm hot. I'm hot.

OLYMPE: You little darling.

PARROT: *(deep)* Let me out!

GEORGES: Did you hear that? The little darling wants to go out. He wants to be free. Maybe we should open a window.

PARROT: *(squawking)* Free! Free! Man is born free and is everywhere in chains.

GEORGES: At least take him in the other room.

PARROT: *(langourously)* Take me! Take me!

(From far away there is the low sound of a drum beating.)

OLYMPE: *(sitting up)* Listen.

(The drum grows louder. Suddenly the piercing sound of the tocsin rings throughout Paris.)

The alarm bell!

GEORGES: *(trying to pull the resisting Olympe back into bed)* Don't pay any attention to it. Every day it's something new. Listen to me. I'll talk to you again— just the way you like.

(The door bursts open. Two Market Women rush in, their hair streaming, their eyes wild. One carries a long pike, the other a pitchfork. A large drum is strapped around her neck. Georges leaps to his feet, reaches for his sword.)

FIRST MARKET WOMAN: *(stepping in front of him and brandishing her pike)* No need for that, my pretty man. We're the ones who are armed today.

OLYMPE: What do you want?

SECOND MARKET WOMAN: *(pointing her pitchfork at Olympe)* You. Every woman in every house—we're taking them all.

FIRST MARKET WOMAN: The alarm's ringing all over Paris, *ma belle.* And every woman is heeding its call.

SECOND MARKET WOMAN: *(putting her foot on Olympe's bed)* Every woman who cares for her own, that is. Who cares for the starving children of France.

FIRST MARKET WOMAN: It started on the breadlines this morning at dawn.

SECOND MARKET WOMAN: It will lead us all the way to Versailles! We will not lack for bread in the future. We're marching to Versailles to ask the King for bread. At prices we can afford, my friends. He's the baker, isn't he? The only one who can give us our daily bread.

OLYMPE: *(thoughtful)* Big thick loaves, crusty on the outside, spongy on the inside—right out of the oven, all hot—just the way—

FIRST MARKET WOMAN: *(overlapping)* Ah yes, we'll talk to the little father—we'll talk to the baker himself!

GEORGES: *(chuckling)* The King? Your little baker doesn't even know you exist. Nor does he care. He'll never talk to you.

FIRST MARKET WOMAN: Don't mock us, man. We've had enough mockery.

GEORGES: To a bunch of women.

SECOND MARKET WOMAN: Look out your window. We're a bigger bunch than you think. *(grabbing hold of Olympe's arm)* Ready to go, my lovely? Those eyes are hungry to go.

GEORGES: *(grabbing Olympe's other arm)* She's not going anywhere. Certainly not on a bread march to Versailles. *(pulling her toward him)* You're no savage! You have nothing in common with these women. *(both hands on her arm)* They don't need you. They have their own people.

(Olympe stares at him, pulls her arm away.)

What's wrong with you? Why should you care what happens to them? You have enough to eat. You're warm here with me. Believe me, Olympe—there's no reason for you to go.

SECOND MARKET WOMAN: *(sitting down on Olympe's bed, her pitchfork in her hand)* There are six thousand of us out there already. Soon we'll be seven.

FIRST MARKET WOMAN: Eight. Nine. A whole army!

SECOND MARKET WOMAN: The women of Paris, Olympe. The women of France. Marching for our rights.

FIRST MARKET WOMAN: Children are dying in Paris. Dying on the streets. Beggars everywhere. Just look. Every day, every hour, France starves a little bit more. When will we have bread, Olympe? When will our children have bread?

OLYMPE: *(rising from the bed, her hair down to her waist. Overlapping)* I'm going.

GEORGES: Are you out of your mind? You're not going to listen to these imbeciles, are you?

OLYMPE: Every word you say, Georges. Every word pushes me out that door.

GEORGES: *(pushing in front of her)* Olympe, don't be an idiot. You have no place out there.

OLYMPE: Every woman has. Didn't you hear what they said?

GEORGES: Are you going to listen to that rubbish? It's

over twenty kilometers to Versailles. *(picking up her delicate satin slippers)* What are you going to march in—these?

OLYMPE: I ran barefoot in the hills of Montauban. I'll find something. *(quiet)* Don't bully me, Georges. I can't stay in this big white bed with you forever. *(stepping forward as he turns away)* Georges.

PARROT: Georges.

SECOND MARKET WOMAN: Who's this?

FIRST MARKET WOMAN: *(laughing)* A talking bird, is it? Where'd you get this character?

PARROT: Let me out! Let me out!

(The Market Women laugh wildly.)

SECOND MARKET WOMAN: He wants to go too. Why don't you take him?

PARROT: *(longingly)* Oh yes. Take me. Take me. I love you.

(The Market Women are beside themselves. The tocsin sounds repeatedly, over and over and over again. The Second Market Woman beats her drum. The First Market Woman throws her heavy jacket around Olympe's shoulders.)

OLYMPE: I'm going, Georges. I'm going. *(She lifts the parrot from his swing.)*

GEORGES: Olympe, you're mad. This is insane. He'll get killed on the way—your beloved Rousseau. And you will too.

OLYMPE: *(tweaking the parrot's beak)* We're going to Versailles, Jean-Jacques, to speak to the baker—the King! He's our little father, isn't he? He's got to talk to us. We may even bring him home—all the way back to Paris, where he belongs!

PARROT: Back! Back! Bring him back.

(Laughing, the Market Women leave.)

OLYMPE: Goodbye, Georges. *(She kisses him. Holding the parrot, she follows the Market Women out.)*

GEORGES: *(calling after her)* Olympe, wait! You'll never speak to him. You'll never even get near!

(There is no response. Georges runs to the window, throws it open. Outside, the sound of marching feet grows louder.)

Listen to me! You're marching for nothing. Getting yourself killed for nothing! Nothing, Olympe! You'll never speak to the King!

(Light comes up immediately on Pierrot, the street singer.)

PIERROT: *(sings)* THE KING HAS GONE OUT HUNTING AGAIN
ON A FINE FALL MORNING
WITH ALL OF HIS MEN
WHILE ALREADY IN PARIS AWAY FROM HIS KEN
THE WOMEN ARE MARCHING
AT A QUARTER TO TEN.

THE FIFTH OF OCTOBER, SEVENTEEN EIGHTY-NINE
TEN THOUSAND WOMEN WALKED IN A GREAT LINE

AND SOME WALKED AHEAD
AND SOME WALKED BEHIND
A KNOWN DESTINATION
BUT WHAT WOULD THEY FIND?

VERSAILLES, VERSAILLES,
THAT GLORIOUS PLACE
ADORNED GENERATIONS BY A PRIVILEGED
RACE
A COURT OF CORRUPTION BEHIND A GOLD
FACE
INTRIGUE AND EXTRAVAGANCE
RED RUBIES AND LACE.

THE FIFTH OF OCTOBER, SEVENTEEN
EIGHTY-NINE
THAT ARMY OF WOMEN
HALF STARVING, HALF BLIND
ARRIVED AT THE PALACE AND CRIED OUT
THEIR MIND
THEY CRIED FOR THEIR CHILDREN
AND ALL OF MANKIND.

THE KING MUTTERED FINE WORDS
BUT NOTHING WAS SAID
SO THEY BROKE THE QUEEN'S DOOR DOWN,
THEY RANSACKED HER BED
AND ALL THROUGH THE COURTYARD AND
THE SKY OVERHEAD
A SINGLE CRY CARRIED
"JUST GIVE US OUR BREAD!"

"BREAD; BREAD: WE'RE BEGGING FOR BREAD
WITHOUT IT WE'RE STARVING
WITHOUT IT WE'RE DEAD
AND ANY MORE PROMISES ARE BETTER
UNSAID
WE DON'T WANT YOUR PROMISES
WE JUST WANT OUR BREAD."

(There is the sound of heavy rain, marching feet,

shouts, screams. Light comes up on Olympe's empty apartment. There is the sound of footsteps, heavy, dragging. Olympe comes in, bedraggled and wet, soaked from the pouring rain. Her white shift is torn, her boots are falling apart, the huge heavy jacket is ripped and smeared with mud. The parrot, his feathers covered with dirt, sits on her shoulder. Around her neck is the broken drum of the Second Market Woman. Around her head is a wreath of oak leaves.)

PIERROT: *(sings)* THE SIXTH OF OCTOBER
SEVENTEEN EIGHTY-NINE
A GREAT BAND OF WOMEN
MARCHED OUT IN A LINE

(Absently, Olympe strokes the parrot's feathers. Her face has a triumphant look. Softly she begins to hum.)

OLYMPE: They shall not lack for bread in the future. We are bringing back the baker, the baker's wife, and the baker's boy.

PIERROT: *(sings)* AND SOME WALKED AHEAD
AND SOME WALKED BEHIND

PARROT: The baker's boy. The baker's boy. The baker's little boy.

PIERROT: *(sings)* AND THEY BROUGHT BACK THE BAKER
THAT MORNING OF MORNINGS
THAT MORNING DIVINE.*

---

*Copyright © 1990, "October Days." Music and lyrics by Wendy Kesselmen.

ACT II
SCENE 1

PIERROT: *(sings)* WOMEN HANG THEM FROM THEIR EARS
  WEAR THEM HOME AS SOUVENIRS
  VENDORS HAWK THEM ON THE STREET
  CHILDREN GET THEM AS A TREAT
  EVERYBODY WANTS A TOY
  SOMETHING WE CAN ALL ENJOY
  WIND THEM UP—SO QUICK, SO CLEAN—
  WHACK! THAT'S IT—LA GUILLOTINE!
  BUT WHEN HEAD FROM BODY GOES
  WHO KNOWS WHAT THE HEAD STILL
  KNOWS?*

> *(Light comes up on the Executioner's Wife and the Grandmother, examining several large drawings. The Grandmother uses a magnifying glass. The Executioner is watering a large red hibiscus.)*

EXECUTIONER: It's perfection, I tell you! It works like a charm. *(standing over his wife's shoulder)* The body goes there. The head goes here. The blade comes down like so—*(letting his hand fall)* And it's all over in a second. In less time than it takes you to wink, as Dr. Guillotin says. *(smiling)* The victim feels nothing. Just a momentary shiver of ice on his neck before the blade sets in.

WIFE: Ah.

EXECUTIONER: Neat. Clean. Impeccable. There's never been anything like it. No more accidents. No more mistakes. But not until you've seen it with your own eyes will you understand its absolute simplicity, its incredible precision.

WIFE: And when will that be?

---

*Copyright © 1990, "What The Head Knows." Lyrics and music by Wendy Kesselman.

EXECUTIONER: Soon. We're doing the first experiments with sheep right now. You'll see. The whole thing will happen so fast, only the thump of the blade will tell the people the victim is no longer alive.

GRANDMOTHER: *(looking up)* Too fast. The people will be disappointed.

EXECUTIONER: Nonsense.

GRANDMOTHER: Absolutely. *(leaning forward)* They won't be able to see. *(silence)* What about the rack? The rope? The wheel? The sword? Hot poison? Burning oil? You think they won't be missed? *(She pauses.)* And the four ordeals? Ordeal by fire, by the cross, the iron, the—

EXECUTIONER: *(breaking in)* All gone. All abolished. None of them will ever be necessary again.

GRANDMOTHER: Don't worry—they'll be back. The people must see. The people must know. They must witness the punishment. They have that right. Believe me—they'll soon be clamoring for the old ways.

EXECUTIONER: They're no longer practical, Mother. They weren't humane. This, beyond everything, is a humane invention. Before, the common criminal got the rack, the wheel, the rope. Only the nobleman got the sword. But the Revolution has made all citizens equal before the law. *(looking straight out)* Now it gives them the same privilege before death. From now on it will be the same for everyone. For all of France! *(He goes back to watering his hibiscus.)*

WIFE: *(holding up a drawing)* And the color?

EXECUTIONER: Red.

Scene 2

(A bridge. Night. Darkness. A hooded figure in a black cape emerges from the shadows, carrying a stack of posters. The figure looks around, hurriedly begins putting up the posters beneath the bridge. A second figure, also in black, wearing a mask, stands hidden in the shadows. The First Figure puts up poster after poster. Silently, the Second Figure glides toward the first.)

SECOND FIGURE: Stop where you are!

(Clutching the posters, the First Figure draws back into the shadows. The Second Figure advances.)

Stop, I tell you! Any posters denouncing the King are forbidden.

FIRST FIGURE: *(in a disguised voice)* These posters do not denounce our beloved Louis.

SECOND FIGURE: Just as I thought—they defend the traitor!

FIRST FIGURE: Louis's no traitor!

SECOND FIGURE: Traitor to the people of France! *(advancing even further)* Hand them over at once.

FIRST FIGURE: Never! These posters have nothing to do with the King.

SECOND FIGURE: No? That's something I'll see for myself.

(He draws his sword. The First Figure hesitates, then also draws a sword. Their swords clash as a rapid duel ensues in the shadows beneath the bridge. At one

point, the Second Figure drops his sword. Quickly, the First Figure bends down, picks it up, and throws it back to him. The duel continues.)

SECOND FIGURE: *(pinning the First Figure to the wall)* Now I'll see who I'm dealing with—who this expert swordsman is. This generous soul who gives me back my sword!

(With the tip of his sword, he lifts the hood off the head of the First Figure. A mass of luxuriant hair comes cascading down. It is Olympe. The Second Figure quickly draws back, releasing her. Then, abruptly, he rushes forward and, for just a moment, takes her in his arms and kisses her. Olympe flees, leaving her sword behind. The Second Figure picks it up and starts after her.)

Wait! Please! Forgive me. Come back. I didn't mean— I didn't know—

(But she is gone. The Second Figure gazes after her, then rips a poster from the wall and begins to read. Light comes up on Celeste, the Executioner's Daughter, standing before a black trunk. She looks around her. Quietly, cautiously, she bends over the trunk, gingerly begins removing pieces of clothing. It is an odd assorted mixture. There is a man's elegant jacket, a long flowing scarf, a pair of worn green trousers, heavy wooden shoes, delicate pointed slippers, a child's bonnet, a finely embroidered vest, a woman's long flowered dress. There are several white cambric shirts, several pairs of gloves, a few handkerchiefs, rough ragged shawls, a floppy wide-brimmed hat. Celeste takes each item of clothing carefully out of the trunk, folds it neatly, lays it before her. She looks up, listens, goes to the door. She stands very still, then tiptoes back to the trunk again. She examines each piece of clothing

minutely, makes a selection, and begins dressing up. Everything she puts on is much too big on her. When she is finished, she wears an odd combination —the long flowered dress, the embroidered vest, the heavy wooden shoes, a rough ragged shawl, a pair of long white gloves. Each item of clothing is deeply stained with blood. She picks up the floppy wide-brimmed hat and puts it on. For a moment she stands still. Then she pulls off the long white gloves and takes one of the men's large white handkerchiefs from the pile of clothing. She ties a knot in it. She places her hands behind her back and fits the handkerchief around them. The handkerchief is also stained with blood. Awkwardly, her hands bound behind her back, she tries to walk around the room, but the heavy wooden shoes do not allow her to go very far. She trips and falls. She gets up and starts again. Her hands still bound behind her back, she continues clumsily to walk in the heavy shoes. Again she trips. Again she falls. The large floppy hat slips from her head. Her Grandmother comes in.)

GRANDMOTHER: Celeste!

(Celeste looks up from the floor.)

Get up from there immediately.

(Celeste tries to stand, but can't get her balance. She struggles to undo her hands from the knot of the white handkerchief, but she has bound them too tightly.)

Are you listening to me, young lady? I will not have disobedience in my house.

(Without untying the handkerchief knot, Celeste somehow manages to stand up.)

Now come here.

(Celeste backs away slightly.)

(emphatic) Come here.

(Awkwardly, her hands still bound behind her, Celeste, barefoot, walks forward, stands before her Grandmother.)

How many times have I told you not to dress up in those clothes. *(quiet)* Your father would kill me if he found out. He would kill you. *(eyeing Celeste up and down)* You must understand. This clothing is sacred. After every execution, it has always been our right to take it away and keep it. *(sudden)* Now take it all off and put it back in the trunk where it belongs.

(Celeste stumbles over to the trunk, her hands still bound behind her back. She stands still, her back to the audience, quietly trying to get the handkerchief knot undone.)

Must I count to ten as if you were still a baby? *(gradually becoming aware of Celeste's movements)* Just a minute.

(Celeste stops moving.)

What are you doing behind your back?

(Celeste, her head bowed, is silent.)

I saw you doing something with your hands. Moving them in some way. Celeste—what are you hiding from me?

(She advances on Celeste. Celeste circles around her Grandmother, trying to keep her bound hands out of sight. Swiftly, the Grandmother follows her, tries

to stop her. Finally, she blocks Celeste against a wall.)

Now. *(her hand on Celeste's shoulder)* I will look.

(She looks down and sees Celeste's hands bound by the white handkerchief. Twisting Celeste's face toward her, she points to her bound hands. In a violent gesture, she rips off the handkerchief. They stand as if frozen together. Light comes up on the Second Figure, reading Olympe's poster.)

SECOND FIGURE: "To each of us, from the beginning, the Revolution held out a promise, a hope. But what advantage have we gained from our glorious freedom? The new Declaration of the Rights of Man and Citizen says that men are born free and must remain free and equal under the law. What does it say about—"

(Light comes up on Olympe, standing on a table in a women's club in Paris.)

OLYMPE: *(her voice blending into the voice of the Second Figure)* About women! Are we free? Are we equal?

(The Grandmother abruptly slaps Celeste's hands, pushes her over to the black trunk. The women in the club lean forward, listening to Olympe.

We have the right, the terrible right, to mount the scaffold—have we the right to mount the podium too? The right to speak out, to be heard?

(Celeste slowly begins taking off the bloodstained clothing, gathers the shoes, the gloves, the floppy hat and places it all inside the trunk. She picks up the clothing she has folded and carefully lays it back in. The Grandmother stands over her throughout.)

We can't even write our own names! We must sign with an X—as if we didn't exist. And do we exist, my sisters, my friends?

(The women in the club move closer.)

I come from Montauban. French is not my mother tongue. Neither is it the mother tongue of over half the population of France. I can't spell. I have no grammar. I write in a barely legible hand. I am one who signed with an X! *(She draws a large X in the air.)* But tonight I bring you this—*(She takes out a freshly written manuscript. Celeste stands up from bending over the black trunk. She stares straight out. Olympe reads from her manuscript. Exuberant)* Declaration of the Rights of Woman and the Female Citizen. Article One. "Woman is born free and lives equal to man." *(looking up)* It took us a long time to find the courage to write, the courage to speak. But we have that courage now! Give us our rights! In all the great things that are happening, all the great things yet to come, the change, the growth, every hour, every day, are we the ones to be left behind?

(Celeste stands still. Her Grandmother sits very straight in a high-backed chair. The Second Figure tucks the poster under his cape, rushes off.)

GRANDMOTHER: Don't try to hide anything from me. I can see right through you.

CELESTE: See what, Grandmother?

GRANDMOTHER: Remember this. *(pausing)* Obedience has always been the first virtue of our family. *(eyeing Celeste)* Obey him. Do as he decides. Whatever he tells you will always be right. There's no reason to be unhappy. This is a family like any other. We have our heritage, that's all. Our tradition. *(quiet)* Your father is in a noble profession. One of the noblest of all. *(Watching, as Celeste looks away.)* Mind you, you're not the first. Many people have been unhappy in this house.

CELESTE: You, Grandmother?

GRANDMOTHER: Ah no. Not me. Ever since your grandfather brought me from Normandy, I've been very proud to be a member of the household. When I saw those paintings at the top of the stairs—*(She stops, gazing out.)*

CELESTE: The family portraits. *(urging her on)* Go on, Grandmother.

> *(Light comes up on the Second Figure entering a studio filled with primitive paintings of wild animals—animals being released, breaking free, escaping from cages and restraints. An unfinished painting of a hand releasing a lynx from a golden cage stands on an easel. The Second Figure stares at it for a moment, then takes Olympe's poster from under his cape and pins it on the easel beside the unfinished painting.)*

GRANDMOTHER: *(slowly)* Yes. Ah yes. Such a noble gaze. Such precision. Such grace. So different from my own family. Growing up in Normandy, I saw scenes— indescribable—in our village square. My own father, my grandfather—*(She pauses.)* And then of course... the old man.

> *(Celeste looks at her.)*

My great-grandfather. Famous in his day. He did things—*(She hesitates.)* To his own daughter, even. When she wanted to run away. They kept the instruments at home those days—the rack, the rope, the black boot. The boot that broke the bones. And when she tried—*(cutting herself off)* Ah, the old methods. The old ordeals. All gone now.

CELESTE: She tried to run away?

GRANDMOTHER: With someone completely out of the question. Someone who wouldn't do at all.

CELESTE: Who was that, Grandmother?

GRANDMOTHER: An old story. Forgotten long ago.

CELESTE: But who was he? What was wrong with him?

GRANDMOTHER: He didn't belong. Ours is an inherited profession, Celeste. You know we cannot marry outside. If he had known, if he had learned—*(pausing)* Let's just say, he wasn't one of us. *(watching Celeste's face)* He wasn't one of the family.

Scene 3

(Music. Glowing lights. A costume ball at a women's club. Women greet each other, embrace, dance. There is much laughter and applause, as they exclaim on each other's costumes. Some have come dressed as women, some as men. There is a sansculottes woman, a sans-culottes man. Someone is dressed as Robespierre, someone as Marat. One woman comes as Messidor, another as Ventôse—two months in the new Revolutionary Republican calendar. There are women dressed as Revolutionary playing cards and chess pieces. One woman, dressed as Red Riding Hood, wears an enormous tricolored cape—the left side blue, the right side white, the back and the hood bright red. Olympe appears, dressed as Jean-Jacques Rousseau, the parrot sitting on her shoulder. She immediately meets two women she knows, stops and talks with them. A new dance begins. Several of the women start to dance, moving from partner to partner. Olympe eventually finds herself paired with the woman dressed as Red Riding Hood, wearing the Revolutionary tricolored cape.)

OLYMPE: *(taking Red Riding Hood by the hand)* And which path are you taking tonight—the path of thorns or the path of stones?

RED RIDING HOOD: *(in a deep voice)* How about you?

OLYMPE: *(looking up. Startled)* Oh, I'm taking the path of thorns.

RED RIDING HOOD: *(looking up. Startled)* Well, then I shall take the path of stones.

(They move on to the next partner. The dance continues, with the women going from one partner

to the next. Again, Olympe and Red Riding Hood meet.)

Ah, we meet again.

OLYMPE: What a deep voice you have.

RED RIDING HOOD: The better to talk to you, my dear. The better that you might hear me.

(They dance a few steps together. Red Riding Hood accidentally steps on Olympe's foot.)

OLYMPE: And what big feet you have.

RED RIDING HOOD: The better to—

OLYMPE: *(interrupting, looking down at Red Riding Hood's feet)* Enormous feet, in fact. *(looking up)* For a woman. *(peering closer)* What are you hiding underneath that great cape? And why are you wearing your hood?

RED RIDING HOOD: *(quiet)* Wouldn't you like to see?

OLYMPE: *(soft)* There are no men allowed here tonight.

RED RIDING HOOD: I know that, Olympe de Gouges.

OLYMPE: You know me?

RED RIDING HOOD: We've met before. *(a pause)* Under a bridge.

(Olympe steps back.)

You were disguised that night. You could have killed me, but you gave me back my sword. I came disguised tonight to find you. To warn you. *(drawing her into a corner)* You're in danger, Olympe de Gouges. Come with me.

OLYMPE: Come with you? I don't even know your name.

RED RIDING HOOD: *(pulling down the great hood, revealing a striking face)* Michel. *(Drawing her even closer, he opens his cape slightly, revealing a pistol.)* Trust me.

> *(A new dance begins. Swiftly, Michel closes his cape, draws his hood back over his head and, pulling Olympe close, begins the dance. Light comes up on the Executioner and the Grandmother, eating dinner. Light comes up on Pierrot, the street singer, standing on a Paris corner, a few spectators surrounding him.)*

PIERROT: *(sings)*
I WILL NOT MARRY AN EXECUTIONER, FATHER
NO MATTER WHAT YOU DO
I'M NOT CONTRARY
I'M SIMPLY WARY
I'D RATHER STAY HERE WITH YOU.

> *(The spectators laugh.)*

SO MANY PEOPLE COME CALLING, DEAR FATHER
PEOPLE YOU SEE EVERY DAY
EACH HOLDING HIS HEAD
EACH WANTING A BED
THEY HAVE NO PLACE THEY CAN STAY.

THEY WANT TO LIE DOWN BESIDE ME, MY FATHER
THEY WEREN'T GIVEN A GRAVE
THEY MAKE A GREAT DIN

BUT I WON'T LET THEM IN
FOR WHO KNOWS HOW THEY MIGHT
BEHAVE?

(The spectators begin to act out the song, following the words. They stage a mock execution, mimic scenes between the Executioner and his daughter, the daughter on her knees, her hands in a gesture of prayer, pleading with her father, her father's refusal. They perform these scenes with mock seriousness, ending with wild bursts of laughter. Celeste appears, stands at a distance, watching and listening, as Pierrot, noticing her, continues to sing.)

AN EXECUTIONER NO MORE THAN A KING,
MY DEAR FATHER
CAN ABDICATE HIS THRONE
I WON'T BE HIS BRIDE
AND SIT BY HIS SIDE
I'D RATHER LIVE ALL ALONE.

(Celeste, no longer even noticing the spectators, and more and more enrapt in the song, moves even closer. The spectators, suddenly aware of her, stop their play-acting and move away.)

FOR THE BLOOD ROLLS DOWN IN THE
BASKET, MY FATHER
IT ROLLS DOWN A GREAT BLACK HOLE
DOWN EACH PARIS STREET
OVER CITIZENS' FEET
LIKE A RIVER RIGHT INTO MY SOUL.

(He stops singing. Celeste, aware of being left alone with him, starts to leave. But Pierrot begins singing again and she stops as if mesmerized, listening. It is almost as if he is singing for her alone.)

ONE DAY I'LL WAKE UP IN A WIDE OPEN
FIELD
WITH THE SUN ON MY FACE LIKE A FLOWER
AND THE SKY BREATHING DOWN
AND THE WIND BEATING ROUND
AND GAIN BACK MY LIFE BY THE HOUR.

SO DON'T MAKE ME MARRY AN
EXECUTIONER, FATHER
NO MATTER WHAT YOU DO
I'M NOT CONTRARY
I'M SIMPLY WARY
I'D RATHER STAY HOME WITH YOU.*

> *(There is silence. Celeste doesn't move. Pierrot stands perfectly still, looking at her. Moments pass. Celeste bows her head and cries. Pierrot still doesn't move, watching her. Celeste wipes her tears away with the back of her hand, like a child. Pierrot walks up to her, gently lays his hand on her shoulder. She raises her tear-stained face and looks directly into his eyes. Pierrot smiles. Light comes up on the Executioner, finishing his meal, the Grandmother sitting beside him.)*

EXECUTIONER: *(wiping his mouth with his napkin)* Well, what is it?

GRANDMOTHER: Your daughter.

EXECUTIONER: *(looking up)* What about her?

GRANDMOTHER: She's seeing someone. I'm sure of it.

> *(Light comes up on Olympe and Michel, dancing a minuet.)*

MICHEL: *(drawing her aside and whispering urgently)* You know why I carry a pistol? Because the Royal Family is plotting to leave the country! Marie-

---

*Copyright © 1990 "The Executioner's Daughter." Lyrics and music by Wendy Kesselman.

Antoinette's brother is Emperor of Austria. Let the King escape and he'll call the emigrés and Austrians to his side, march right back into Paris and reverse the Revolution—order an invasion of France!

OLYMPE: I don't believe it!

MICHEL: I didn't think you would—knowing your attachments. You're totally divided, Olympe de Gouges. No matter how passionate you are about women's rights, slaves' rights, the rights of the poor, you won't give up your most dangerous attachment—to Louis, King of France! A King about to leave Paris any moment. Abandon his people. Spit in the face of the Revolution! *(raising his pistol. Quiet, fierce)* A King who must not be allowed to go!

OLYMPE: Louis came back with us from Versailles to be part of our Revolution. He believes in it as much as we do. If he leaves now, goes back on his oath to the new Constitution, it will be treason. High treason. And the punishment for treason is—

MICHEL: Death! I'm warning you. Anyone loyal to the King will be a traitor too.

EXECUTIONER: *(overlapping. Staring at the Grandmother)* A boy? You must be mad. She doesn't even know about boys.

GRANDMOTHER: All girls know about boys. *(pausing)* I watch her, give her her lessons. She's dreaming about someone. I feel it.

EXECUTIONER: Impossible. She's never even met anyone except within the family.

GRANDMOTHER: Whether she's met someone or not, she's ready for it. Ripe. And—*(pausing)* It has got to be made clear that there is no one she is allowed to meet. Unless, of course, he's one of us. *(looking at him)* Someone within the family.

EXECUTIONER: *(after a long pause)* She's very young.

GRANDMOTHER: Fifteen. I was younger than that. *(after a moment)* I can think of only three. His Grace, Monsieur de Lisieux, Monsieur de Chartres, and of course, your young nephew, Monsieur de Dijon. Now that would be a great match. A new breed. A new race. What more could she ask for?

EXECUTIONER: I was hoping to keep her at home for a while.

GRANDMOTHER: She's not like her brothers. She never was. She has a rebellious streak, a mind of her own. The only place she's safe is here at home. *(She pauses. Gently)* Or in Dijon. You can't keep her here forever, you know.

EXECUTIONER: Maybe you're right. Maybe it's time. *(after a pause)* I'll arrange for him to come. In a few months.

GRANDMOTHER: Oh, I wouldn't wait that long if I were you. Couldn't you use some extra help these days?

(The Executioner stares at her, stands up abruptly.)

What is it?

EXECUTIONER: I heard someone. Didn't you? *(He opens the window. A single voice floats up.)*

WOMAN'S VOICE (V.O.): The King has fled!

VOICES (V.O.): *(repeating the cry)* The King has fled! The King has fled!

(Light comes up immediately on Olympe, Michel and the dancers at the costume ball. The door bursts open. The dance comes to an abrupt halt, as several people rush in. Some are shouting, some weeping uncontrollably.)

PEOPLE: *(repeating the cry that has begun outside)* The King has fled! The King has fled!

(Michel draws Olympe close to him.)

MICHEL: Come with me, Olympe. Now. Tonight. You're in danger.

(Olympe, frozen, disoriented, gazes around her at the frenzied group.)

Please. Just say yes, Olympe.

OLYMPE: Yes.

MICHEL: Michel.

OLYMPE: Michel. *(after a moment)* Yes.

(Quickly he enfolds her under his huge cape. Together, they go out. The people crowd together, clutching each other, crying, yelling. A woman runs in from outside.)

WOMAN: Gone! Gone! They've all gone away. He's left us, abandoned us. The Tuileries lies silent. The great house is abandoned. Someone's hung a huge sign on the door. The palace is empty. He's betrayed us all!

(Light comes up instantly on Pierrot.)

PIERROT: *(sings)* HOUSE TO LET
OWNERS AWAY

LEFT NO ADDRESS
MAYBE THEY'LL STAY

GARDENS IN FRONT
MAGNIFICENT
LARGE FURNISHED ROOMS
NOT TOO MUCH RENT

RIVER IN BACK
AND THE THEATER NEARBY
VIEWS OF ALL PARIS
TO RAVISH THE EYE

IF YOU WILL PROMISE
TO JUST KEEP IT TRIM
NEVER DESERT IT
WE MIGHT LET YOU IN.

PETS ALLOWED
CHILDREN ARE FINE
LONG WINDING STAIRCASE
WOOD FLOORS THAT SHINE
NORTHERN LIGHT
NICE QUIET STREET
WE JUST WANT PEOPLE
WHO'LL KEEP IT NEAT

THE LAST ONES WERE CARELESS
THEY LEFT TOO MUCH DUST
THE SORT OF PEOPLE
YOU JUST COULDN'T TRUST

WE KNOW THEY LEFT US
WE JUST DON'T KNOW WHEN
LAST THEY WERE SEEN WAS
A TOWN CALLED VARENNES....*

Scene 4

(A Paris rooftop. Olympe wears a white dress. Her long hair is loose. Beside her stands Michel. A sweltering summer day. A deathly quiet. Olympe steps to the edge of the roof.)

MICHEL: See anything?

OLYMPE: Not a sign of them. *(a pause)* Maybe they won't come.

MICHEL: Oh, they'll come all right. All Paris is waiting.

OLYMPE: *(low)* God, this quiet. This unearthly quiet. As if no one will ever speak again. As if it's a funeral.

MICHEL: *(looking over the edge of the roof)* It is a funeral. Every window, every roof, every tree filled with faces. Silent faces. A black sea. *(soft)* Betrayal.

OLYMPE: Why did he do it? Why did he leave us? Didn't he know the whole country would be looking for them? Now all Paris would kill them if it could.

MICHEL: None of us want to be deserted, do we? Especially when we're children. And we're all children now, Olympe—waiting for our lost King to come home.

A VOICE (v.o.): Vive la Nation!

MICHEL: Hear that?

(As Olympe nods.)

Get used to it. "Vive le Roi!" will never be heard again.

OLYMPE: *(grabbing his arm. Pointing)* They're coming.

(Silence.)

Closer. So close. I can almost see them through the window of the carriage! There's the little Dauphin with all his golden curls. *(peering over the edge of the roof)* Michel—he's waving to us!

MICHEL: He's waving to everyone. It's what he's been taught. To wave to all his subjects. They haven't yet told him, he doesn't yet know that this time the gesture is a mistake. Perhaps it's a gesture that no longer even exists.

OLYMPE: Oh Michel, Michel. We've lost our King. Our only King. We have no more King, Michel. *(She kneels at the edge of the roof.)*

MICHEL: *(stroking her long hair)* We lost him long ago. Long before he took that coach to Varennes. Only you didn't know. You couldn't see. *(He turns her face toward his. Light comes up on Pierrot.)*

PIERROT: *(sings)* NOW THEY'RE BACK
   TOOK DOWN THE SIGN
   FILLED UP THE ROOMS
   WE CHANGED OUR MIND
   THOUGH THEY'RE BACK
   THEY MIGHT NOT STAY
   FOR ALL WE KNOW
   THEY'LL VANISH TODAY

      SOMEONE BETRAYS YOU
      AND DOESN'T EXPLAIN
      HOW CAN YOU KNOW
      IT WON'T HAPPEN AGAIN?

      OUR HOUSE STOOD EMPTY
      FIVE DAYS OF DESPAIR
      MAYBE IT'S BETTER
      SUPPOSE IT'S BETTER

WE THINK IT'S BETTER
IF NO ONE LIVES THERE.

(Celeste appears, holding a red rose. She stands on the opposite corner from Pierrot, her face eager, expectant. She is waiting for him. Light comes up on Olympe and Michel coming into Michel's studio. Olympe moves about the room, gazing at his paintings, overwhelmed.)

OLYMPE: Animals. Animals everywhere. Animals escaping. Animals being freed. *(looking up)* But only animals. Do you paint nothing else?

MICHEL: I grew up in a house of privilege, Olympe. One of the most important was the privilege to hunt. A nobleman's right. In the name of God, honor and the family, I was forced to learn the tracks of animals, how to find their lairs, sniff them out by the direction of the wind. Eagles, stags, wolves, wild boar! *(soft)* Peacocks. Fawns. Doves. One night I woke up choked with blood. I locked my door and refused to go. They broke it down and set me on my horse. I rode straight to the forest and never came back—gave up all my privileges. Wild animals snuffled round me. I watched them, studied them, freed them from their traps and cages. Their anguished cries trailed me all the way to Paris. Each night I saw them in my dreams. I began to paint. Every animal I murdered rose up on my canvases. Every animal who never got away. I can never paint anything else.

(Olympe is silent, gazing at the paintings.)

OLYMPE: I've seen your animals in the hills of Montauban. *(picking up an empty wooden frame and holding it to her face)* Maybe you'll paint me one day, Michel.

MICHEL: You, Olympe? Capture you on canvas? How could I? You're transparent. You're like water. A child of nature—luminous, cloudless, you light up from within—the child we once were, the child we recapture only in dreams.

OLYMPE: Like your animals? Don't study me too much, Michel. Don't watch me too closely. *(stepping back, the empty frame around her face)* I've never been in a cage.

MICHEL: *(snatching the frame away from her face)* I'll never put you in one.

    (He breaks the frame in two. She draws back. He grabs hold of her wrist. She lifts her other hand. He grabs that too. Olympe laughs.)

Did you really think I would? *(Quickly he releases both her hands. Olympe throws her arms around his neck, covers him with kisses.)*

Scene 5

(Light comes up on the Executioner standing at a long table elaborately set for dinner. Silver gleams, glasses sparkle, candles glow. Five men dressed in black sit at the table, their backs to the audience. The Executioner faces out, holding a glass of champagne. The men look toward him. They are all Executioners.)

EXECUTIONER: It's a rare opportunity that brings our family together. Some of us, of course, couldn't manage to come. The lists were too long, the hours too short. But although we may not be graced with our entire family, I think we can rest assured that most of France is represented tonight.

(There is laughter.)

So without further ado, I would like to welcome— *(raising his glass)* my brother, Monsieur de Lyon, His Grace.

(At the far end of the table, Monsieur de Lyon rises, bows. There is a round of applause.)

My son, His Grace of Rouen.

(Monsieur de Rouen rises to stand beside Monsieur de Lyon. He bows low to another round of applause. The Executioner smiles.)

My first cousin, Monsieur d'Orléans, His Grace.

(Monsieur d'Orléans stands, bows gracefully to more applause.)

Another brother—*(The Executioner chuckles.)* Lucky we're such a big family these days—His Grace of Marseilles.

(Monsieur de Marseilles rises and bows to much laughter and applause.)

And last, but certainly not least, my young nephew, our own extremely capable Monsieur de Dijon, His Grace.

(At the opposite end of the table, Monsieur de Dijon stands and bows. There is a rousing round of applause. And now all the Executioners stand together and raise their glasses high in a toast to the Chief Executioner.)

EXECUTIONERS: Monsieur de Paris! His Grace!

(Everyone clinks glasses, then sits down, except for Monsieur de Paris, who remains standing.)

EXECUTIONER: In these times, these troubled times, our work calls on us to perform ceaselessly. There was a dog today. One of the men had a dog. She ran after us all the way to the scaffold, jumped on her master's shoulders to be petted, to be stroked. He had to push her down. But she leapt right up those ten steps again, sat right next to him and began to howl. A pitiful, terrible sound. A sound to break your heart in two. Finally, a gendarme pinned her with his bayonet. And then the crowd, which stands there watching people being murdered every day, suddenly took the dog's part. They spat curses at the gendarme. Then they started throwing stones. *(He pauses.)* We live in sadness, we live in grief. In isolation, sometimes in despair. But if we are lucky, sometimes we are blessed, and there is one light which shuts out the darkness and makes death disappear. *(pausing)* I am lucky, gentlemen. I am blessed. In my life I have such a light. Just to see her when I come home every night makes me forget the day's dark and terrible beginnings. *(quiet)* We may live in the midst of death, gentlemen, but tonight I offer you my life. I offer you my joy. I offer you—*(a pause)* Celeste.

> *(He holds out his hand. Celeste appears, all in white, white ribbons in her hair. Hesitant, shy, she walks unsteadily up to the long table.)*

And the man who is to take her into the world, the man who will carry her away—*(pausing)* Her betrothed, my future son-in-law, Monsieur de Dijon, His Grace.

> *(He reaches out his other hand to Monsieur de Dijon. Celeste averts her eyes. Monsieur de Dijon rises, comes forward, and bows gracefully to Celeste. She curtseys deeply, lowers her head. The Executioner smiles.)*

May they live together happily, forever in the light.

> *(The Executioners all begin to clap, then are suddenly still, as Monsieur de Dijon takes Celeste's trembling hand in his and, just for an instant, brings it to his lips. Of all the Executioners, his is the only face we see—intense, magnetic, almost beautiful. He looks, in fact, like an angel. Celeste turns pale, then blushes violently. Monsieur de Dijon stands still, watching her, as the President of the Assembly begins to speak.)*

PRESIDENT (V.O.):   Citizen Cambon, what do you say?

CAMBON (V.O.):   The will of the French nation is to abolish all privilege. Today I must pass judgment on one of the privileged convicted of treason. I would consider myself guilty if I restricted myself to deportation. I vote for death.

PRESIDENT (V.O.):   Danton.

DANTON (v.o.): One must never compromise with tyrants. One can only strike at Kings through the head. I vote for death. Death unconditional!

PRESIDENT (v.o.): Robespierre.

ROBESPIERRE (v.o.): Do you want a Revolution without a Revolution? The Revolution begins with the death of the tyrant. Death within twenty-four hours!

(The Executioner pulls a black hood over his head. All the other Executioners do the same.)

VOICE (v.o.): The National Convention decrees that Louis Capet, last King of the French people, shall suffer the death penalty. Within twenty-four hours he shall be taken by a company of the National Guard to the Place de la Révolution and there—

(The light dims, then comes up immediately on the small window of a chateau. Le Franc de Pompignan sits at his desk, writing with a long feather pen. A girl's hand darts in, grabs the pen from his hand. Abruptly, Le Franc stands up, puts his head out the window and, in a violent gesture, with both hands pushes someone down from the ledge. There is a piercing scream, then silence, then the sudden crash of the window coming down on Le Franc's head. Light comes up on Olympe in bed with Michel. She is screaming. The parrot sits on his swing. On the wall hangs a primitive painting of the parrot in flight.)

MICHEL: *(holding Olympe)* Olympe. Shhh. Shhh, my darling.

OLYMPE: *(overlapping)* The same. Always the same! He sits at the little window, writing with his feather pen. The pen I stole, Michel! The little window of the guillotine!

MICHEL: *(lighting a candle)* Hush. Hush now. He died in his sleep. Long ago in Montauban. It had nothing to do with you.

OLYMPE: He smiles. He throws me out. He wants nothing to do with his bastard child.

MICHEL: I won't throw you out, Olympe. No matter what you do.

(Olympe is silent.)

You believe me, don't you? *(pausing)* Olympe? Where are you?

OLYMPE: *(after a moment)* Here. With you.

MICHEL: No. Not with me. Somewhere else. Far away.

OLYMPE: He never even read anything I wrote. He threw it away. Like he throws me away every night in my dream.

MICHEL: Suppose he didn't love you, does that mean I can't? Why won't you let me, Olympe?

(Olympe puts her hands over her ears. Michel pulls them away.)

Why won't you listen to me?

OLYMPE: Why didn't he listen to what I said, what I wrote?

MICHEL: Maybe you said things he didn't want to hear.

OLYMPE: *(broken)* Why isn't anyone listening to me now?

MICHEL: People still don't want to hear. You're ahead

of your time, Olympe. Nothing's harder.

OLYMPE: Maybe I should stop trying.

MICHEL: You have a right to be heard. A right to be loved. You believe that for everyone else. You speak about it, write about it all the time. Why don't you believe in it for yourself? *(a pause)* If you don't, how will you ever believe I love you? Will nothing I say, nothing I do convince you?

(Olympe is still. Michel stands up.)

OLYMPE: Michel?

MICHEL: You'll always say things people don't want to hear. Keep saying them. Keep writing. No matter what they say, Olympe. No matter what they do to you. You will. I know you. It's who you are. *(He moves to the door.)*

OLYMPE: Where are you going?

MICHEL: *(looking back at her)* In a duel once you gave me back my sword. You were generous. You were kind. You didn't even know who I was. *(smiling)* You know now. If you want to, you'll find me.

OLYMPE: You're leaving. You're throwing me away!

MICHEL: Am I? Am I, Olympe?

(He turns to go. Olympe does not move. He leaves. Olympe sits still a few moments, then turns and blows the candle out. Silence.)

OLYMPE: *(suddenly)* Michel! Wait!

(But he is gone. She does not stir. Quiet.)

Forgive me.

Scene 6

(Light comes up on Celeste, smiling, dancing by herself. Moving effortlessly, she almost seems to float around the room. Ange appears, tenderly holds out his arms to her. She rushes into them, takes his hands in hers, pulling him into the room. They dance together, perfectly in step—a peaceful, dreamlike dance.)

Scene 7

(*Light comes up on Olympe running, a batch of posters in her arms. She looks over her shoulder, drops a few posters, bends down to pick them up, drops several more. There is the sound of footsteps. Olympe grabs the fallen posters, stumbles on. The footsteps grow louder. A figure appears, rushes toward her, enveloping her in a huge cape. Olympe tries to pull away, but the figure hurries her along, stops beneath a tunnel, takes down his hood. Olympe steps back, then leaps forward, embracing him.*)

OLYMPE: Pierrot, you old rascal—how did you find me?

PIERROT: I never lost you, Marie Gouze. I've been right here in Paris, keeping my eye on you. Just as I always did.

(*Coming close as Olympe laughs.*)

But I won't be able to keep an eye on you anymore. There isn't a street corner in Paris where I'll be safe. They smashed my drum today.

OLYMPE: Why?

PIERROT: For singing the wrong songs. But which are wrong and which are right these days? All songs are dangerous now. (*urgent*) No one is safe. And certainly not you, Olympe de Gouges. Leave. Leave while there's still time. We're country folk, you and I. We don't belong here. Come home with me to Montauban —we'll find all our old haunts.

(*There is silence.*)

OLYMPE: *(turning away. Smiling)* Say hello to all of them for me. Say hello to my old Nounou.

PIERROT: You won't come?

OLYMPE: I write for the Revolution and only for that. All my work is here. Without it I could not exist. You think they'd listen to me out there in the provinces? That was all I wanted to escape from. Would they listen to what I have to say?

PIERROT: Are they listening here? *(following her as she turns away)* You're working in complete isolation. *(He turns to go. Turning back)* If you change your mind, meet me in Dijon. I'm going there first. There's someone I want to see.

OLYMPE: Ah Pierrot, Pierrot. Are you leaving me too? Will nothing—nothing bring you back?

(They stand still, looking at each other. Pierrot smiles.)

PIERROT: I'll swim naked in the Tarn for you. I'll climb the ragged mountains. I'll tell them all about you, Marie Gouze. *(embracing her)* They won't believe a single word.

SCENE 8

(Light comes up on the Executioner, exhausted, sitting in a chair. His wife stands behind him. She takes a white towel, plunges it into a basin, wrings out the water and places it on his forehead. They stare straight ahead. Light comes up on Celeste, standing before a basin of water. She is holding a large black glove. She lifts it to her face, rubs it against her cheek, kisses it. Gently, she drops the glove into the water, begins washing it. She wrings it out, stares at it for a moment, then abruptly throws it down in the water again. Silently, Ange glides in behind her, slides one hand around her waist, with the other smooths back her hair. Celeste recoils, almost pulls away, then is suddenly still as Ange slowly places his hand inside. Celeste leans back against him, a look of ecstasy filling her face. The Executioner picks up his cello bow, fingers it absently, then, taking his cello tenderly in his arms, slowly begins to play. The Wife stands still for a few moments, then goes to a high shelf and takes down a long narrow box. She opens it, stares at the contents inside. Slowly, she takes out a long white ribbon, a small lace cap, a pair of baby shoes, a silver spoon, a folded piece of paper containing a lock of Celeste's hair. She examines them all, carefully puts them back inside. Finally she takes out Celeste's thin black dress, holds it before her, brings it to her face, smells it. She sits down, the dress pressed against her body, and slowly begins to rock. The Executioner plays more and more intensely. The sound of the cello gradually blends into the sound of carts clattering down the street.)

(Light comes up on Olympe, leaning out the window of her room. There is the sound of carts clattering down the street below. Shouts, screams, cries for mercy. Olympe backs away from the window. She is trembling. She grabs a battered suitcase and hastily begins throwing in her belongings, gathers posters, pamphlets, plays and throws them in too. She forces the suitcase closed, fragments of clothing and paper sticking out. She drags the overstuffed suitcase to the door, rushes to take the parrot from his swing, hurriedly looks around the room. She runs to her desk, grabs the feather pen. Halfway back to the door, she stops, looks down at the pen in her hand. She stands still, smoothing the feathers across her mouth, then throws the pen on the floor, leaving it behind. She runs to the door, grabs the suitcase, rushes out. Silence. Olympe steps back into the room. From the darkness, a figure emerges. Nounou, in rags, stands at the door.)

NOUNOU: *(desperate)* Where shall I put my apron? Throw it on the fire—you won't need it anymore. My bodice? Throw it there too. My shirt? My petticoat?

OLYMPE: Nounou!

NOUNOU: Throw it all in! You won't need any of it anymore. *(wildly looking around)* Watch out! Look behind you! *(suddenly very clear)* The big bzou. Which path did he take? Can you tell me, Marie Gouze? Tell me which path he took.

OLYMPE: *(clutching her)* Nounou. My sweet Nounou.

(Blackout)

Scene 10

(Dijon. Celeste and Ange stand facing each other. Celeste is wearing a white nightgown. Ange's shirt is soaked with blood.)

ANGE: I came as quickly as I could. *(stroking her forehead)* Feeling better, little Celeste? Are you feeling better now?

CELESTE: *(stepping back)* Your clothes are soaked through.

ANGE: *(moving toward her)* You'll have to stop, you know. You can't keep fainting in public. In the middle of the day. *(smiling)* It's becoming embarrassing.

CELESTE: I can't help it. *(soft)* I can't stand the sight of blood.

ANGE: Strange. You think you'd be used to it by now.

CELESTE: I never got used to it. *(urgent)* Please don't make me go again.

ANGE: *(gently)* I can't do that. You're my wife. Things are different in the provinces. They expect it of you. *(stroking her hair. Tender.)* Don't worry. You'll get used to it.

(Light comes up on Pierrot, standing on the corner of a dark street in Dijon.)

PIERROT: *(sings)*
FOR THE BLOOD ROLLS DOWN IN THE BASKET, MY FATHER
IT ROLLS DOWN A GREAT BLACK HOLE
DOWN EVERY LAST STREET
OVER CITIZENS' FEET
LIKE A RIVER RIGHT INTO MY SOUL.

ANGE: My mother called me Ange, Celeste. Do I look like an angel to you?

(*Celeste is silent.*)

Why don't you call me Ange anymore? It's my name.

PIERROT: (*sings*) ONE DAY I'LL WAKE UP IN A WIDE OPEN FIELD
WITH THE SUN ON MY FACE LIKE A FLOWER
AND THE SKY BREATHING DOWN
AND THE WIND BEATING ROUND
AND GAIN BACK MY LIFE BY THE HOUR.

CELESTE: Forgive me for today. It was the women. All those women.

ANGE: Ah yes, the women. They always ask for me. The laundresses, the lacemakers, the prostitutes, the nuns. Even the young lady aristocrats. They all want me. The last shoulder to cry upon, the last hand to squeeze. They expect everything, they want everything from me. (*looking at Celeste*) Thirteen today. The biggest batch ever. And all the time I was cutting off their heads, you were here at home, waiting. Waiting so patiently.

CELESTE: Shhh.

ANGE: For me to come back to you. Weren't you, Celeste? Don't you always wait?

(*Celeste is still.*)

In your beautiful white nightgown.

CELESTE: (*quiet*) I wish I'd never met you. Never seen your face.

ANGE: Ah, but you did. And now you love me, don't you, Celeste? *(gentle)* Now you love only me.

(Celeste bows her head. She is crying.)

PIERROT: *(sings)* THEY WANT TO LIE DOWN
   BESIDE ME, MY FATHER
   THEY WEREN'T GIVEN A GRAVE
   THEY MAKE A GREAT DIN
   BUT I WON'T LET THEM IN
   FOR WHO KNOWS HOW THEY MIGHT
   BEHAVE?

ANGE: Yes. You love me. With all the immense love in your immense heart. You can't help it. *(brushing away her tears)* Any more than you can help fainting at the sight of blood. *(in a whisper)* I dare you not to say it. I dare you not to scream it. In a moment you'll be down on your knees.

(He lifts the wide lace strap of her white nightgown, pulls it down over her shoulder. Celeste trembles visibly. Ange continues softly, urgently.)

I have very little time. They just condemned six more. It's a long way, living where we must—at the edge of town. *(his mouth at her ear)* But I wanted to come. I told you. I came as quickly as I could. *(He places one hand on her shoulder, presses his fingers gently in.)* Celeste.

CELESTE: *(quiet)* Take you hand away.

(He does. The imprint of his bloodstained hand is left on her shoulder.)

ANGE: Ah, that name. Celestial lips. Celestial eyes. Celestial flesh. Celeste, Celeste. Please. Let me. Will you let me, Celeste?

CELESTE: Tell me. *(hesitant)* The—women you spoke of. The laundresses, the lacemakers—

ANGE: Prostitutes? Nuns? Young lady aristocrats? What about them? What is it you want to know? *(his face close to hers)* Ask me, Celeste. You can ask me anything.

(She looks away.)

PIERROT: *(sings)* SO DON'T MAKE ME MARRY AN EXECUTIONER, FATHER

(Ange laughs.)

ANGE: The answer is yes. Of course. Ah yes. *(lifting her chin)* What did you think?

(Celeste closes her eyes.)

PIERROT: *(sings)* NO MATTER WHAT YOU DO

CELESTE: But didn't they know—

ANGE: What?

CELESTE: Who you are.

ANGE: Of course they knew. *(smiling)* They know.

PIERROT: *(sings)* I'M NOT CONTRARY
I'M SIMPLY WARY
I'D RATHER STAY HOME WITH YOU.

(Celeste stares at Ange.)

ANGE: What is it now? What are you asking me?

CELESTE: *(soft)* When?

ANGE: *(softer)* When I cut their hair. *(delicately lifting her long hair)* When I come to cut their hair. In their cell. In their last moments.

CELESTE: *(violently pulling away)* Go now, why don't you? Hurry. You mustn't be late.

ANGE: *(following her)* Little girl. Little little little girl. *(lightly touching her neck)* Anything. Anything you want. You know that. I told you once—you can make me do anything.

CELESTE: *(pushing him away)* You wouldn't want to miss it, would you? After all, you love what you do.

(Ange smiles.)

ANGE: It's my job. I do what I'm told.

CELESTE: But you would do it anyway, wouldn't you— if you could. You love it so much, you would do it without any orders.

ANGE: Perhaps. But I'm not a butcher. I'm not one of those monsters who slaughtered people right and left in the September Massacres. I don't dip my bread in the blood of the victims while they're still warm, and gobble it up with gusto. I'm not the man who roasted and ate the heart of the Princesse de Lamballe. I don't eat hearts.

(Celeste smiles.)

CELESTE: No? *(after a pause)* You're eating mine.

ANGE: Yours? *(He laughs, pulling her toward him.)* Yours, my darling? *(pushing her hair back from her face)* The heart of my fair, my beautiful Celeste. The heart which will never beat for anyone but me. Dare I dream of it? Dare I fondle it? Dare I even touch it?

(In a single gesture, he rips the other lace strap off her shoulder, so that her nightgown falls to the floor. He runs his bloodstained hands along her body. Celeste does not move.)

Eat your heart, my love? Your tender, throbbing, delectable heart? Eat it? *(gathering her up swiftly in his arms)* I'll devour it whole.

Scene 11

(Light comes up on Olympe, dressed in black. Exhausted, she collapses onto a chair. Michel comes in, also in black. The parrot is sitting on a swing.)

MICHEL: *(Stroking Olympe's hair)* I'm glad you came. Glad you found me.

OLYMPE: *(desolate)* She was my last link. There's nothing to go back to now. What's happening down there—*(She pauses.)* It's a graveyard there for me.

(Michel pulls her toward him.)

MICHEL: Then let's go somewhere else.

OLYMPE: Oh Michel, Michel, if only I could. But people are dying—innocent people—persecuted, hunted down. Everywhere living in terror. I can't leave now. *(looking away)* Nounou came all the way to find me. All the way here for me. I couldn't save her. But—*(She pauses.)* I've written something. Something—this time—people will have to listen—*(She grabs a poster from a huge stack on the floor.)* Please. I want you to read it. I want you to—

MICHEL: *(overlapping)* There isn't time. Leave with me now. Now, Olympe. Before it's too late.

OLYMPE: I can't. *(She stands before him, unmoving, the poster in her hands.)*

MICHEL: *(watching her)* You're so absolute. Nothing in between will do, will it?

OLYMPE: Nothing. No.

MICHEL: No matter where it takes you. No matter how many mistakes you make.

OLYMPE: I'd rather live my life fully with all my mistakes than die with the secret of what I always wanted to do. *(She holds the poster out to him. He steps forward, takes it from her.)*

MICHEL: *(reading it quickly)* Olympe! No. You can't do this! You won't.

> *(A doorbell jangles loudly. Light comes up on Celeste, wearing wet disheveled traveling clothes, her hair wild all around her.)*

EXECUTIONER: All right, all right. Who's at the door this time of night?

> *(He appears, wearing his nightclothes, carrying a candle.)*

CELESTE: I had to come.

EXECUTIONER: Celeste!

CELESTE: I've been traveling three days.

EXECUTIONER: *(embracing her)* Celeste. My little Celeste.

CELESTE: *(quiet)* I've come to tell you something.

EXECUTIONER: Take your time, my angel. Don't look so distraught. Nothing can be that terrible. *(He takes her by the hand.)* Come, dry yourself by the fire.

CELESTE: *(still)* How do you live with it? How do you manage?

> *(He stares at her, then begins putting logs in the grate.)*

EXECUTIONER: I live with it. I've always lived with it.

CELESTE: You never thought of running away?

EXECUTIONER: Where could I run? There's no place to run. *(pausing)* To have run anywhere. To have done anything else in this world...But what could I do? Who would have taken me?

(Celeste is silent.)

I wear a black coat. I wear a black mask. I cause fear wherever I go. Who will touch me? Who will come near? Even the host at Mass is given me with gloved hands. *(He pauses.)* In the Norman farmlands, there's a stream they call "the stream of dirty hands." Once the water was pure. But ever since my grandfather washed his bloody hands there, after decapitating someone from the village nearby, the water will be forever unclean. Isolated in birth, isolated in death, we live, we die in darkness and shame. My family was all there was, Celeste. All there is. You... are all there is. The blood that stains my hands does not permit me anyone else.

CELESTE: But you healed people, Father. Ever since I was little, people came to the house to be cured.

EXECUTIONER: Don't you know everything that causes horror also has the power to heal? People knock on my door, they enter my lair—people whom doctors refuse to treat. I set bones, I know all the old remedies, the old cures. They know that I can heal.

CELESTE: Everything, Father?

(He is silent.)

Father?

(He stares at her.)

EXECUTIONER: Not everything, Celeste. *(pausing)* The day of my first execution, my father woke me at dawn. "Get up," he said. "It's time." *(pausing again)* That day, and every day since then, I feel I am being sentenced to my own death, I am going to my own execution. I am the condemned man. As condemned as he! I kill others in the name of the law, in the name of the people of France. But I am the man torn out of sleep—"It's time. It's time." The man doomed to die every day for the rest of my life.

CELESTE: *(slowly)* Yes. Yes. You tell me what I came to hear. And everything you say—*(a pause)* reassures me, comforts me, makes me know that this is right. It will be right.

EXECUTIONER: Good. I'm glad. *(He goes back to the fire.)*

CELESTE: Father.

EXECUTIONER: Celeste? *(turning toward her)* What is it?

CELESTE: I'm pregnant. *(She smiles.)* I'm going to have a child.

(Light comes up on Olympe and Michel.)

OLYMPE: *(reaching for a long green coat. Gently)* I'm going now—before it gets light. You can come with me if you want. *(smiling)* Help me paste them up.

MICHEL: *(taking the top poster from the huge stack on the floor)* Are you mad? These are dangerous words, Olympe. Posters calling for a vote on the form of government France should have? We have our form of government—the Republic—one and indivisible! You believe in it yourself.

OLYMPE: I hate every form of tyranny! No one should be forced to follow one way of thinking, of being. People should be allowed to choose.

MICHEL: *(waving the poster in her face)* There is no choice! These posters will be seen as treason. Treason, Olympe!

OLYMPE: *(reaching for a floppy wide-brimmed hat)* Just a few words.

MICHEL: Enough to kill you!

OLYMPE: If I can't write them, why should I live? *(She moves toward the posters. Michel blocks her path.)*

MICHEL: No! I cannot let you go! *(He grabs her by the shoulders.)* Don't look at me like that. Like a woman possessed.

OLYMPE: How should I look at you? *(gazing at him demurely)* Like this? *(smiling seductively)* Like this, Michel? *(tearing off her hat, her coat)* Is this better? Is this what you want? *(ripping open her dress)* This? This? This?

(She circles him, glaring.)

But not this. Never this. Possessed, you said. Like a woman possessed. You mean like a witch?

MICHEL: No, Olympe. No.

OLYMPE: A witch. A wild thing. That's what I am. Look at me. We women are witches. We women are possessed. Our hair curls like serpents, our eyes blaze like cats' eyes, our teeth have the grip of corpses. Why, if we are angry, must we be seen as monsters? Have we not reason, have we not rights the same as you? I say we have. Curse and condemn us! We shall carry our curses like banners and raise our condemnations to the sky! *(a pause)* Now you say I cannot go. All my life people have said, you cannot, you must not, you won't be able to. But you loved me for speaking my mind, Michel. For speaking the truth. "No matter what they say, Olympe. No matter what they do to you."

MICHEL: I still love you, Olympe. I always will.

OLYMPE: Then let me go.

> *(She turns away from him and reaches for her posters. But Michel gets there first, grabs half the stack in his arms, and in a rapid gesture, opens the window and throws them out. As he turns and takes another armful, Olympe runs forward and leaps onto the ledge.)*

Go ahead, Michel! Go on. But if you throw them out, you throw me out too. You throw my life away!

> *(For a moment Michel stands still, hesitating. Then he holds the posters out to her. Olympe stands very tall, very straight, clutching the posters to her breast. She speaks after a moment.)*

Look at the Seine. The light on the water. The barges coming in under the bridge.

MICHEL: *(picking up Olympe's long green coat)* Where are you going, little girl, little girl?

> *(Olympe smiles.)*

OLYMPE: To my grandmother's—with a loaf of hot bread and a bottle of wine.

MICHEL: Ah...And which path are you taking? The

path of thorns or the path of stones?

(Olympe is silent.)

Which path, little girl?

(Olympe laughs.)

OLYMPE: *(stepping off the ledge into the room)* The one I always take.

MICHEL: *(wrapping the long green coat around her. Laughing too)* Which one is that?

(For a moment there is silence.)

OLYMPE: The path of thorns, you big bzou. It's the shortest way by far. *(smiling)* I go right down the path of thorns.

(Michel steps closer, touches her mouth, her hair. He moves even nearer, his long hair falling in her face. Olympe lets the posters fall. Gently, she pulls him toward her. They lie down on the floor together, beneath the long green coat.)

MICHEL: *(soft)* Closer. Closer yet. Even your breath inside mine.

(Olympe moans in the darkness.)

Nothing between us. Ever.

(Light comes up on Celeste and the Executioner.)

EXECUTIONER: *(his head buried in his hands)* I can't, Celeste. It's impossible. Never. Not even for you.

CELESTE: *(urgent)* You've got to. You have the means.

The medicines. You're the only one who can. *(moving closer)* Listen.

EXECUTIONER: I can't listen. I won't. Please don't ask me this.

CELESTE: *(quiet)* I've tried myself.

(The Executioner looks up.)

Many times. It doesn't work. Nothing works.

EXECUTIONER: Of course it doesn't. Why should it? A baby in the family. It should be a joy.

CELESTE: Papa, please. I beg you.

(The Executioner covers his ears.)

Listen to me! *(pulling his hands away)* He's a murderer! Do you understand? A killer. He kills.

EXECUTIONER: We all kill, Celeste. Every one of us.

CELESTE: But he loves it. The sight of blood excites him. The sound of it, the smell of it. I know. He takes me to every execution. In Dijon they're held at noon in the public square—in the suffocating heat, in the icy cold. The crowds are enormous. And when he holds up the head, when the blood drips from the roots of the neck—he smiles. *(She pauses.)* This baby will be born of blood, Father. A blood baby. Born of the blood that has spattered my face, stained my shoes. I have washed it off, but it has entered the mouth with which I eat, I have felt it on my tongue, I have swallowed it. It is my mother's milk, my father's sweat. It has been passed on to me for generations, but I in my turn will not pass it on. I have seen the portraits at the top of the stairs. Their faces have looked down on me all my life. So dark, so gloomy, so full of grief. They didn't want to live their lives. No one has the right to be so cursed!

EXECUTIONER: You come from a long line of executioners, Celeste. We go on. We go on. We are known to all. On the street they recognize us. Everywhere we go. But we must submit. We are necessary.

CELESTE: No! The blood that has stained me all my life, that has stained you and Mother and Grandmother, over and over from son to son, daughter to daughter, shall never stain my child. Those hands shall never have blood on them. *(pausing)* No more murderers!

EXECUTIONER: Celeste. Little Celeste. I should never have let you go. I didn't want to! I wanted to keep you here forever. *(silence)* But now—

CELESTE: What?

EXECUTIONER: It's time.

> *(Light comes up dimly on Olympe and Michel, asleep under the long green coat. Olympe awakes, sits up for a moment, then lies down again, her arms around Michel. The Executioner begins to get dressed.)*

CELESTE: *(stepping close to him)* Don't go, Father. Please. Just this once. Stay with me. *(soft)* I'm afraid.

> *(Slowly Olympe sits up again, bends over Michel, strokes his hair, kisses him on the forehead.)*

EXECUTIONER: I can't, Celeste. They're waiting for me. *(a pause)* Please. Don't hold onto me like that.

> *(Celeste steps back. She is not touching him.)*

I can't bear it.

(He turns away, puts on his long black redingote, then swiftly turns back and embraces her.)

Forgive me.

CELESTE: You won't do it then?

EXECUTIONER: You're my child. And the child to come. How can I? *(quickly)* I must go. I must. *(He does not let her go.)*

CELESTE: Go then. You'll be late.

(Olympe stands up. She is wearing a white chemise. Her long hair is loose. She reaches down to take her long green coat, then draws it even more closely around Michel. Silently, she crosses the room, wraps a shawl around her shoulders. She gathers the remaining posters in her arms and goes to the door. She hesitates, turns back, looking at Michel. The light dims.)

EXECUTIONER: *(cradling Celeste in his arms)* It will be all right, Celeste. You'll see.

CELESTE: No. *(gentle)* Promise me. Please, Papa. *(pausing)* Please.

(He is silent.)

Don't worry. Never mind. *(She smiles.)* Papa... Papa, I love you.

(For a moment he clings to her, then leaves. Celeste does not move. Light comes up on Olympe crossing a bridge, her posters in her arms. Two men appear on the other side. Slowly, Celeste begins taking off

her clothing, hanging it in front of the fire to dry. She remains in a white chemise. On the bridge Olympe stops. The two men continue toward her. Celeste drags the black trunk into the room. Quickly, she begins taking out all the clothing. At the bottom of the trunk is a long thick rope. The two men reach Olympe, take the posters from her arms, draw her hands behind her back. Light comes up on Michel, waking under the long green coat. It is dawn.)

MICHEL: *(calling out)* Olympe!

(Celeste draws a chair into the center of the room. She sits on the chair in her white chemise, brushing her long hair. There is the sound of a cart rumbling along cobblestones. The sound of thunder.)

OLYMPE!

(Light comes up on Olympe's face, wet with rain.)

OLYMPE: Michel, don't worry. Whatever happens, don't despair. I have done more than I ever dreamed. Me—the little savage from Montauban! So many obstacles nearly kept me from myself. I always felt I was failing. I always wanted to be praised. But I always wanted to live, Michel. And was there ever a more glorious time to be alive? *(She pauses.)* Do you know— the other day—why I was so late? I was crossing the Seine, my eyes shut, dreaming of the moment I would see you again. When I opened them, I thought I had lost my way. Overnight, the name of your street had been changed! Fourteen hundred Paris streets had new names! Every day things are changing. The clothes we wear, the measurements we use, the very map of France! The Revolution has touched everything. It has given us the freedom to make our own mistakes. Even if those mistakes are enormous. Even if they lead to death itself.

(Light comes up on the Executioner setting up the scaffold. Celeste takes out a pair of scissors and slowly begins cutting her hair. Olympe appears at the bottom of the scaffold, her white chemise pulled down over her shoulders, her hands bound behind her back. Awkwardly, she mounts the ten steps of the scaffold. She stops, looks up. The Executioner is waiting for her. She almost falls. The Executioner holds out his hand, helps her up the last step. At the top of the scaffold, he takes out a pair of scissors and begins to cut Olympe's hair. Celeste hangs the rope from the ceiling. Olympe steps forward. The morning light glints on the blade of the guillotine. Celeste ties a noose at the end of the rope. She climbs on top of the chair. Gently, the Executioner lowers Olympe's body onto the plank, clamps the lunette around her neck, holding her head in place. Celeste places her head in the noose. Slowly the Executioner raises his arm. Olympe and Celeste gaze straight ahead, their eyes wide open, unafraid. Light comes up on Pierrot, standing on the bridge.)

PIERROT: *(sings)* THERE ARE THREE SOUNDS
I'LL REMEMBER FOREVER
THREE SOUNDS I'LL HEAR ALL MY LIFE
THE PLANK SWINGING DOWN
THE LUNETTE SWIVELING ROUND
THE DULL THUMP OF THE KNIFE.

(The sound of the Executioner playing the cello blends with Pierrot's singing. Light comes up on the parrot sitting on his swing.)

THAT MONTH OF NOVEMBER
SEVENTEEN NINETY-THREE
TWO TREASURED WOMEN WERE TAKEN
FROM ME
TWO HEARTS, TWO BODIES

TWO SOULS ALL COULD SEE
WILL SING OUT FOREVER
WILL ALWAYS BE FREE.

(Light dims on Pierrot and comes up brightly on Olympe's face.)

OLYMPE: Some things will last, some will disappear. Some will blossom, some will be suppressed. But that first hot breeze blowing in our faces, that first fire will never again go out. The seed that has started, the spark, the hope will not die. It will burst through barricades and betrayals and grow and grow till it changes the face of the world.

∽

Klaus Mann
adapted by
Ariane Mnouchkine

MEPHISTO

Translated from the French by
Timberlake Wertenbaker

Mephisto was premiered by the Théâtre du Soleil on May 15, 1979, at the Cartoucherie of Vincennes, with the following cast:

Klaus Mann, then Sebastien Brückner	Christian Colin
Hendrik Höfgen	Gérard Hardy
Carola Martin	Lucia Bensasson
Hans Miklas	Jonathan Sutton
Theresa von Herzfeld	Marie-Françoise Audollent
Otto Ulrich	Jean-Claude Bourbault
Magnus Gottchalk	Yves Gourvil
Madame Efeu	Louba Guertchikoff
Knurr	Roland Amstutz
Juliette	Myrrha Donzenac
Myriam Horowitz	Anne Demeyer
Alex	Norbert Journo
Erika Brückner	Joséphine Derenne
Nicoletta van Niebuhr	Nicole Félix
Theophile Sarder	René Patrignani
Lorenz	Julien Maurel and Pierre Fatus
The Waiter	John Arnold
Thomas Brückner	Jean Dupont
Emelyne	Odile Cointepas
Ludwig	Claude Forget
Hans Josthinkel	Georges Bonnaud

At the Peppermill

Hitler	Christian Colin
General Fonnesique	Jonathan Sutton

At the restaurant

The Maitre d'	Georges Bonnaud
The Officer	Jean Dupont

Adapter and director: **Ariane Mnouchkine**
Set: **Guy-Claude François**
Costumes: **Nani Noël**
Daniel Ogier
Music: **Jean-Jacques Lemêtre**
Assistant director: **Sophie Moscoso**
Masks: **Erhard Stiefel**

"Immortal Sacrifice" was sung by **Martine Rouvières.**

ARIANE MNOUCHKINE studied at the University of Paris and Oxford before founding the Théâtre du Soleil in 1964 with a group of friends who had worked together in university theater. The theater company had a cooperative structure; the tasks and responsibilities of running a theater were shared. Committed to drama that dealt with both social and personal issues, in 1967 the group performed *The Kitchen*, the first Arnold Wesker play to be enacted in France. After the events of 1968, the company began to create its own plays through a collaborative system of collective creation. In 1970 they moved into a disused cartridge warehouse at Vincennes, which became the Cartoucherie, the Théâtre du Soleil's home. They produced three landmark works, which began to establish them as the most important innovative theater company in France: *1789* (1970), *1793* (1972), and *L'Age d'Or* (1975). Mnouchkine later directed a film based on the play *1789* and, in 1976-77, wrote and directed the acclaimed film *Molière*. She returned to theater direction in 1979 with *Mephisto, The Novel of a Career*, which was performed at the Cartoucherie, the Avignon Festival, and the Theater Workshop of Louvain-la-Neuve and, in 1980, toured Lyons, Rome, Berlin, Munich, and Lons-le-Saulnier. In 1981, Mnouchkine embarked on a Shakespeare cycle: *Richard II, Twelfth Night,* and *Henry IV, Part I.* The company toured the 1984 Olympic Arts Festival in Los Angeles, the Avignon Festival, and the Berlin Festival. These productions were followed by epic plays written by Hélène Cixous and directed by Mnouchkine, *Norodom Sihanouk* (1985) and *The Indiad, or The India of Their Dreams* (1987). In 1989 Mnouchkine and Cixous collaborated on *La Nuit miraculeuse,* a television film. Timberlake Wertenbaker's translation of *Mephisto* was premiered by the Royal Shakespeare Company in April 1986.

TIMBERLAKE WERTENBAKER was resident writer at the Royal Court during the 1984-85 season. Her plays for the Court are *Abel's Sister, The Grace of Mary Traverse,* and

Our Country's Good, for which she received the Evening Standard Award for Most Promising Playwright and the Olivier Award for the Best Play of 1988. Her other plays include *The Third* (Kings Head), *Case to Answer* (Soho Poly), *New Anatomies* (ICA), and *The Love of the Nightingale* (RSC), for which she won the Eileen Anderson Award in 1988. Her translations include Marivaux's *False Admissions, Successful Strategies,* and *La Dispute;* Anouilh's *Leocadia;* Maeterlinck's *Pelleas and Melisande;* and Ariane Mnouchkine's *Mephisto* (RSC). Wertenbaker's screenplay of Edith Wharton's *The Children* has been filmed for Channel 4. Her original screenplay *Do Not Disturb* is to be filmed for BBC2.

Pitiful, abject nations, you have taken leave of your senses! You cling stubbornly to evil and are blind to what is good! You allow the best part of your income to be taken from you, you let your farms be pillaged, your houses despoiled and stripped of your ancient ancestral possessions! You can claim nothing as your own, and it seems you would be glad to be allowed to rent from someone else your possessions, your families and your very lives. And all this devastation, this misfortune, this ruin is not visited upon you by an enemy—or rather, it does come from an enemy, and from the man to whom you give the power he has, for whom you so courageously go to war, laying down your lives without hesitation to make him more powerful. Your oppressor has but two eyes, two hands, one body, and has nothing that the least of your infinite number of citizens does not have—except the advantage you give him, which is the power to destroy you. Where did he get those eyes which spy on you, if you did not give him them? Would he have all those hands to strike you with, if he did not get them from you? Those feet which trample upon your cities, where did he get them if they are not your own? What power has he over you, if it is not the power you give him? How would he ever dare attack you, if you were not his accomplices? What could he do to you, if you were not receivers of the goods this thief plunders from you, the companions of this murderer who is killing you, traitors to yourselves? You sow your fruit so that he can destroy the harvest. You furnish your houses, so that he can pillage them. You bring up your daughters to sate his lust. You bring up your children so that (at best) he will take them off to fight his wars and be butchered, or make them ministers to his greed and instruments of his vengeance. . . . You make yourselves weak so that he can be strong and oppress you ever more harshly. . . . Resolve to be slaves no more, and you are free!

—Estienne de La Boétie, *Discours sur la servitude volontaire*, translated by Malcom Smith, in *Slaves by Choice*, Runnymede, Egham, England, 1988

CHARACTERS

KLAUS MANN, then SEBASTIEN BRÜCKNER
HENDRIK HÖFGEN
CAROLA MARTIN
HANS MIKLAS
THERESA VON HERZFELD
OTTO ULRICH
MAGNUS GOTTCHALK
MRS. EFEU
KNURR
JULIETTE
MYRIAM HOROWITZ
ALEX
ERIKA BRÜCKNER
NICOLETTA VON NIEBUHR
THEOPHILE SARDER
LORENZ
THE WAITER
THE MAITRE D'
THE OFFICER
HITLER
GENERAL FONNESIQUE
THOMAS BRÜCKNER
EMELYNE
LUDWIG
HANS JOSTHINKEL

PROLOGUE

(Voice on tape.)

THE VOICE OF THE PUBLISHER: May the 5th, 1949. Dear Sir. Thank you for sending us your manuscript of *Mephisto*. Unfortunately, we are unable at the moment to fit your novel into our budget. You cannot be ignorant of the leading part Mr. Höfgen is once again playing in German affairs, and your book could be construed as a personal attack. Had we been in East Berlin, we wouldn't have hesitated to launch such an operation, but West Berlin presents too many difficulties. It is with great regret that we've relinquished all thoughts of publishing *Mephisto,* but we cannot risk a ban which we fear would be unavoidable in the present political climate. Yours sincerely, etc.

(Another voice rises. This one is alive, indignant, furious.)

Sir. Your letter of May the 5th boggles the imagination. Publishing a book in your house is now called "launching an operation." And when this "operation" presents certain difficulties, you abandon it. Why? Because Mr. Höfgen is once again playing a leading part in Germany. And you call that reasonable. Responsible citizenship. Honoring a contract. I don't know which amazed me more: the baseness of your thinking or the artlessness with which you've confessed your baseness. Höfgen is successful: why then publish a book "which might be construed as a personal attack"? Indeed. Why? We mustn't take risks. We side with power. We swim with the current. You know as well as I do where that leads: straight to the camps, those camps no one is supposed to have known even existed. I am taking the liberty of asking you to send *Mephisto* back by return of post. And please refrain from ever writing to me again. Yours, Klaus Mann.

THE ACTOR: *(to the audience)* For Klaus Mann, the story of this novel began on a November evening of 1923, in the city of Hamburg. The stage will begin by representing the Hamburg Theater. The members of this company will play all the people Klaus Mann met and who became caught up in his story, as well as those people Klaus Mann chose to invent.

SCENE ONE

> *(The Hamburg Theater. Thunderous applause. The curtain goes up as an entire company comes onstage for the call. The officer, a worker, a priest, a whore, a minister, all of Germany is taking the call. The star of the evening is Carola Martin. She takes several bows with her two leading actors in full evening dress. A news item has been traveling backstage and is adding to the usual emotion of a first night. One of the actors, Hendrik Höfgen, decides to make an announcement. He steps forward, to cheers and applause.)*

HENDRIK HÖFGEN: *(at the microphone)* Friends. Dear friends, ...something has happened to put this applause, these actors' vanities, into more sober perspective. Listen to me,... This morning, November the 9th, 1923, a coup took place in Munich. The coup was led by Hitler and his storm troopers.

> *(The audience goes silent. Hendrik continues solemnly.)*

It gives me the greatest pleasure to be able to tell you that...it failed. The police remained loyal to our young republic and opened fire. The rats have fled. Hitler has been arrested. Goering is on the run. The National Socialist party has been outlawed. That's all I wanted to say. Goodnight,...thank you,...thank you,...goodbye,...thank you....

(He bows again and again. Little by little, the applause dies down and the theater empties.)

HENDRIK: *(to Otto)* Friend. Brother. Comrade. What a victory! Hitler's done for.

(Congratulations all around, kisses, embraces. Carola is made much of, petted. She sits at the make-up table. Knurr, the caretaker, brings a bottle of champagne and glasses.)

HENDRIK: Champagne! Carola is offering us all Champagne.

CAROLA: I'm afraid there's only one bottle, but it did cost a fortune. And you can't expect more from a Jew.

THERESA: Champagne! To drink a glass of Champagne in times like these. Hold me back, someone, or I'll misbehave. No one loves Champagne more than I do.

CAROLA: *(to Hans Miklas)* And here's my handsome little soldier. I must tell you how much I admire you, Miklas. You're quite an actor. You were simply marvelous in that border scene. I wasn't at my best there, but you managed to save us both from mediocrity.

MIKLAS: I did my best, Miss Martin, but you didn't help. You were supposed to let go of my hand after saying, "Remember me."

CAROLA: Yes, and you tore your hand away as if I'd set fire to it.

MIKLAS: You ought to have let go of my hand, Miss Martin, and when you didn't, I pulled my hand away.

CAROLA: I ought to have let go,.... yes, yes. Instead of

which I held onto that hand a little too long. And it's such a stiff little hand, too....

MIKLAS: If you don't like the contact of my hand.... If you find the contact of my hand displeasing.... *(He stops.)*

CAROLA: I never suggested such a thing, Hans Miklas, you know that very well. I simply felt that such a brutal gesture was unnecessary.

MIKLAS: That's for the director to decide and no one else. Especially not you, Miss Martin; you only came for the last week of rehearsals.

CAROLA: Do have a taste of my Champagne, Miklas, and let's put an end to this silly quarrel.

MIKLAS: I refuse to drink French Champagne worth its weight in gold when the rest of Germany is starving.

CAROLA: That's enough now. I'm a patient woman, but this is really too much.

(Sebastien Brückner comes in. He is played by the same actor who was Klaus Mann in the Prologue.)

SEBASTIEN: Carola. You were wonderful. What a success! *(He stops, thrown by the tension in the air.)*

CAROLA: Sebastien, my dear. What a pleasure to see you! I completely forgot you were coming.... Let me introduce you to the actors of the Hamburg Theater: Miss Theresa von Herzfield. Miss von Herzfield is also an excellent stage designer. Hans Miklas.

SEBASTIEN: I found you very moving, Mr. Miklas.

CAROLA: Wasn't he? Wasn't he just. Otto Ulrich. I fear

Mr. Ulrich is one of those dangerous communists. Hendrik Höfgen, the greatest actor in Hamburg, and soon, no doubt, in all of Germany. Magnus Gottchalk, our director, the artistic director of the theater, in a word, God. And his wife, Myriam.

MAGNUS: Delighted. I believe we're seeing each other tomorrow. You're reading me one of your plays, aren't you? I'm looking forward to it with much pleasure. And curiosity. I'm a great admirer of your father.

SEBASTIEN: Ah yes,...my tremendous Papa....

HENDRIK: *(to Otto)* I think there were quite a few communists in the audience tonight. They were overjoyed.

CAROLA: You triumphed, my dear.... It was as if you'd routed Mr. Hitler and his storm troopers all by yourself. That's an art....Yes, they'll like you in Berlin, you see. And now, please forgive me, all of you. We're invited to a dreadful reception and I have to put in an appearance. Those people are paid in dollars and it'll be lavish.... I'll steal some Champagne. *(to Miklas)* Don't make such a face, little soldier. Your Mr. Hitler will soon be out of prison.

(She leaves, followed by Sebastien.)

MIKLAS: Champagne. Dollars. There's a kike for you.

MAGNUS: No. I do not allow that kind of thing in my theater.

MIKLAS: What's wrong. Isn't she a Jew?

HENDRIK: Yes. Carola Martin is a Jew. Everyone knows that. Just as everyone knows that Hans Miklas is a Na-tio-nal So-cia-list. And he's not the only one, either.

Mr. Knurr, who's making himself look very small over there, is also a great admirer of Adolph Hitler. Don't hide, Mr. Knurr, we all know you have a swastika sewn on the inside of your jacket.

MR. KNURR: I'm not hiding, Mr. Höfgen. I'm sweeping your corner.

HENDRIK: You don't like me very much, do you, Knurr? You hoped filthy reds like me would be the first to hang when Adolph came to power, but you've been unlucky, Mr. Knurr. It's your Hitler who almost got himself hanged this afternoon. *(to Miklas)* And you, my lad, if you want to stay on here, let me advise you to—

OTTO: That's enough from you, Hendrik. *(to Miklas)* As for you, why don't you try to think with your own brains? Because believe me, all these friends of yours ever do is trumpet through their assholes.

(Miklas goes. Hendrik sits and takes his make-up off. Otto is about to leave.)

OTTO: Are you coming? We're rehearsing tonight. I can wait for you.

HENDRIK: No,...you go. You can start without me.

MAGNUS: Listen, Otto, you and my wife are getting me into trouble with this revolutionary cabaret of yours. I want to talk to you. *(to Hendrik)* Do me a favor and sit in for me tomorrow morning. Frankly, the minor pieces of this century's spoiled children get on my nerves.

HENDRIK: What spoiled children?

MAGNUS: Brückner junior.

HENDRIK: Was that him? Brückner's son?

(Magnus follows Otto out. Hendrik contemplates himself in the mirror and enjoys what he sees. Of the actors, Theresa alone remains.)

THERESA: What are you thinking about?

HENDRIK: Carola Martin. "They'll like you in Berlin," she said. Berlin, will I ever get to Berlin, Theresa? I'm a provincial actor. I'll never be anything more than an obscure actor from the provinces. It'll kill me. Can you understand how much that hurts, Theresa?

THERESA: There's always a price to be paid for hurting others. And you're hurting so many people around you, you're bound to have to atone for it, one way or another.... *(As she's about to leave, she throws off)* Goodnight, Comrade.

(Theresa leaves. Mrs. Efeu, the dresser and prompter, is also getting ready to leave. Hendrik calls her back.)

HENDRIK: Darling Mrs. Efeu. Help me. Don't abandon me now. I'm exhausted.

(Mrs. Efeu helps him dress and puts away the clothes he drops on the floor. He puts his cap on carefully, studying himself in the mirror, combs his hair, and leaves.)

HENDRIK: Heil...,what was his name?

MRS. EFEU: He's made me miss my last tram again.

KNURR: There's no hurry, then. A little something?

(Miklas plays the violin. Mrs. Efeu sits down.)

MRS. EFEU: So the Nazis made a mess of it, did they? Shame. They might've brought down the price of swedes. *(She drinks.)* What's in here?

KNURR: Shit. A Jew's discovered how to distill shit. He's a millionaire now.

(Mrs. Efeu laughs.)

MRS. EFEU: And how much does he pay for it, that's what I want to know. I've got some to sell and I'm sure you do, too, Mr. Knurr. The one thing Germany isn't short of these days is shit. Haha. Well, give us another glass, then. I need a good treat.

MIKLAS: *(playing)* Armchair communists. Höfgen, the Martin woman and their little clique. But the Jews haven't won yet; no, the German people will recognize its true savior. It won't succomb to the lies of the Jewish Marxists nor to the lies of the middle classes who suck out its blood. Hitler isn't hanging at the end of a rope yet. The Germans have lost their honor, but Hitler will give it back to them. He'll wipe his ass with the treaty of Versailles. Our movement will win. Our revolution is nigh.

MRS. EFEU: Well, you tell this revolution of yours to get a move on, because tomorrow I'm selling myself for a slice of bread.

SCENE TWO

(The dressing room of a dingy nightclub. Hendrik watches Juliette shave her legs.)

HENDRIK: Can't you hold yourself straight?

JULIETTE: Ppph. I'm exhausted. I had to do that number three times tonight, twice in a row for just those five drunks. Well, at least I had a full house for my entrance.

HENDRIK: Did you do the "woman with a lasso"?

JULIETTE: No, thank you. Thank you very much. Not that one. You made me sweat over it for weeks and when I did it, they pissed themselves laughing. That lasso, let me tell you.

HENDRIK: That's because you didn't feel confident enough with it.

JULIETTE: Not confident? Not confident?

HENDRIK: I choreographed you a very good number. I know what I'm talking about.

JULIETTE: You should've seen me. There was my arse pointing straight up at the ceiling, my lasso twirling and twirling round my head, while I rolled my great big ferocious African eyes and yelped a lot. And all they said was, "Just show us your bush, doll, cut the monkey business."

HENDRIK: What did you expect? They laughed because they found it disturbing. It *is* disturbing.

JULIETTE: Yeh, well. Maybe it's disturbing for you, all that stuff, the lasso, getting slapped around....But them, they prefer the rumba, it's more advanced. You know, the blokes who come here, they wouldn't mind giving you a good thrashing but they'd never dream of taking one.

HENDRIK: Do hurry up. I missed the revolutionary cabaret to come and get you.

JULIETTE: Yeh. Well. It's not the first time you've missed your revolutionary cabaret. *(She drinks straight from a bottle.)* What piss. Want some? What is it you do exactly in this revolutionary cabaret of yours?

HENDRIK: Nothing to interest little girls. I'll tell you about it when you grow up.

JULIETTE: Bollocks, I've seen revolutionary theater before, let me tell you, in the street. I know exactly what happens. They bring out a big loudspeaker and someone shouts: "Down with the bourgeoisie. Long live communism." And then the police come and arrest everybody. But what exactly is it, communism?

HENDRIK: Look at my hands,...how ugly they look next to your legs. I shouldn't even be allowed to touch you.

JULIETTE: Yeh. Hands, feet, everything of yours is ugly. Your soul, everything. Why don't you let me come to the theater when you're acting? I know what I'm going to do. One night, you'll come out onstage and you'll see me, right there, in the middle of the stalls. Yes. And I'll be laughing very very loud.

HENDRIK: That's not funny! I forbid you to come to the theater, do you hear!

JULIETTE: Every time you're onstage, I'll point my finger at you. I'll twirl my lasso and roll my great big beautiful eyes and I'll shout: "Look at the handsome monkey, ladies and gentlemen, look at dat monkey dere. Dat's me own little monkey and me be his she-monkey."

HENDRIK: *(taking her in his arms)* Ah. I love you. You're smooth, you're hard, you're strong. You're the love of my life, do you know that?

JULIETTE: Yeh. But seriously, Hendrik, teach me communism. I want to learn something that's good.

HENDRIK: "You walk on the dead, Beauty, with mockery. Horror glitters brightly among your ornaments and mingling casually with your expensive baubles murder dances lovingly on your belly's proud curve." Murder dances lovingly on the proud curve of your belly.

JULIETTE: Dancing in a dockland nightclub doesn't do much for your brain, let me tell you. Doesn't do much for your heart either. Hendrik, teach me something.

(He takes her hand and slowly makes her slap him harder and harder.)

HENDRIK: You don't need to know anything; it's all in your blood. My Beauty, my Africa, my Torment, my Savage.

JULIETTE: No,...Hendrik,...let me go. I don't feel like it. Hendrik, I like you. Stop. Please. You're hurting me.

Scene Three

(The Peppermill, a revolutionary cabaret. Otto, Alex, and Myriam are rehearsing. An exhausted Magnus, who's been waiting hours for his wife to finish, watches them. A short musical overture.)

THE M.C. (ALEX): Dear Audience. Thanks to the exquisite courtesy of the official censorship which has condescended to be amongst us tonight and has had the exceptional graciousness of allowing us to act before you, the Peppermill is proud to present its great modern epic-lyrical verse drama in the form of a mystery play in seventy-five scenes. Scene the first: Myriam at the Department of Social Security. *(He lowers a drop.)*

THE WOMAN (MYRIAM): It's now six times I've been here, and every time I have a form missing. Could you please tell me, Mister the Employee, Sir, if this time I have everything you need?

THE EMPLOYEE (OTTO): What I need. What I need? Wait. Why are you asking me what I need? You're the one who has to have everything you need. I don't need anything.

THE WOMAN: I was told I'd find the information I need at the Department of Social Security.

THE EMPLOYEE: Yes.

THE WOMAN: Yes what?

THE EMPLOYEE: That's probable. The Department of Social Security will give you the necessary information.

THE WOMAN: I've been sitting here an hour and you still haven't given me any information.

THE EMPLOYEE: You didn't ask for information. You kept asking me what I needed.

THE WOMAN: Now I'm asking you for some information.

THE EMPLOYEE: The office is closed.

THE WOMAN: What are you doing here, then?

THE EMPLOYEE: I'm waiting for it to open.

THE WOMAN: When does it open?

THE EMPLOYEE: When I open it.

THE WOMAN: When do you open?

THE EMPLOYEE: When it's time.

THE WOMAN: Will that be a long time?

THE EMPLOYEE: Ah. Time is relative. Let us suppose I'm lounging on the soft cushions of a velvet sofa eating a bowl of chicken consommé with little balls of chopped liver in it, then a minute will pass as quickly as lightning. But if you're shivering by a coalless stove, then that same minute will last more than a century. So you see, my dear lady, knowing nothing about the circumstances of your life, I'm in no position to give you any answers. *(He takes off his hat and puts on a cap.)*

THE WOMAN: Why are you putting on a cap?

THE EMPLOYEE: I wear a cap when I work.

THE WOMAN: Are you working now?

THE EMPLOYEE: Surely that's obvious.

THE WOMAN: Right. Now can I have some information, please?

THE EMPLOYEE: Stop. Halt there. This is the Department of Social Security, not the Department of Information. If you're looking for the Department of Information, you'll find it at number Seventeen The Treaty of Versailles Is a Filthy Insult Avenue. Whereas this department is at number Twenty The German Army Never Lost the War, It Was Stabbed in the Back by the Bolsheviks Square.

THE WOMAN: But it's social security I need.

THE EMPLOYEE: Any special kind of social security?

THE WOMAN: Yes.

THE EMPLOYEE: Stop. Halt there. Special cases are at number Twelve If Germany's on the Shitheap It's Because Wages Are Too High Street.

THE WOMAN: How the hell do I know if I'm a special case or not?

THE EMPLOYEE: You mean you don't even know what kind of a case you are? You're not by any chance trying to cheat the system, are you?

THE WOMAN: I'm expecting twins, my husband was badly wounded in the war, I can't find work and I don't have anywhere to live.

THE EMPLOYEE: Sounds like you need some social security. Let's begin at the beginning. What's your address?

THE WOMAN: I told you I'm on the street.

THE EMPLOYEE: Where's your permit?

THE WOMAN: What permit?

THE EMPLOYEE: Your street permit. Where do you expect me to send you the forms?

THE WOMAN: Send them to my sister at number Fourteen Everything Was Better under the Emperor Lane.

THE EMPLOYEE: When did you lose your housing?

THE WOMAN: On November the 20th.

THE EMPLOYEE: Now that's a shame.

THE WOMAN: Of course it's a shame.

THE EMPLOYEE: If you'd lost it on the 21st, you'd be entitled to special benefits because of the legislation passed on the 31st, which took effect retrospectively on the 21st but not on the 19th.

THE WOMAN: What about my twins? I've been told I'm entitled to a swede allowance.

THE EMPLOYEE: Certainly. Everybody's entitled to a swede allowance. But stop. Halt there. It's not here. It's at One-Twenty-Seven Everybody's Ganging Up against Germany but That's Because They're Jealous Alley.

THE WOMAN: What kind of help can you give me here, then?

(The employee looks at his watch. He takes off his cap and puts on his hat. Then he goes to sit next to the woman.)

THE EMPLOYEE: Listen to me, little lady. You'd better

hurry up and decide what it is you want. I've been listening to the three of you for more than an hour now.

THE WOMAN: What are you doing?

THE EMPLOYEE: That was my last day of work. Now I'm unemployed, so I'm joining the queue at the Department of Social Security. Do you think they'll be able to give me some information?

THE WOMAN: What's your address?

THE EMPLOYEE: Number Seven Fuck German Bureaucracy Circus.

MYRIAM: *(taking off her false nose)* And now: beddyby.

OTTO: *(stubbornly)* What about the next scene, the scene about inflation? It isn't ready yet. We haven't found an end for it. We have to find an end.

MYRIAM: What's wrong with my idea?

OTTO: What idea?

MYRIAM: You have the capitalist here and he holds up one gold coin. The worker comes on with a big shopping bag full of notes, then he brings on a wheelbarrow, but it's still not enough to buy his kipper. *(She stops and looks at the others questioningly.)*

OTTO: So?

MYRIAM: So there's your scene about inflation.

OTTO: And what has it explained?

MYRIAM: That you need three million marks to buy a kipper.

OTTO: Everybody already knows that. It's something everyone experiences every day. What we need to show is the why, the how, who's making this happen and in whose interest.

MYRIAM: So how should I know? I don't understand the first thing about it. It's too complicated.

OTTO: In that case everything we do here is too complicated. Is that what you're saying?

MYRIAM: Yes. For a piece of theater, it's too complicated.

OTTO: You're saying theater is incapable of portraying our society.

MYRIAM: Well, sometimes I have my doubts, yes.

OTTO: That is something we must never accept. Never.

(Silence.)

MAGNUS: *(condescendingly)* Look. There's nothing in the least complicated about inflation. Inflation is simply a huge legalized fraud, which allows big business to pay off its debts in devalued marks. You're a big businessman: the state offers you big loans in good money. You buy nice new machines. Then inflation spirals and you pay back the state with peanuts. Wages drop, the price of exports drops. You start dumping on the market and you get yourself paid in foreign currency, which you stash safely...somewhere abroad. Old-age pensioners are ruined; so are the small proprietors, tenants. Heavy industry gets fat and the working class pays. There. Simple.

MYRIAM: Simple it may be, but I didn't understand a word of it.

MAGNUS: What didn't you understand?

MYRIAM: I told you: anything. Why is it good for heavy industry? What about light industry? Why are exports cheap when everything here is so expensive?

MAGNUS: Because exports are paid for in foreign currency. You'd think 700 generations of unadulterated Jewish blood would make you able to understand something as simple as that.

MYRIAM: Here we go. The Jews and money. So I'm the Jewish bank, am I? I'm married to him for fifteen years and now he tells me he's antisemitic.

MAGNUS: You don't want to understand, that's all. If you owe somebody one thousand marks and ten years later one thousand marks is worth one mark, then when you pay back that thousand marks, you're in fact only paying back one mark. Your net profit is nine hundred and ninety-nine marks. Do you understand now, my little Mymichik?

MYRIAM: You're getting on my nerves.

(She leaves, followed by Magnus. Carola Martin has come in and watched some of this. She's silent. Otto has remained alone. He sees her.)

OTTO: The great star from Berlin in our little Peppermill. To what do we owe such an honor?

CAROLA: I can't find my way around Hamburg at night. I only know the way to the theater and back. I came to ask you if you'd walk me to the hotel.

OTTO: How was the reception?

CAROLA: Rotten. I brought you some canapés.

OTTO: No, thank you. It's daylight now; you'll be able to find your way back alone.

CAROLA: Come with me anyway. On the way, you can tell me what it is about me you so dislike. Rehearsing with you was...painful, to say the least.

OTTO: Please accept my apologies.

CAROLA: No. I don't accept your apologies. You're a wonderful actor, Otto; what are your plans?

OTTO: Plans?

CAROLA: For your career.

OTTO: I don't have any plans for my career and I don't want any, either.

CAROLA: What about the theater?

OTTO: *(provocatively)* I'm not interested in the theater.

CAROLA: Liar!

OTTO: I'm a communist. Communism is my profession and my vocation. The theater is nothing more than a roof over my head and a hot meal on the table. Now I've told you everything there is to know about me.

CAROLA: A roof over our heads, yes. A meal on the table, yes. And a light in our darkness? Isn't it? Your theater is beautiful.

OTTO: Come. Let me offer you a cup of coffee.

CAROLA: A big one?

OTTO: A big one.

CAROLA: And a slice of poppy-seed cake?

OTTO: And a slice of poppy-seed cake.

SCENE FOUR

(The Hamburg Theater. Hendrik is ready to listen to the "reading" of Sebastien's play. Sebastien gives the last stage directions. Mrs. Efeu and Knurr hover, intrigued.)

SEBASTIEN: So. Now. The children of the boarding school can be heard singing in the distance. The scene is a large hall of dark wood. Stage right, there's a majestic door which leads to the Western dormitories. Stage left, the door leading to the Eastern dormitories. Through the windows can be seen statues on the lawn. On the wall, a large crucifix, or possibly a palm branch. Anja and Esther come on. No, one moment. *(He runs to the wings, stage right, then stage left, and comes back.)* Anja and Esther come on.

(He sits next to Hendrik as Nicoletta and Erika appear. They're barefoot and dressed in little girls' nightgowns. Each holds a candle.)

ESTHER (NICOLETTA): Anja, Anja, where are you?

ANJA (ERIKA): Esther?

ESTHER: I've been waiting for you. I jumped out of the lavatory window. And you? How did you get out?

ANJA: It was difficult. The housemistress was lying across my door. I leapt over her body.

ESTHER: Oh. You're so brave. I wouldn't have dared do such a thing. That housemistress is frightful.

ANJA: She's ugly; she's old.

ESTHER: She's mean.

ANJA: She's bearded.

ESTHER: She prickles.

ANJA: She has hair on her bottom.

ESTHER/ANJA: *(laughing)* She has a hairy bottom.

ESTHER: You're so funny, Anja. You make me laugh.

ANJA: It's hot. My nightie's clinging to my body.

ESTHER: What a dreadful August! I'm boiling.

ANJA: The moon burns like a sun. It's hot.

(Erika lifts up her nightdress and shows herself to be naked underneath, as is Nicoletta.)

ESTHER: Yes. I'm hot.

(They improvise a little game to see who can shock the two men most.)

ANJA: Listen. I hear it.

ESTHER: Oh god.

ANJA: It could be the ghost.

ESTHER: No. Don't say that. I'm afraid of ghosts. Don't play games.

ANJA: I'm not playing games. There is a ghost. A ghost there is. It's the ghost of the former headmistress. They say she used to bite her favorite pupils on the throat. Here. *(She shows her neck.)*

ESTHER: I'm frightened. You always frighten me. You're wicked.

ANJA: Oh. I feel ill. Suddenly. Something...someone ...bit me. Oh my god. What if the poison's deadly?

ESTHER: I'll suck it out. It's what you're supposed to do.

(Nicoletta slides herself under Erika's nightgown.)

HENDRIK: Drop the curtain, Knurr; someone might come in.

(Mrs. Efeu leaves, outraged.)

ESTHER: Do you feel better now? Much better?

ANJA: Yes. Thank you.

ESTHER: Sometimes I feel afraid for you. It's as if you might die, quite suddenly. And if you died, what would become of me? I have a feeling I'm capable of horrors.

ANJA: You have a little crease. Did you know that? And your skin is shining. *(She looks into Nicoletta's nightgown.)*

ESTHER: What cold hands you have! Have you looked at the stars?

(During this exchange, a man walks onto the stage. It's Theophile Sarder. He walks towards the two actresses, who see him and jump.)

SARDER: Please don't stop.

NICOLETTA: Who is that?

ERIKA: Theophile Sarder. He calls himself the greatest living German playwright. My father thinks he's right.

NICOLETTA: Oh. If your father thinks so.

(Sebastien signals for them to continue. He wants to prompt them, but the two women ignore him and continue their acting.)

ANJA: I must go now.

ESTHER: *(running after her and holding onto her)* Wait. Wait. One more little moment. I believe you are a saint. You are so gentle. You are more gentle than any other human being. Even when you say no, you do it gently. You are a saint, a dark and silvery saint. Everything you touch, you purify. Everything you do is sanctified. Everything we do together is sanctified. Anja, Saint Anja, my saint, my Anja.

ANJA: Let's not go and join the others. Come. Come with me. Come into the garden. Come into the night.

(They kiss. The kiss lasts and lasts. Sebastien becomes embarrassed and tries to interrupt them but meets with no success. He insists. The two women pull him to the floor and tease him.)

SEBASTIEN: No. No. Please forgive me, Mr. Höfgen, they make me laugh. They're always making me laugh.

SARDER: Erika. How is your father?

ERIKA: Well.

SARDER: And your grandmother?

ERIKA: Well.

SEBASTIEN: The whole tribe's well.

SARDER: I'm afraid there isn't much skill in what

you've shown us there, my boy.

SEBASTIEN: Thank you. I was thinking the same thing.

ERIKA: Don't listen to him. He can't bear anything he hasn't written himself. There are only three writers he admires: Shakespeare, Schiller, Sarder. The immortal S's.

SARDER: What are you doing for lunch?

ERIKA: I'm having it with them.

SARDER: I'll come, too, if that's all right.

ERIKA: Yes, but you'll have to take us.

SARDER: Of course.

ERIKA: It'll have to be an expensive restaurant where you pay in dollars.

SARDER: Why dollars?

ERIKA: Your American royalties. Don't they pay you in dollars?

SARDER: As they do your father.

ERIKA: Leave my father out of this. You're not fit to—

SARDER: All right. All right. I'll pay in dollars.

(He goes, dragging a surprised Nicoletta after him. Sebastien follows.)

ERIKA: *(to Hendrik)* Aren't you coming?

(They go. Mrs. Efeu, Knurr, and Miklas appear suddenly from the darkness of the wings.)

MIKLAS: It won't be long before we can throw all that into the sewers, Mr. Knurr.

(They're about to eat when a young boy comes in. He's dirty, thin, and very hard.)

MRS. EFEU: Who's that?

MIKLAS: He was hanging about near the theater. He's hungry.

MRS. EFEU: I'll get you a slice of bread.... I've hidden some in the.... I'll be right back.

(She goes out, leaving the two men with the boy. He looks at them defiantly. Knurr feels uneasy.)

KNURR: How old are you?

THE CHILD: Fifteen.

KNURR: What's your name?

THE CHILD: Lorenz.

KNURR: Lorenz what?

LORENZ: Lorenz Lorenz.

KNURR: Lorenz Lorenz what?

LORENZ: Prattface.

KNURR: Listen to me, boy. If that's the way you talk, you won't get any bread and butter here, is that clear?

LORENZ: Why? I don't have the right to be called Lorenz Lorenz Prattface?

KNURR: If you think I don't know what your game is, young man.

LORENZ: If you think I don't know what your game is, you old turd burglar. The woman's off. Leaves the men. Time to set out my stall. You want to see my arse, you tell me. I drop my trousers, you do our business, I get my bread and butter. *(He takes down his trousers.)*

KNURR: What's he doing? What the hell is he doing? Get him out of here. Quickly.

(Knurr slaps Lorenz, who picks up his trousers.)

LORENZ: I want my bread and butter.

MIKLAS: Look. You can eat bread and butter here without having to—

(Mrs. Efeu comes back with two slices of bread and butter in a greasy paper. Lorenz and Miklas start to eat greedily.)

LORENZ: The other day two French tourists gave me a whole meal. For just two blow jobs. They were nice. They took me rowing on the lake. Seems there's deprivation here. That's what they said.

MIKLAS: Yes, there's a lot of deprivation here, Lorenz, but it's all going to change. And we're the ones who will change it: you,...me,...Mr. Knurr,...Mrs. Efeu. We'll make it change, you'll see. The time has come for the German people to stop dropping their trousers. The time has come for the German people to make others drop their trousers.

(Lorenz laughs.)

Yes, but in order to do that we all have to unite around a strong leader. Do you understand, Lorenz? If you want, I'll introduce you to some other boys like you tomorrow. They'll make you feel welcome, you'll see, and you'll eat a bowl of soup every day.

LORENZ: *(incredulously)* Every day?

MIKLAS: Every day. What about it?

LORENZ: Why not?

(The four of them drink.)

MIKLAS: To our Germany!

KNURR: To the future!

MRS. EFEU: To peace!

LORENZ: What time is it, Knurr?

(Knurr looks for his watch.)

KNURR: Where's my watch!

(With a malicious little smile, Lorenz finds the watch in Mrs. Efeu's cleavage. They all laugh and a party begins, during which Lorenz demonstrates his conjuring tricks and Mrs. Efeu plays the piano.)

Scene Five

(The restaurant. Sarder, Sebastien, Nicoletta, Hendrik. A large and glittering table. There is another small table next to it. The maître d' places an immense menu in Sarder's hands. The orchestra plays discreetly. A little waiter brings the lobsters, which Sarder chooses with infinite care.)

SARDER: The lobsters. Let us study the lobsters. We'll have this one, that one, and that little rogue over there, and that naughty one over there. And the one there, not that one, the one with the plump thighs. Vulger it might be, but I detect a promise of sensuality. *(to Nicoletta)* And I presume the little friend of the family won't refuse a glass of Hock. What do you think of this place, Höfgen? It's the only restaurant in Hamburg where you can still find a decent meal.

ERIKA: Hendrik feels ill at ease in a place like this. He's angry with me for having brought him here.

HENDRIK: I'm not angry with you.

SARDER: Oh, dear. I have a feeling we're about to embark on the subject of Revolution. It can't be helped. Höfgen, let us hear about your Revolution. But first, the lobsters. Waiter: the lobsters.

(They drink heavily.)

NICOLETTA: I believe it is already a revolutionary act to eat lobsters which are being paid for by an old reactionary for whom one feels nothing but contempt.

SARDER: Wrong. Wrong again. It was the reactionaries who first invented contempt. It is an item of which they have a surplus. Believe me when I tell you, my dear girl, that you'll never feel as much contempt for them as they already feel for you.

(The orchestra begins a slow dance. Sarder gets up and drags Nicoletta onto the dance floor. Hendrik musters up the courage to invite Erika. Sebastien, left alone at the table, watches them and drinks. Suddenly Nicoletta leaves the dumbfounded Sarder in the middle of the floor and takes Erika in her arms. The two women dance together. No one has noticed the maître d' slapping the little waiter.)

SARDER: What a shame! Freaks. We long for real women and we have to make do with freaks. Look at them. Half creatures. And they're doing it on purpose, to taunt us. I'd like to pay one of those waiters to take down their pants and give them the lesson they deserve. And look at this little runt here: the flotsam spawned by genius. He's part of it all. Do you know it's for him those two save themselves? It's for him they keep their full and beautiful mouths, their silky limbs, their ravishing little white breasts. You must have been aware of that, Mr. Höfgen; everyone is talking about it, so it must be true. The beautiful Brückner twins and the family friend. The shocking little galaxy. It's disgusting.

(Sebastien laughs at his indignation and leaves the table to join the two women. They welcome him with great tenderness. He's pleasantly drunk.)

HENDRIK: I'm surprised by what you've just said, Mr. Sarder. Aren't there scenes in your own plays which are as shocking...and possibly less tender?

SARDER: Art can never be shocking. The poet purifies his most demonic creations. But what is daring on the stage becomes crude and disgusting in real life.

HENDRIK: Yes, but what about the scene in Sodom and Gomorrah, with the man and the two children...?

SARDER: Chastity! That scene is about chastity! The crudeness of all that's said and done in that scene only serves to highlight its fundamental chastity. It is because that man is so different that he becomes worthy of our love.

SEBASTIEN: Blah, blah, blah.

HENDRIK: But why does it irritate you when life itself offers something different, and equally chaste?

SEBASTIEN: Yes, Sarder, why?

SARDER: Real life does not come into my plays, Mr. Höfgen. I don't have such vulgar ambitions; no, my plays have absolutely nothing to do with real life. Theater floats in the realm of the impossible.

SEBASTIEN: I want my plays to be real life, nothing but life, inner life, exterior life, art, politics, love, this wine....

SARDER: How banal you are, Sebastien! And I suppose you agree with him, Höfgen.

HENDRIK: Yes, I do. It is the duty of the theater to portray life. And it becomes a political force when it deals with human progress. That's what we're looking for at the Peppermill.

SARDER: The Peppermill?

HENDRIK: It's the name of a cabaret I manage with some friends. We practice a very different kind of theater from yours, Mr. Sarder. It's a theater of the future, which will belong to the working class.

SARDER: The working class.

SEBASTIEN: Yes, Sarder. The working class.

SARDER: And so Anja and Esther is a play for the working class.

SEBASTIEN: Yes. Why not? Just because it isn't good enough for you doesn't mean—

SARDER: If it isn't good enough for me, it's not good enough for the working class.

HENDRIK: The working class doesn't need a bourgeois theater.

SEBASTIEN: Did you hear that, Sarder, the working class doesn't need you.

SARDER: While the working class is waiting for you with bated breath. The working class doesn't need Shakespeare; it doesn't need Goethe, Chekhov, Molière; it doesn't need Sophocles; but it needs you, and him.

HENDRIK: (solemnly) The working class needs a revolutionary theater.

SARDER: The working class needs the truth. We all need the truth, and God knows that's a rare enough commodity these days.

(The Officer comes on.)

SEBASTIEN: There's a man. Look at that. Isn't he handsome? What an air! How he carries himself! There's civilization for you. Alas, alas, alas.

SARDER: Alas what? Have we produced anything better than that recently? Are your physical abilities greater than those of that soldier? Are your moral qualities superior to his? Isn't our age infinitely more drab and despairing than his ever was?

ERIKA: Eat your lobster, Theo, and stop drinking. You're being silly. You're all being silly.

SARDER: *(drunk)* I am the only one sitting at this table who has the right to judge our times. And I tell you that this vulgar, this superficial age can't begin to compare with the age in which I grew up. And yet, I reviled it. I poured on it all the poison I could dredge from my being. We were a nation of soldiers and poets. That's bad enough, I admit, but we're now becoming a nation of shopkeepers. It makes me sick. And that silly old man who sits there so stiffly, at least he has a spine. You,... Mister Höfgen, did you fight in the war?

(Höfgen hesitates.)

HENDRIK: No. Obviously not. Thank God.

SARDER: There you are. No discipline and hence no personality. No breaking-in.

SEBASTIEN: *(sarcastically)* Sarder, I'm crushed. I'm crushed by all you've said. We're all crushed.

SARDER: And I'm crushed by what I see around me. Look at him. A relic, yes, but the relic of an eagle. He and I are eagles in a population of rats. We're ridiculous, yes, we're the rats' jesters, but you want a Germany populated with mice. *(He begins to cry.)*

ERIKA: Theo, shut up and eat your lobster.

SARDER: We're heading for the abyss. Our age is rotting away before us. It's already stinking and I'm the only one who notices the stench. I can see the catastrophe that's looming; it will be unbelievable. All that is will collapse, and we'll lie buried in tombs of excrement. I feel so sorry for you, my children. You won't live out your lives. You're already decomposing on the spot, like flowers in a sunless spring.

(He bursts into sobs. He's about to break down completely. Sebastien and Hendrick take him out. Nicoletta is obviously upset. She begins to follow them.)

ERIKA: Where are you going?

NICOLETTA: I love that man. Passionately.

ERIKA: You've gone mad.

NICOLETTA: Yes. Just now.

ERIKA: Let me tell you something.

NICOLETTA: About the stars?

ERIKA: About that man. He's dangerous.

NICOLETTA: Why?

ERIKA: He's desperate.

NICOLETTA: Then I'm lost. Let me go, Erika.

(She goes out. Erika is alone. She's beat. Hendrick comes back in.)

HENDRIK: Nicoletta von Niebuhr asked me to give you a message.

ERIKA: What are you waiting for?

HENDRIK: She asks you to remain her friend. She threw herself into the car and took the wheel. The poor chauffeur was left standing on the pavement. He kept saying, "But it's a kidnapping, she's kidnapping him." I thought the same. Was she your best friend?

ERIKA: She is my best friend.

HENDRIK: Of course.

(Silence. The Officer leaves. The maître d' salutes him.)

HENDRIK: Yesterday...since yesterday...what a life! The first night's a resounding success. I meet the son of Germany's greatest living author. Then I meet Germany's greatest living playwright. The dollar is worth 50 billion marks. I'm invited to an exclusive restaurant where my meal costs 500 billion marks. I watch the inexorable power of love at first sight. I'm still young, I'm full of promise. I think I'll ask Gottchalk for a raise and after that, I might fall in love. At the thought of falling in love I can feel my heart beat faster. I'm not used to the thought of being happy.

ERIKA: Our evening is making you think of happiness, is it?

HENDRIK: I know you're unhappy tonight, Erika, and yet you're the one who's making me think of happiness. You've dazzled me. I've been waiting for this meeting since I was a little boy. I used to watch my mother and father in their slovenly dress, drinking beer in a sitting room that hadn't one book in it. And I swore then that one day I'd be elegant, frail, seductive, and I'd mix in the company of delicate and learned people. Someone will come, I used to say to myself, Saint Nicholas, or a gangster, a woman, an angel, someone will come and take me away from this sad, dark and stupid Dresden backstreet. Your unhappiness tonight is making me hope for prodigious things. ....what have they put in this bottle? It's not wine we've all been drinking, it's a love potion. Erika, I saw you drink out of that glass. Look at me quickly or you'll fall in love with the maître d', who's coming our way, or maybe even with that lobster. Erika Brückner, why don't you fall in love with me? Do you have anything more interesting to do tonight? *(He's on his knees, in front of her.)*

ERIKA: What's happening to us? Sarder is right; the world's turning too fast, it's upside down.

(Sebastien comes in and watches them.)

HENDRIK: I need you, Erika. I'm bad. Take what's good in me and make it grow. I'm lost if you don't. Save me, Erika. You're an angel. You're a witch. You're all-powerful. If you don't love me, it'll be the end of me. I'll never come to anything.

ERIKA: Let's try. Yes, let's try since you want it so much. What else is there for us to do?

(Sebastien goes to Erika. The maître d' signals the orchestra to play a slow dance, and the three dance together. Sebastien wipes Erika's tears as the maître d' empties the glasses with great dignity.)

SCENE SIX

(A rehearsal at the Peppermill. A musical overture. We see Hitler in prison. Clowning.)

OTTO: Visit for you, Sir. Mr. Fritz Thyssen, cannon manufacturer. *(He puts on a mask and comes forward.)*

THYSSEN (OTTO): Have you heard the election results of May the 4th, 1924? No? Why not? It's the 5th today, isn't it? The communists held four seats. They now hold sixty-two. What do you make of that? Do you know on what kind of a scrap heap I'll find myself if you don't stem this Bolshevik tide? And you haven't helped with your despicable failure. When I think of Mussolini.... The march on Rome. Now there's a man. You should be ashamed of yourself. God knows there are enough officers in the German army willing to lend a hand. In fact, I'm waiting for....

AN ACTOR: The Head of Staff of what's left of the German army, Sir.

(Clowning entrance of Fonnesique)

FONNESIQUE: *(lost in thought)* Buggered. They buggered us. It's the Jews.

THYSSEN: My dear Fonnesique, allow me to introduce one of your most fervent admirers.

FONNESIQUE: Sissies. Poor Germany. Nothing but sissies. The real Germans are dispersed over the face of the earth.

THYSSEN: Quite. My young friend here shares your feelings, and—

FONNESIQUE: Austria. Full of Germans, Austria. We'll annex Austria.

THYSSEN: That's exactly what my young friend was saying. Would you—

FONNESIQUE: Poland. Crammed with Germans. We'll annex Poland.

THYSSEN: Precisely, but before you—

FONNESIQUE: Lorraine, Alsace, Czechoslovakia, all Germans there. Switzerland, Belgium, Spain, the Canary Islands. Nothing but Germans. We'll annex.

THYSSEN: If we could just look at the election results—

FONNESIQUE: And Panama. What about Panama? A million oppressed Germans in Panama. We'll annex Panama.

THYSSEN: (shouting) The Bolsheviks! What are you going to do about the Bolsheviks?

FONNESIQUE: There are Germans in the USSR. We'll annex the USSR.

THYSSEN: Save yourself the trip. There are Bolsheviks right here in Germany.

FONNESIQUE: Jews. Hang them.

THYSSEN: Assuredly. I have here in my office a young man—

FONNESIQUE: All women are whores.

THYSSEN: I understand your legitimate grievances, my dear Fonnesique, but to come back to the Bolsheviks—

FONNESIQUE: What's the name of that general who executed ten thousand soldiers for insubordination?

THYSSEN: Petain. Philippe Petain.

FONNESIQUE: We'll annex Philippe. It's the communists who stabbed the German army in the back. I have that from the socialists themselves.

THYSSEN: My young friend and I hate the communists above all.

FONNESIQUE: Long live Bismarck. Long live Frederick the Great. Long live the 15th century. Long live the Stone Age. The Republic's a dung heap. What?

THYSSEN: Personally, Frederick the Great leaves me cold. I don't want to find myself sweeping the floor of my own factory for ten rubles a month, that's all. Now listen to me, my dear Fonnesique, what you need are the mercenary and paramilitary organizations of Mr. Hitler. Right?

FONNESIQUE: Wrong!

THYSSEN: Listen, Kurt, I've got him well in hand. As soon as he's finished with the Bolsheviks, we'll ditch him. Right?

FONNESIQUE: Right! They can have the sleeping bags.

THYSSEN: *(to Hitler)* That's a deal. You've already got the sleeping bags. We'll talk about the big money when you get out of this place. Heil Hitler. Guard! Hurry. Out of here, we're getting....

(They bang on the door. The guard (Alex) comes to open it. But he hesitates, pushes the two men back, and closes the door.)

OTTO: What are you doing?

ALEX: I'm not letting them out.

OTTO: But—

ALEX: I think we need to present a positive figure.

MYRIAM: Have I heard this? It's two o'clock in the morning and he wants to start discussing the role of the positive figure. Now is that wise? Is that wise?

OTTO: All right. You don't let them come out. Go on. Improvise. Let's go back.

FONNESIQUE/THYSSEN: Air. Of air in need ve are. Or suffocate ve will.

(Alex pulls the bolts across the door.)

ALEX: *(striding to the front)* And that, Comrades, is the end. You know who's in there: the capitalists. Down with the bourgeoisie. Down with international capitalism. So, Comrades, come rally and the last fight let us face. Long live the Revolution. Greetings to the Soviet Union. There. The message is clear, optimistic, positive.

MAGNUS: Yes, but if you show the positive figure of the guard you also have to show the negative figures of the bosses. They'll kick you in the behind and say, "Open that door immediately or we'll put a bullet through your brains." *(This he demonstrates.)* And frankly, when I see an actor who claims to be politicized shout and salute the Soviet Union with his eyes closed, I say that isn't an actor, that's a vulgar propagandist. A brainwasher.

ALEX: I am a communist worker.

MAGNUS: That doesn't have to be synonymous with brainwasher.

ALEX: I am a communist worker and I am aware of the fact that the person addressing me is nothing more than a bourgeois social-democrat. And I'm tired of all this clowning. We're not creating revolutionary theater here, we're simply imitating the same old forms of bourgeois entertainment.

MYRIAM: What's he saying? What's he saying now? Enlighten me, my son. Tell me just what it is I have to do to be allowed entry into the heaven of revolutionary theater. What? What?

ALEX: Why can't we have a theater that's as concise as our pamphlets? In any case, Hitler's now in prison. The Germans aren't the same people as the Italians. The German working class is much too politicized for fascism to be a serious threat in Germany. The real danger we face and have always faced is the continual betrayal of the social-democrats. We mustn't forget it was Noske who ordered his friends to be shot, not Hitler. The domination of the bourgeoisie is always the domination of the bourgeoisie, whether you call it fascism or social-democracy.

MYRIAM: *(to Otto)* How long are you going to put up with this?

OTTO: I don't know. I'm confused. I'm tired. If fascism isn't a serious threat, then we should forget about Hitler and do something else. Anyway, I'll show you the backdrop.

> *(Alex lowers the drop. It's been wrecked. There's an inscription: JEWS, COMMUNISTS, SOCIAL-DEMOCRATS...BE PATIENT...WE'LL GET ALL OF YOU. Blackout.)*

(A few hours later, still at the Peppermill. Otto and Theresa are finishing the repairs.)

THERESA: That's it. Now they can start again.

OTTO: And we'll repair it again.

THERESA: Until they take to their axes and hack the words on our faces. I'm frightened. If only you knew how frightened I am. I don't understand. I'm the only one who seems to feel so frightened. I feel sick with fear.

OTTO: Come and work with us, Theresa. Fear is best cured by the struggle.

THERESA: And so on and so forth. I don't like you when you talk like a pamphlet. I'll come when Höfgen comes.

OTTO: Höfgen is here. He may not be rehearsing at the moment, but he's still with us. He's a true socialist, Theresa; you're unfair.

THERESA: That's because I want to go to bed with him. I'm going. Are you coming? You're not? Why? Are you waiting for someone? Who? I'm so nosy. Come on, Theresa, come along. It's time to go home.

(She goes out. Otto turns off the lights. Carola comes on.)

CAROLA: Otto?

OTTO: Is that you, my lovely star...?

CAROLA: Yes. It's me. Otto. I have very bad news. I feel so sad for you, Otto.

OTTO: What is it?

CAROLA: Lenin is dead.

(Silence. Otto repeats like a child.)

OTTO: Dear God, please make it not be true! Please make it not have happened. It mustn't...not now...later...please make it not now, dear God, please, not now. What's to become of us?

SCENE SEVEN

(The verandah of Thomas Brückner's house. It's a warm September evening. Some are reading, others daydreaming. Nicoletta is playing a game of patience. The atmosphere is pleasant and gentle. Sebastien sings, accompanied on the piano by his father.)

THOMAS: Ah. You sing Schubert so well, my boy, and I play so badly. Whenever I hear those *lieder* I'm reminded of that sentence of Dostoyevsky's: "The world will be saved by beauty." Is that from *The Brothers Karamazov* or *The House of the Dead*? What do you think, Theo? You must remember.

SARDER: No.

ERIKA: *(curled up in a chair)* It's from *The Possessed*.

(Sebastien is taking photographs. Emelyne, the servant, follows him, holding an inspection lamp.)

SEBASTIEN: No it isn't. It's from *Crime and Punishment*.

ERIKA: Not at all. It's in *Anna Karenina*.

THOMAS: Well, wherever it's from, it's a very great thought.

HENDRIK: *(to Erika)* Doestoyevsky didn't write *Anna Karenina*.

ERIKA: Really? Are you sure?

NICOLETTA: Sebastien, come and take a picture of Erika and me together.

THOMAS: *(to Hendrik)* Come and sit next to me for a photograph, Hendrik. You come, too, Erika. Are you still working on your poems and songs? I hope so. Ah, my little girl, my little girl with her thin little legs always covered in scratches. She looked like a boy with her cropped hair and she used to come to me at night and say: "Father, father, you who are a great magician, you must tell that animal on my dresser to go away and not to frighten Sebastien." Ah, little traitor, you've found yourself another magician now and I shall have to disappear in a puff of smoke. And he's put on such an elegant suit, too. So,...my dear son-in-law,....

HENDRIK: *(embarrassed)* Sir,....It's strange having a piano on the verandah.

THOMAS: Yes, that piano gives us a lot of trouble; it's very demanding. When we cook pancakes or fritters, we have to bring it with us into the kitchen. I have to go away tomorrow,...it's such a shame. We were just getting to know each other.

SEBASTIEN: You're going tomorrow? Why?

THOMAS: They're having a festival in Goethe's honor in Frankfurt. I must go and honor Goethe. It's exceedingly tedious, but what can I do? And I have a strange conviction I'll miss my train.

ERIKA: Ah, yes. By the way. Where is the train time-table? Hahaha. There's trouble brewing. I can feel it. *(She goes out.)*

HENDRIK: *(to Nicoletta)* I'm bored.

NICOLETTA: We're carnivores in a house of herbivores. It's not that easy for the wolf to sleep with the lamb. Theo, take a picture of the two of us.

SARDER: I can never make those machines work.

ERIKA: *(coming back)* Where, but where is the time-table?

SEBASTIEN: Where it always is, on top of the magazines in the lav.

ERIKA: No. Damn. It isn't. I've just been there and the timetable is not there anymore. No one ever puts it back in its place. Theo, what have you done with the timetable?

THEO: *(irritated)* The last time I saw it, it was in the lav. I haven't touched it.

(Emelyne comes in and serves raspberries, with the help of the chauffeur, Ludwig.)

THOMAS: The very last raspberries of the season. Smell them,...it's the scent of passing time. Emelyne, my dear, have you come to a decision yet? Are you going to marry Ludwig or will you let him stew in his misery?

EMELYNE: I'll let him stew a little and when he's really desperate, I'll give in and marry him.

THOMAS: That's very wise of you, Emelyne, very wise. Ludwig, you're a good-looking lad, but you're not worthy of her, do you understand?

LUDWIG: Yes, Sir. I'm not worthy of her.

ERIKA: Emelyne, my darling Emelyne, will you come to my new house with me? Father, please give me Emelyne; I couldn't think of a better wedding present.

THOMAS: Emelyne, are you willing to leave me and go with Erika to her new home?

EMELYNE: Yes, if I can go with Ludwig.

THOMAS: You've broken my heart, Emelyne,...but there we are. *(to Sebastien)* And you, my boy, tell me, where have you been? Where are you going? What are your plans?

SEBASTIEN: I've been nowhere, I'm going nowhere and I have no plans. Raise your head, father, or you'll have a shadow across your face.

ERIKA: He's lying, Father. He's written two plays and we acted them in Hamburg and Munich.

THOMAS: I didn't know,...yes, the world can be full of malignant stupidity,...one gets used to it.

SEBASTIEN: You and I have the honor of featuring in a "Simplicissimus" cartoon.

THOMAS: Ouch.

SEBASTIEN: I actually find it quite amusing. I'm standing behind your chair, leaning a little over you, just like this, and I'm saying, "I am told, Father, that the son of genius cannot be a genius himself. Therefore you are no genius."

THOMAS: Sebastien, my accomplished colleague,...I am a most promising father,...I have total faith. Theo, why are you sulking over there? I find you exceedingly tedious this evening and so does your charming wife.

SARDER: I'm not sulking.

THOMAS: Go and amuse him, Sebastien.

SEBASTIEN: I can't, I make him angry. I'm against an amnesty for the Nazis; he's for it. We get nowhere.

SARDER: All I said was that if the youth of Germany wants this amnesty, we must be understanding.

THOMAS: We mustn't be understanding about everything. We mustn't be complacent.

SARDER: I understand today's youth and its disgust with our continual politicking. I've put my faith in our country's youth.

SEBASTIEN: But....

THOMAS: The young don't always point to the future.

SARDER: The young are becoming radical, at last.

SEBASTIEN: You used to be in love with the sabre; now you're content with the truncheon.

SARDER: I'm content with a little psychology.

SEBASTIEN: Yes, you can justify anything with a little psychology, including the use of the truncheon. Hitler is about to be given an amnesty. In less than nine months, he'll get out of prison and reorganize the Nazi party. And that's all going to happen because people like you are quaking before a couple of youth organizations. And what really kills me is that I'm talking to you about my own generation.

SARDER: But—

THOMAS: That's enough, Sarder, you're being exceedingly tedious. Do you know I have to cut down our lane of elm trees?

ERIKA: The elm trees! Why?

THOMAS: It's a disease. And there's no cure for it. All

the elms of Germany will die soon and after that, those of the whole world. Do you know that in 1983, '4, or '5, there won't be a single elm left in the world?

(A silence)

ERIKA: *(acting)* Mama asks you not to cut down the trees until she's left.

SEBASTIEN: Friends, my dear friends, now that I'm about to leave this house forever, I can't remain quiet, I can't refrain from expressing my deepest feelings....

ERIKA: Theo, do Trofimov.

SARDER: Humanity is marching towards the supreme truth, towards the greatest happiness, and I'm at the forefront.

SEBASTIEN: There isn't much time left. We must go. Who's smelling of herring here?

ERIKA: Goodbye, dear house, dear ancestor. Winter will pass, spring will come and you'll no longer be here. They'll have pulled you down.

HENDRIK: *(to Erika)* Do you know the whole of *The Cherry Orchard* by heart?

ERIKA: I've known it since I was ten.

HENDRIK: You, too, Sebastien?

SEBASTIEN: We used to say all of Act Four on summer evenings with Nicoletta. Erika and I always ended up in tears.

ERIKA: Just one more little moment. I'm going to sit down. I feel as if I've never seen these walls before, this ceiling....And now my eyes feast on them and I feel such tender affection....When we're gone, there won't be a soul left here.

SEBASTIEN: My friends, let's get into the carriages. The train will be in soon.

NICOLETTA: Goodbye, house. Goodbye, old life.

SARDER: Greetings to the new life.

ERIKA: They go. Liouba and Gaiev are left alone and throw themselves into each other's arms. They cry silently, trying desperately not to be overheard.

SEBASTIEN: My sister, my sister....

ERIKA: My orchard, my dear, my beautiful, my treasured orchard. My happiness,...goodbye.

NICOLETTA: Mama!

ERIKA: We're coming.

SEBASTIEN: They go. There is a sound of footsteps and Freers, the old servant, appears through the door on the right. He's ill.

THOMAS: It's all locked. They've gone,...they forgot me. It doesn't matter,...I'll rest here. Life's already over and it's as if I never lived. I'll lie down. There's no strength left in you, you useless old lump, none at all. In the distance, a sound is heard, as if coming from the sky, the sound of a chord snapping slowly and sadly dying away. Then nothing is heard but the dull thud of the axe against the trees far away in the orchard.

Second Prologue

THE ACTOR: *(to the audience)* 1925, 1926, 1927, 1928, 1929. The years went by and they paid too little attention to those years. Even the depression of 1929 and its brutal repercussions could be explained away as part of the natural upheavals of modern society. And upheavals, they said to themselves, were self-contained. They didn't necessarily provoke other upheavals. And indeed, 1929 didn't provoke anything new, because everything was already there, lying in wait. And then, at last, the rats came out of their hiding and they saw that they were many. And in September, that warm September of 1930, they were forced to open their eyes and count the numbers. A pale Germany, a red Germany, a dark Germany had given birth to a putrid carcass, and even their delicate nostrils had to breathe in the stench.

Scene Eight

(Hendrik and Erika's home. Breakfast. Hendrik has just finished reading a letter and puts it down on the table.)

HENDRIK: They want to see me in Berlin. Several theaters are making me very...interesting offers. Even Reinhardt wants to meet me. You're not interested, are you? You're not even interested in what I'm going to say to them.

ERIKA: Are you going to accept?

HENDRIK: Of course not. I'll turn them all down. Because I've given my word....

ERIKA: When do we get the results?

HENDRIK: *(distracted)* What results?

ERIKA: Hendrik. The elections!

HENDRIK: Otto's waiting for them at the printers. I'll
have them before they've even reached the newsstands.
(Pause) I'm stuck here,...tied down by my word of
honor. Mind you, there isn't really anything to keep
me in Hamburg after *Faust*. I haven't committed
myself to anything for next year. What?...The
Peppermill. What did you say? What?

ERIKA: I didn't say anything.

HENDRIK: I have to turn my thoughts to the Peppermill.

ERIKA: You might do a little more than turn your
thoughts to it.

HENDRIK: Would you mind explaining to me precisely
what you meant by that remark?

ERIKA: Nothing. You know, as far as I'm concerned,
world revolution—

HENDRIK: Darling, when I need advice on revolutionary
tactics, I'll go to someone who knows something about
it.

ERIKA: Otto's so fond of you, he melts my heart.

HENDRIK: You don't understand a thing, do you?
Otto's a Comrade. We are part of the same struggle; we
share the same ideology. Feelings don't come into it. It
doesn't make any difference whether he's fond of me or
not. *(Hendrik is having difficulties with his egg.)*

ERIKA: You should try it my way. Break the egg into a
glass, add a lot of pepper, a pinch of salt, *sauce
piquante* and a drop of lemon.

HENDRIK: Would you do me an enormous favor, my darling, and try not to make fun of me every time I behave differently from your venerable Papa? In the Brückner household eggs are eaten in crystal goblets with a clove from Zanzibar and sprinkled with Siamese pepper. In my house, we ate them with salt. Please forgive me for displaying such appalling lack of originality. You see, I'm only a simple human being.

ERIKA: I have some letters to type. Give me your letter; I'll answer it for you.

(She takes the letter from the table, but Hendrik snatches it away.)

HENDRIK: Leave it. It's not that urgent. I can dictate an answer tomorrow. We have more important things to worry about today.

(At this moment, Emelyne brings in Otto and Theresa.)

ERIKA: Sebastien! Hurry up! Otto's here.

(Sebastien comes in, wearing his bathrobe. Otto has all the newspapers and the table is cleared for them. He sits. Magnus and Myriam come in.)

OTTO: *(reads)* "Total number of registered voters: 43,000,000. Total votes cast: 39,260,000. Or 82 percent."

MAGNUS: That's the best turnout since the first elections of 1915.

OTTO: *(reads)* "Social Democrats: 143 seats. 24 percent of the vote."

MAGNUS: We've lost ten seats and more than 5 percent of the vote.

OTTO: *(reads)* "Communists: 77 seats. 14 percent of the vote."

MAGNUS: They had 54 seats and 10 percent of the vote. They must be pleased.

OTTO: *(reads)* "National Socialist Party: 107 seats. 6,407,000 votes. It becomes Germany's second-largest party." *(softly)* They too must be pleased.

(Silence. They freeze. Ludwig comes in and joins Emelyne.)

MYRIAM: *(coming to herself, to Magnus)* So what's happened to the walking encyclopedia? Come on, numbers! Numbers! How many seats did they have, how many are they taking, how many of them go to bed before midnight? What are you waiting for?

MAGNUS: They had twelve seats. 810,000 votes.

OTTO: *(reads)* "German National Party: 41 seats. Probable coalition of Nazis and Nationalists: 148 seats."

SEBASTIEN/ERIKA: It's not possible, it's just not possible.

THERESA: It's like trying to run in a bad dream.

SEBASTIEN: *(reads from a paper)* "6,400,000 men and women of voting age have added their voice to the dullest, most empty and vulgar charaltanism imaginable."

THERESA: *(reads from another paper)* "The Fifth Reichstag of the German Republic is the most despicable parliament this country has ever elected. Let us hope its existence will be brief."

OTTO: *(from another paper)* "3,336,000 unemployed as of last week. Ten million Germans are currently affected by unemployment. Those who remained silent about those figures yesterday have no right to make an outcry today."

MAGNUS: *(opening the last paper)* "The Red Flag, official organ of the Communist Party: September 16th, 1930. The final victory of communism has been confirmed by the present socialist defeat. The social-democrats will never recover from the blow they received on September 14th. Not only did they lose 600,000 votes, they also had to forgo their majority in Berlin. Of even greater significance are the clear indications that the Communist Party is at last making inroads into the working class, which was once totally dominated by the socialist camp." They really do seem pleased. *(to Otto)* Well, Comrade, are you pleased?

HENDRIK: I don't understand. I don't understand any of it. Could you please explain to me, Comrade Otto, where is the victory of your party? Because I'm desperate, you see, I'm desperate.

THERESA: So what? We're not interested in your despair, Hendrik. Leave him alone.

SCENE NINE

(The Hamburg Theater. Theresa, Myriam, Magnus, Erika, Hendrik, Otto, Mrs. Efeu. The whole company are there for the rehearsal of Faust.* Hendrik plays Mephisto; Otto, Faust.)

MEPHISTOPHELES: Good friend,
  You view things as they're generally viewed;
  We must do better, ere the joys of life
  Escape us.
  So up!
  Quit thought, and out into the world with me!
  I tell thee, sooth, a carle who speculates
  Is like a beast upon a barren heath
  Led in a circle by an evil sprite,
  While beautiful green pastures lie all around.

FAUST: And how do we begin?

MEPHISTOPHELES: We just go out.
  Why, what a place of martyrdom is this?
  Is this to be call'd life— to bore to death
  The youngsters and thyself? Leave that, I say,
  To neighbour Paunch! Why should'st thou vex thyself
  With threshing straw? The best that thous canst know,
  Thou dar'st not tell the lads. Even now I hear
  One o' them in the passage.

FAUST: I cannot possibly see him now.

MEPHISTOPHELES: Poor boy! he has
  Waited long while, and should not go away
  Uncomforted, Give me thy cap and gown!
  The mask will suit me excellently.
  Now leave me to my wit! I only want
  A quarter of an hour; meanwhile thyself
  Prepare for a fine journey!

---

*Translation by James Adey Birds, 1880.

Mephistopheles (in Faust's long gown.)

Reason and Knowledge do thou only scorn,
The very highest strength of human kind;
Do but allow thyself to be confirm'd
In blinding magic by the Prince of lies;
Then shall I have thee unconditionally.
Him hath Fate gifted with a spirit which
spurning all bounds, forever forward hastes,
One whose o'er-rash impetuous impulses
Overleap all the pleasures of the earth.
Him will I trail thro the wild ways of life,
Thro weary ways of Inutility;
Sprawl shall he, be benumbed, cleave to the dust;
And for his insatiety shall float
Viands and drinks before his greedy lips;
Refreshment shall he supplicate in vain;
And even tho' he had not to the Fiend
Render'd himself up, still he must be lost!

(Miklas, who is playing the student, comes on, carrying his script.)

STUDENT: I am but just arrived here, and I'm come—

HENDRIK: Aren't you off the book yet?

(Miklas gives his script to Mrs. Efeu.)

STUDENT: I am but just arrived here, and I'm come Full of devotion—

HENDRIK: Stand in for me, Otto, will you? Now let's try to lift this scene from the quagmire of boredom we fall into every time we do it. And whatever happens, let's not blame Goethe. For once, it isn't the writer's fault.

MIKLAS: I am but just arrived here, and I'm come Full of devotion to address and make

Acquaintance with a man whom all do name
With reverence.

MEPHISTOPHELES: Your courtesy delights me
You see a man like many more. Have you
applied elsewhere?

MIKLAS: I beg you will receive me!
I come with all good disposition,
Moderate means, and innocent young blood;

HENDRIK: Start again.

MIKLAS: From the top?

HENDRIK: From the top. Why? Already tired? Stop
there. Go back one step; take a half step to your right.
That's where you stand. Now start.

(Miklas goes off and comes on again.)

MIKLAS: I am but just arrived here—

HENDRIK: I thought I showed you where to stand.
That's your place. There.

MIKLAS: I am but just arrived here, and I'm come
Full of devotion to address and make
Acquaintance—

HENDRIK: Again.

MIKLAS: I am but just arrived here—

HENDRIK: Again.

MIKLAS: I am but just—

HENDRIK: That's awful. Again.

(Miklas remains silent.)

I thought I told you to start again.

MIKLAS: Tell me at least what I'm doing wrong, Mr. Höfgen.

HENDRIK: Wrong? What are you doing right? Start again.

MIKLAS: I'm waiting for your instructions, Mr. Höfgen. You're the director. It's your job to help me.

HENDRIK: I'm trying, Miklas, I'm trying. It's very difficult.

(Miklas goes off and comes on again. He's about to open his mouth.)

HENDRIK: Where do you stand?

(Miklas corrects his place.)

MIKLAS: I am but arrived here—

HENDRIK: That's not what Goethe has written.

MRS. EFEU: *(prompting)* I am but just arrived—

HENDRIK: Who asked you to prompt? Miklas, we're all waiting for you.

(Erika leaves. Miklas tries.)

MRS. EFEU: I am but just arrived—

HENDRIK: I thought I told you not to prompt. You're not running the theater yet, Mrs. Efeu, whatever you may think. It's not because you've managed to get a few more votes for your cretinous party of beef-wits that you can start ruling the country, my poor woman.

MIKLAS: May I ask what party you mean, Mr. Höfgen? Is it the National Socialist party?

HENDRIK: He's awake!

MIKLAS: I am a member of the National Socialist party, Mr. Höfgen. The National Socialist party is the party of the working class and I will not allow it to be criticized. No one in this Jew-infested theater has a right to speak against the Party. I will not tolerate it.

HENDRIK: You won't tolerate it? Well, you can thank me for not having to tolerate anything anymore in this Jew-infested theater. Magnus, I formally request that the Nazi Hans Miklas be excluded from this company.

MRS. EFEU: No! You can't do that!

HENDRIK: We've heard rather enough from you, Mrs. Efeu.

MRS. EFEU: Half the theaters in the country are closed. If you throw him out, he'll have nowhere left but the doss house.

HENDRIK: What have you decided, Mr. Gottchalk?

MAGNUS: (after a silence) I don't like the idea of throwing him out to join the three million unemployed. I won't ask him back next season, that's all.

MRS. EFEU: Can't you see how sick he is?

HENDRIK: Sick? Sick? The whole of Germany will be

sick if we don't do something about it soon. *(to Magnus)* You're the perfect illustration of social-democratic cowardice in the face of the Nazi threat. When are we going to show those thugs they can't get away with it? When are we going to show them they have to stop somewhere? When? Gottchalk, make up your mind.

OTTO: Magnus has already given you his answer, Hendrik. Given the present political situation I really think we should avoid turning Hans Miklas into a martyr. He's nothing more than a little creep who'll wake up one day crying and screaming that everyone's tricked him.

MIKLAS: Stalin's a murderer.

(Hendrik spits in Miklas' face. Miklas goes for him. The others try to separate them. Otto intervenes and ends up fighting with Miklas.)

MRS. EFEU: Leave the poor boy alone, leave him alone. He's sick. You're all so sure you're right, but you're blind, all of you, you're blind.

HENDRIK: It's simple: He goes. Or I go. Choose, Magnus.

MAGNUS: Don't be stupid. Miklas is going. *(to Mrs. Efeu)* And so are you, Mrs. Efeu, if I hear one more word from you.

Scene Ten

> *(The Railway Bridge. It's night. Otto, Hendrik, Theresa.)*

THERESA: What about Magnus?

HENDRIK: I adore Magnus, Theresa. I admire Magnus. Magnus has taught me everything I know; well— almost everything. I love Magnus. But I feel he's beginning to get on. And our political views are so different. And he's seen better days. And—I need to feel free. What a night! Look at the stars.

> *(A train goes by.)*

The train to Berlin. Will I ever be on that train? Oh God, when will I take the train to Berlin? Hendrik Höfgen: The great leading actor—of Hamburg. What a joke! And it's the same for you, Otto. Even the Peppermill would be more effective in Berlin; they're ready for that kind of work there. Listen, Otto, I have an idea: I'll go up to Berlin, and when I've made a name for myself I'll bring you all there and we'll start another Peppermill. Well? What do you think?

THERESA: Magnus has already announced the next season and we're all in it.

HENDRIK: Which is more important? The Hamburg Theater season or the Struggle? In any case, the rest of you will stay on. It'll take me some time to get everything ready. I'll have to find the right café or restaurant for the Peppermill. Make some money,... films,...you can make films in Berlin. Otto, Otto, I know it's a cruel decision to make. If only you knew how painful it was for me to make it. But it's time to break off and we must break off. And since we have to go to Berlin, let us go to Berlin.

(As the train goes by, Hendrik embraces Otto and Theresa and leaves. The train moves away. Theresa looks carefully at Otto's face. He turns his head away. He's in tears.)

THERESA: "God knows we needn't blush at our tears, they are like rain on the dry dust of our hearts." I like Dickens. Time for you to go home, Comrade, and get a good night's sleep.

(Otto goes. Erika comes on.)

THERESA: *(coldly)* I suppose you're looking for your husband.

ERIKA: I've just met him.

THERESA: And you aren't already on your way to Berlin?

ERIKA: I'm looking for Otto.

THERESA: "Theresa von Herzfield, let me ask you something: I do a little writing: songs, pamphlets, short scenes. Is there any way I could make myself useful at the Peppermill?"

(The two women embrace.)

SCENE ELEVEN

(A rehearsal at the Peppermill. Carola, Sebastien, Nicoletta, Magnus, Otto.)

OTTO: *(singing)*
I'm the prince of lies
in the country of lies
I make the trees bloom blue
and the sky rain green.
My lies are fantastic
my lies buzz like flies
in the hot air.
It's already november
and summer is here
the trees are in flower
the violets bright yellow
and at the front
no one will be wounded
no one no one
hahahaha.

(Refrain)

Lies, lies, lies
lying's so good
lying's so fair
makes you lucky
makes you healthy
makes you rich
makes you famous
and then it's easy
because at the front
no one will be wounded
no one no one
hahahaha.

(Refrain)

What I want
I lie for
and the world
applauds
because after all
I'm the prince of lies
in the country of lies
lies are soft
lies are delicate
lies make you quiet
rock you to sleep
make you dreamy
make you still
as death

Wake up quickly and throw the truth at the vile mask of lies. Only truth can triumph over adversity.

(The deafening ring of a telephone. Mrs. Grunt-boum (Erika as a clown), the landlady, enters with a newspaper under her arm, the Volkischer Beobachter*)*.

MRS. GRUNTBOUM (ERIKA): Coming. Coming. Never a moment's peace around here. I can't even go to the neighborhood rallies anymore. Look at this bunch of shifty-eyed sheep, look at these vegetarian vegetables. What a country! What are you doing here, anyway? Why aren't you at your neighborhood rally? Well? Why? Why? You get a free lecture, you learn something there, grass-brains. It's going to change, that's what they said. About time, too. Quick turn of the screw. That's what they said. About time they took things in hand, that's what I say. *(She reads her paper.)* You don't mind if I read, do you? Aohh. Look at that. Isn't that nice. Yes. Ohh, and what about this now. I didn't know that. Did you? You didn't, did you? Do you know what's wrong with this country? No? Can you guess? Come on, guess. No? Well, my little darlings, it's those telephones. You didn't know that, did you? I didn't either. I knew absolutely nothing about it when I came here, but now I know, I'm sure, I'm smothered in sureness, it's written right here: The telephone is at the root of all our problems. That's right. Well, actually, I had my suspicions the first time I saw one, didn't you? It's obvious. And when I think that some people still don't know that all our troubles have their root in the telephone, that we're poisoned from the root up by the telephone, that the telephone has been poisoning our roots for millions and millions of years,...oh, really? That's a long time, isn't it. Millions of years,...but it's written here and yet, it's true, it's absolutely true. Is there anyone here with a telephone? Raise your hand if you're harboring a telephone and come and see me in my office later. I'll take down your names. I'm in charge of taking down names now. It's like that with them; one day you're a nobody and next day you're in charge of names, you're petrified with importance. *(The telephone rings.)* Listen to that. Just listen to that. It has the gall to call me right here in my cozy polished sweet little German home. No manners. Disgusting. Just rings when it wants without so much as a by-your-leave. And me, with Germany's fate here on top of my two shoulders, I'm expected to get up and answer it. And mark my word, it's going to ring until dawn, with its filthy foreign habits, polluting my pure little home; listen to it, damned cosmopolitan race of dangerous insinuators trying to wriggle itself into a proper German home. *(Pause)* That was well put. And they're all over Germany now, breeding like rabbits, taking over our nice clean pure little country; foreign trash. I hate them. Anyone here have any objections to hate? No? Good. *(The ringing stops)* See? That shut it up. A little authority and it stops. I always knew telephones were cowards. Not like us. *(It rings.)* What! *(She shouts. Silence.)* See? I don't even have to say anything. One look and it stops. *(She reads.)* Ohh, really? Yes,... mmm, oh? Extermination? Isn't that going a little far? No, no. They're right. Absolutely right. *(She reads.)* Think what will happen to us if we don't stop them now. Yes. *(The phone rings.)* I'm collapsing with fear. No. Steady. Steady. Bang, bang, bang. *(It rings again.)* Boom. *(Silence)* Got it. *(She reads.)* Yes, yes. What are we coming to? Well, it's a good thing to be well informed. And you out there, you mutton-heads, drugged up to your earlobes, you'd better read this and find out what kind of danger you're in. Well. What are you waiting for? What? What?

(Miss Linnamuck, the cleaning lady, comes in.)

LINNAMUCK (MYRIAM): Dear, dear, dear, what's happening here? I've never heard such screaming and shouting! But you're alone, Mrs. Gruntboum, what's happening?

GRUNTBOUM: It's because it's true. It's all true, absolutely true. Linnamuck, you're a woman swimming with intelligence, you're sinuously subtle, sensationally sensible, sensually senile. In a word, you're a pure German, your ancestors were pure German from the beginning of time, your descendants will be German till the end of time. From one pure German to another, answer me this: Do you have a telephone?

LINNAMUCK: Well, no, you see, I've been thinking of getting one, but—

GRUNTBOUM: Ah Linnamuck, you poor starry-eyed little ewelet, ah, you narrow-minded dumb blonde, repeat after me: "The telephone is a fiend."

LINNAMUCK: "The telephone is a fiend."

GRUNTBOUM: "The telephone is a fiend."

LINNAMUCK: "The telephone is a fiend." Is that so, Mrs. Gruntboum?

GRUNTBOUM: Yes. It's written here. Just go and look at its mug if you don't believe me.

LINNAMUCK: You know, I think you're right. The other day the telephone rang me to tell me my cousin had broken his foot. It gave me ever such a fright.

GRUNTBOUM: I told you it had a fiendish tongue.

LINNAMUCK: But do you still believe in fiends, Mrs. Gruntboum? You're so educated, so advanced, so modernized.

GRUNTBOUM: I believe in the fiends of progress, Linnamuck; I believe in the fiends of liberalism, the fiends of civilization, of intelligence. Look at us. We're simple ordinary everyday women. We're not related by blood, by friendship, we're not even related by neighborhood, but now we're united. Now we've got hate. Hate. We hate the telephone. Why? Because we know the telephones are ruining this country.

LINNAMUCK: You're such a good speaker, Mrs. Gruntboum, and now that I look at the telephone, I can see it's dirty, it's disgusting, it's smelly; I'm going to throw it straight out of the window.

GRUNTBOUM: Wait. Our time has not yet come.

LINNAMUCK: As typical representative symbolic ordinary middle-of-the-road in-no-way-outstanding city dwellers, we proclaim the telephone a national threat.

GRUNTBOUM: What do we know about the telephone?

LINNAMUCK: That it's shit.

GRUNTBOUM: What do we say about the telephone?

LINNAMUCK: That it's shit.

GRUNTBOUM: The telephone is—

LINNAMUCK: Shit.

(Increasing energy. Theresa, playing the Baroness, comes in.)

BARONESS (THERESA): Heaven above, what is going on, Mrs. Gruntboum? Is this an election?

GRUNTBOUM: Forgive us, your ladyship, but everyone's so excited these days and I myself have become a little nervous.

BARONESS: I too am feeling a surge of excitement, Gruntboum.

GRUNTBOUM: Your worshipful Baroness, in the name of all the honest people of our nation, in the name of the masses that stand behind me, in the name of your respectworthy name, I beg you to lead the way and get rid of your telephone.

BARONESS: *(troubled)* There's something bewitching in your words, Mrs. Gruntboum; they're so exotic, quixotic, idiotic, erotic; yes, yes, I will get rid of my telephone.

OTTO: Blackout!

(The working lights go back on.)

Let's see what the censor finds to complain about in what you've written there, Erika.

CAROLA: My dear, why worry about the censor? No one pays attention to the censor anymore. We're no longer in 1931, unfortunately for us. The S.A. will be in the audience tonight, as they were the other night, but this time they'll smash your heads in, that's all. They've even started to come to the theaters where I play my innocuous Shakespeares. It seems I'm a stinking Jew.

ERIKA: And I'm a flatfooted hyena.

CAROLA: I'm the propagator of syphilitic culture.

THERESA: My ugliness would put off the most determined rapist.

ERIKA: Cosmopolitan hermaphrodite.

NICOLETTA: *(to Erika)* Witless dyke.

CAROLA: Diarrheic ape.

MYRIAM: Turkish-bath spittoon. *(Pause)* Yes. It's written in the *Popular Observer:* Myriam Horovitz is small, fat, ugly and displays as much humor as one might find in a Turkish-bath spittoon.

(They burst out laughing, nervously. Theophile Sarder comes on. He is shaking. Alex follows him in.)

SARDER: Woe to us all! I bring you tidings of woe. Let us sit upon the ground and weep. The light of reason is being extinguished. Dark clouds are gathering over our beautiful country. This morning, the grand master of Hell, Adolf Hitler, was named Chancellor of the Republic. The Nazis are in power. God has turned his face away from our nation and soon torrents of tears and blood will cascade through our streets.

OTTO: *(to Alex)* What now? A general strike?

ALEX: The Red Flag is calling for a general strike but with 7 million unemployed, it's pointless.

OTTO: What are our instructions?

ALEX: To remain calm. *(He reads:)* "The workers must avoid any action which would give the new government grounds for taking measures against the Communist Party. The party must remain unharmed until the next general election, when it is sure to triumph once and for all over the Social-Democrats." And the usual analysis from Moscow: "Nazism is the last phase of a moribund capitalism and will sooner or later cause its final downfall."

MAGNUS: And the Social-Democrats?

ALEX: They're against a general strike. They want to wait for the next elections.

SEBASTIEN: The unions?

ALEX: The confederation of unions refuses to interfere. Management is still management.

(Silence)

SEBASTIEN: What day is it today?

MYRIAM: Monday, January the 30th, 1933. The horoscope says Pisces will receive money from unexpected quarters but must go easy on the drink. I'm a Pisces.

(Silence. Otto suddenly throws up.)

SCENE TWELVE

(Still at the Peppermill. Sarder, Nicoletta, Sebastien, Erika, Carola, Otto, Alex, and Theresa are there. The telephone is ringing, but no one can be bothered to answer it.)

OTTO: Carola, you can't afford to lose a minute. You have to go. You have to go today, do you understand? Not tomorrow. Today.

CAROLA: Yes, Otto. I know. I'll leave...tonight.

SARDER: Can you tell me what our generation was able to offer the young? We're the ones who taught them to despise intelligence. We thought we could make a clearing in the human spirit. But we wrecked it with the carelessness of bad woodsmen, who instead of thinning a forest only succeed in decimating it.

NICOLETTA: You're going, too, Theo. You like the South of France. Go and take a little trip to the South of France.

SARDER: Alone? Are you telling me to go alone? Aren't you coming with me?

(Alex goes to answer the telephone, and the ringing stops.)

NICOLETTA: I'll come and visit you, Theo, but what is there for me to do in the South of France? You're a writer, I'm not. I don't know. We've been sitting here for hours asking ourselves what we can do to change the course of events, but there is nothing anyone can do, absolutely nothing. We will have to come to terms with that. As for me, I'm only an actress.

ERIKA: What does it mean to be "only an actress"?

NICOLETTA: It means I'm not a rich little princess. The earth is turning the wrong way around all of a sudden, but what can we do about it?

(Alex comes back and speaks to Sebastien.)

SEBASTIEN: Erika, we have to go home. It's our father....Some students at the University wrecked his study. They beat him. He's back home now. They burnt his manuscript. He was crying on the telephone.

SARDER: Yes. It will all happen very quickly now. Erika, my little one, we're coming with you.

ALEX: I'm coming, too.

SARDER: Yes. It will all happen very quickly now. Until this moment, I was able to say to myself, this is the twilight, yes, but we can still hope, we can still think, that it's a twilight which presages the dawn. It is a morning twilight. Today, we must resign ourselves to the truth. It was a twilight that presaged the evening that was coming and soon it will be night.

(Blackout.)

(Carola and Otto.)

OTTO: Where will you go, Carola?

CAROLA: To America, I suppose. They've been begging for me to come. I'll make films. My English is good.

OTTO: Carola...?

CAROLA: Yes....yes, Otto?

OTTO: Carola. Go to Moscow. Go somewhere where

this is a new dawn. Join those who have made it happen. You can work there, they have wonderful directors in Moscow: Eisenstein, Donskoi, Poudovkine, Meyerhold. They need people like you there.

CAROLA: Yes, but I'm afraid to go there, I'm afraid. They say things haven't been going well for the last seven years. Apparently, they're throwing artists in prison.

OTTO: It's only propaganda to try and discredit our cause. And even if it were true, all the more reason to go and fight against any betrayal of the revolution. Carola, go to Moscow.

CAROLA: I'm afraid. But yes, my love; yes, I'll go to Moscow.

(The Berlin Opera. Chandeliers dripping with light. Rehearsal of Verdi's The Force of Destiny. *Hendrik appears.)*

HENDRIK: *(to the wings)* The mirror! The mirror isn't straight. The audience must see itself the moment the curtain goes up. It must recognize itself. It's the audience that is acting in this opera. During the whole performance, the audience remains face to face with itself. *(He sings; he strides.)* Lalalala lalalala lalala la lala. Are you ready? Now. Careful. AND—houselights down. Footlights up. Yes, that's right. And now, the curtain. Slowly. More slowly. I said slowly. Now. A spot on the mirror, dim at first, then bright, brighter, burning. Take it up another ten points. Good. And now the character comes on. Excellent. Tomorrow we'll put it all together with the orchestra. And if they play a different tempo from the one on the recording, I'll go and hang myself. Thank you. I'll see you all here tomorrow morning.

(The lights go off, leaving only the work lights. There's a sound in the wings.)

Who's there? I can't see anything. Answer me. Who is it?

(It's Juliette, with a suitcase.)

HENDRIK: *(terrified)* What are you doing in Berlin? You must be mad! And in this theater, too. The way things are now. No, no. Keep out of the light. Someone could see you. What do you want?

JULIETTE: When you left Hamburg, you said you'd bring me to Berlin.

HENDRIK: That was two years ago! Anyway, I wrote to you. I told you to be patient. It was too soon.

JULIETTE: And now?

HENDRIK: It's too late. You'll have to go.

JULIETTE: "Go". Go where, Hendrik?

HENDRIK: Try to understand, Juliette. I love you, you know that. But you could get me into a lot of trouble here. You must try to understand my position. If anybody ever found out that you...that I...that you and I...that I had relations with a non-Aryan, they would—

JULIETTE: Who's "they"? The people you work for?

HENDRIK The people I *have* to work with, Juliette. I have no choice. Please try to understand, Juliette. You don't want to harm me, do you? You don't want to get me into trouble? Serious trouble? And all because of you? You don't want that, do you, Juliette? Then you must leave. Listen to me: Go to Paris. Think of it. A dancer like you in Paris, you'll be the toast of the town in no time. Look at what happened to Josephine Baker. I'll tell you what: I'll even pay for your trip.

JULIETTE: So you're dropping me.

HENDRIK: I'm not dropping you. I'm looking after your safety. I'm sending you to Paris!

JULIETTE: I don't give a pig's ear for Paris. I don't speak a fucking word of fucking French. My father was German. I feel German.

(*Hendrik bursts out laughing.*)

That makes you laugh, does it? You think it's funny. You don't give a shit about me, do you; you don't give a shit about anything except your shitty career. You never cared about me. You never cared about your friends. You never even cared about communism. If you had, you wouldn't be working here today with the people who are killing the communists. Go out into the streets, Hendrik; get out of your precious little theater and have a look. They're killing your friends in the streets, Hendrik. They put their corpses in sacks, sew them up and throw them in the river.

HENDRIK: That's enough now.

JULIETTE: "That's enough now"! For years, let me tell you, I had to play at being your savage. You never even asked me if I wanted to, did you? But now Hendrik Höfgen is big and tough. You don't need me to slap you around anymore, do you; there's enough of that going on in the country for your cravings. Are you happy now, Hendrik; are you getting your satisfaction?

HENDRIK: If you don't leave, Juliette, I'll have you thrown out.

JULIETTE: *(screaming)* Just you try, Superman.

HENDRIK: *(whispering)* Shht. Don't shout. Please. Let's calm down, shall we? I'll write you a check. Here. You can take a sleeper. *(He writes a check and gives it to Juliette.)*

JULIETTE: Seems Paris is really cheap these days.

HENDRIK: I promise I'll send you more. But you must go. Promise me you'll go.

JULIETTE: I don't have any cash. I need cash.

(Hendrik empties out his pockets and gives her what he has. Juliette is about to go.)

By the way, I almost forgot. I saw your friends in Hamburg. Your wife, too. She was much too good for you, your wife, wasn't she? I told her I was coming to see you. I asked her if she wanted me to give you a message, from her or from your friends.

HENDRIK: *(moved)* Well?

JULIETTE: There's no message. *(She goes out.)*

SCENE FOURTEEN

(The Hamburg Theater. Josthinkel, the new theater manager, is there. So are Mr. Knurr, Mrs. Efeu, Otto, Magnus, Theresa, and Lorenz.)

JOSTHINKEL: Knurr: Stage doorman. How long have you held this position?

KNURR: Oh, since the war, Mr. Josthinkel, Sir.

JOSTHINKEL: Have you ever been a member of the Communist Party?

KNURR: No, certainly not, Mr. Josthinkel, Sir. I've been a paid-up member of the National Socialist Party since 1925.

MRS. EFEU: That's right, Mr. Josthinkel, Sir. I can bear witness to that, Mr. Josthinkel, Sir.

JOSTHINKEL: Would you both stop calling me Mr. Josthinkel Sir? I am the new superintendant of the Hamburg Theater and you are to call me by my exact title. Call me Superintendant.

KNURR: Certainly Mr. Superintendant, Sir.

JOSTHINKEL: Mr. Knurr. It has been brought to my attention that you are fond of a joke.

KNURR: Oh yes, I like telling a good joke, Mr. Superindentant, Sir.

JOSTHINKEL: Tell me the one about the Englishman.

KNURR: The one about the Englishman. Well—the one about the Englishman,...no, I can't remember any jokes about Englishmen, no....

JOSTHINKEL: Lorenz, you told me—

LORENZ: Yes, Mr. Knurr. The one about the English-man who goes back home and says what he thinks of the Germans.

KNURR: Oh, that one. Oh yes. It's not a very good joke, Mr. Superintendant, Sir. It really isn't.

JOSTHINKEL: Tell it anyway.

KNURR: Well. There's this Englishman who comes back from a visit to Germany. He meets his friend on the street. "Well," says the friend, "what did you make of the Germans?" "Oh," he says, "the Germans. They're wonderful people, charming, and they have three great virtues. First of all, they're national socialist. Secondly, they're honest. And thirdly, they're intelligent." *(Knurr sniggers nervously.)*

JOSTHINKEL: Go on.

KNURR: It really isn't a very good joke.

JOSTHINKEL: Go on.

KNURR: "The trouble is," says the Englishman, "they never have these three virtues at the same time. If they're honest and national socialist, then they're not intelligent. If they're intelligent and national socialist, then they're not honest, and if they're honest and intelligent, then they're not national socialist."

(Pause)

JOSTHINKEL: Were you aware, Mr. Knurr, when you told this joke, that were spreading filthy propaganda invented by the Jews and the Bolsheviks?

KNURR: Oh no, Mr. Superindentant, Sir, I wasn't aware of that.

MRS. EFEU: He wasn't aware of that at all, Mr. Superindentant, Sir, not at all.

OTTO: Since when are jokes forbidden in Germany, Superintendant? Surely the freedom to express—

JOSTHINKEL: *(interrupting)* Since yesterday, Mr. Ulrich. *(He reads:)* "In order to protect the people and the state against communist acts of violence we decree the suspension of articles 114, 115, 117, 118, 123, 124 and 153 of the constitution. We authorize restrictions on personal liberty, on the right to free expression of opinion and on the freedom of the press. We also authorize, beyond the legal limits prescribed in the constitution, violation of the privacy of postal, telegraphic and telephonic communications." *(He folds the decree carefully.)* Presumably you are aware of the events that led to the signing of this decree.

OTTO: The burning of the Reichstag, I suppose.

JOSTHINKEL: That is correct. The burning of the Reichstag by your communist friends, Mr. Ulrich.

OTTO: Unfortunately, the communists didn't burn anything.

JOSTHINKEL: Withdraw the word "unfortunately" forthwith or I shall report you as an accomplice in the burning of the Reichstag, Mr. Ulrich.

OTTO: I withdraw the word "unfortunately."

JOSTHINKEL: To draw this meeting to a close, let me remind you once again that henceforth your repertory must consist solely of the great German classic or contemporary German plays whose national and political integrity cannot be questioned.

OTTO: Like your own plays, Mr. Superindendant.

JOSTHINKEL: Possibly....The concept of art for art's sake is a perverse invention of decadent bourgeois democracies. Art is valid only insofar as it serves the revolution and its people.

OTTO: *(to Theresa and Magnus)* Have you noticed that there are some statements which act like the belladonna plant? Meant to be a cure, in the hands of murderers they become poison.

JOSTHINKEL: The new management of the Hamburg Theater also notes with concern that it does not presently include among the members of its company a young leading actress of pure Germanic type. Nor indeed does it have an actor capable of playing the heroic roles of the classic German repertoire. The management considers this situation intolerable, Mr. Gottchalk.

MAGNUS: Could you explain to me what you mean by a young leading actress of pure Germanic type?

JOSTHINKEL: You cannot be unaware that your wife, to take but one example, is not a young leading actress of pure Germanic type.

MAGNUS: My wife is not a young leading actress, Superintendant, of pure Germanic type or any other type. My wife is forty years old. One is no longer a young leading actress at the age of forty. What's all this about?

JOSTHINKEL: The management wishes to inform you,

Mr. Gottchalk, that you would be allowed back as artistic director of this theater were life's vicissitudes to separate you from your present wife.

THERESA: In a word, Magnus, divorce your wife and marry a young leading actress of pure Germanic type. It's very simple. Don't make such a song and dance about it.

JOSTHINKEL: I have not yet made a final decision regarding your contract, Miss von Herzfield, as my inquiries are not yet complete, but I am obliged to point out that your irony will not help your case.

THERESA: If there was only my irony wrong with me. When you find the name of my grandmother, Superintendant, you'll be most upset. And since I can't divorce my own grandmother, I prefer to give in my notice now, while I can still afford that little luxury.

JOSTHINKEL: That has saved us both valuable time.

MAGNUS: Laws! Where are the laws forbidding a man to be artistic director of a theater because he's married to a Jew? Where are the laws forbidding Theresa von Herzfield to appear on the stage because her grandmother was a Jew? Where are they?

JOSTHINKEL: You want laws, Mr. Gottchalk, don't worry, they won't be long in coming. In the meantime the management finds itself unable to renew your contracts. Ladies and Gentlemen, you're free. Heil Hitler. Lorenz, return the contracts.

(Lorenz hands out the papers.)

Where will you go, Mr. Ulrich? To Moscow?

OTTO: Moscow? Why Moscow? I am German. And these will be interesting times, even for an unemployed German like myself. No, Mr. Josthinkel, I have no more intention of leaving Germany than you do.

Scene Fifteen

(The Railway Bridge. Alex, Otto, Theresa.)

THERESA: "Theresa," I said to myself, "you never know. There's no dictatorship without an underground, there's no underground without pamphlets, there are no pamphlets without a duplicator." The duplicator is the backbone of the underground. So I decided to steal the theater's duplicator. And you, Otto, what have you decided?

OTTO: I don't know yet. I have to find a way to earn a living, like the rest of you. I've been offered a Shakespeare in Vienna, two months' work. But I'm afraid they won't let me back in if I leave Germany. I'm sure there'll be some kind of resistance organized soon, but at the moment all of my friends seem to be in prison. I don't know where to start, I don't know who to contact, I don't know what to do. Any idea what to write in your pamphlets, Theresa?

THERESA: Listen. It's the train to Berlin.

OTTO: *(imitating Hendrik)* Ah, Berlin. Will I ever be on the train to Berlin, Theresa?

(They smile as the train goes by.)

ALEX: So many things have happened in the last few months, at least you can't complain of boredom. Last night, I went home on foot. It was a warm evening, like this one, so I said to myself: "Don't take the tram, Alex; walk, it's cheaper." I turn down Ferdinandstrasse, to the Blue Café. I open the door. Place is packed with S.A. men. I close the door. I walk. I keep walking. I get to this bridge and stop a moment. I hear a train start up. I look at the time: fourteen minutes past midnight.

There aren't any trains that leave Hamburg at fourteen minutes past midnight. It's a cargo train. It goes by....I didn't understand. I stood here, on this bridge. The train gained speed. And then I did understand. There were screams coming from the cattle trucks. Screams of rage, of pain, of indignation. I stood here. Frozen. "If they're screaming," I said to myself, "it's because they want to be heard. So Alex, Alex, stay here and listen." One carriage after another. Some were shouting their names and addresses. "Alex, Alex, carve those names into your brain." I close my eyes. Out of dozens and dozens I managed to remember four names: Holtz Karl, Stresemann Strasse. Firtz Gigah, Chemitzstrasse. Johan Kralik, Katherinen Strasse. Hans Gusti, I didn't get his address, but I'll find it. Then the noise died down. There was only the night left and the fog beginning to thicken. I stayed here, listening, until the only sound I could hear was the blood drumming in my ears. I stayed here. No one else about. Just me. Alone.

OTTO: A minute ago we couldn't think what to do, but now we know. We have to let everyone know what you've just described, Alex. We have to say to the Germans: listen. Listen to the trains moving across your country every night. Those trains are loaded with men and women. Today it's the communists and socialists. Tomorrow it'll be the Jews and then it'll be you. Block the tracks, Comrades, and refuse to drive the trains. Refuse to mine the coal that fuels the trains. Refuse to lay down the tracks that carry the trains. Refuse to serve, friends, refuse to cooperate. Theresa, my friend, what else is there for us to do but follow you to your house? (He takes the duplicator on his shoulders.)

SCENE SIXTEEN

(The dressing room of the Berlin Theater. Hendrik and Nicoletta are at their make-up tables.)

NICOLETTA: I couldn't bear it anymore....I simply couldn't bear it. He would sit all day long on the terrace, staring out at the cypresses and moan. He moaned every hour of the day, day in, day out. "Nicoletta,...Nicoletta,...stay with me, stay close, it's so awful. I hear the men and women being tortured in Germany. The wind carries their screams to my ears. The executioners play Gramophone records in the torture chambers, but I can still hear the screams of pain." And a lot more nonsense of that kind, a lot of sentimental raving. Theo is a wonderful man; he is a genius. I know that and I love him. But he is also outside of his time, he lives outside of reality, and that's something I cannot bear.

HENDRIK: Yes, I know. All those emigrés playing at being martyrs on the beaches of the South of France. Listen to me, Nicoletta, they're deserters, nothing more, nothing less than deserters. What can they possibly do from over there?

NICOLETTA: I couldn't bear it anymore....I simply couldn't bear it. I kept saying to myself, "Nicoletta, my darling, you're dying in this place. Soon, you'll be dried up. You're an actress, my girl; go home and act." Mind you, it's a good thing you were here.

HENDRIK: Did I tell you they've suggested me for....

NICOLETTA: For what?

HENDRIK: It's a very important position. I don't know....Should I, shouldn't I?...It's so difficult....

NICOLETTA: Of course you should. If you don't, someone else will. And so....

HENDRIK: It might as well be me.

NICOLETTA: Quite. And once you're in power, you can be...you can...help...people....

HENDRIK: I'll be able to stop some of the....

NICOLETTA: Exactly!

HENDRIK: You see, we're the ones at the front. If you want to change things, it's better to be here, on the inside, not in Sanary or Cassis. Are you ready? It's our turn. *(He gets up.)*

NICOLETTA: You never told me in whose honor we're doing this gala.

HENDRIK: I don't really know. But all the greatest German celebrities have agreed to take part and they were so keen to have me, I couldn't turn them down. *(He comes close to her.)* Kiss me,... my beauty, my torment....

SCENE SEVENTEEN

(The Hamburg Theater.)

JOSTHINKEL: *(to Lorenz)* Bring in Hans Miklas.

(Lorenz is about to go.)

Lorenz, let me see your plaything again. It fascinates me.

(Lorenz shows him a weapon consisting of a metal base to which are attached steel balls.)

JOSTHINKEL: And what do you call this?

LORENZ: Steelworks.

JOSTHINKEL: Steelworks. How simple. How poetic. Ah. The masses make us drool with admiration when it comes to violence. Lend me your toy, will you, Lorenz?

(Lorenz salutes and goes out. Josthinkel tries to master the weapon. Hans Miklas comes in.)

JOSTHINKEL: *(reads from a file)* Hans Miklas. Born November the 9th, 1903, in Thalburg. Son of Joseph Miklas, accountant, and Hildegarde Breker. Your father was killed in 1916, as was your older brother. One of your sisters is married to Joseph Strepper, butcher in the suburbs of Hamburg. It is this same Joseph Strepper who sponsors you when you join the party in 1923. You are unmarried. You have never been abroad. And since your arrival in Hamburg you've resided at the same boarding house, the Rosa-Monica. You've often helped your neighborhood detachment of S.A. with propaganda spectacles and with the distribution of food to the unemployed. However, you have never actually joined the S.A. Is there anything else you know about yourself which might be of interest to the superintendant of the theater before whom you now stand?

MIKLAS: Yes.

JOSTHINKEL: What? We've left something out? What could that possibly be?

MIKLAS: I'm an actor. You've left that out.

JOSTHINKEL: So we have. So we have. It's not written anywhere in this file. Hans Miklas: national socialist actor. *(He writes this down.)* You've put yourself up for the part of the student in the Hamburg Theater's next production of "Faust." You will play the student. And I am now in the fortunate position of being able to tell you that we will be honored with a special guest appearance by Hendrik Höfgen, whose extraordinary interpretation of Mephisto has earned him such renown. You will have the privilege of playing opposite our greatest national-socialist actor. Heil Hitler.

(Miklas begins to leave. Josthinkel calls him back.)

But I see you've already worked here and were dismissed at Mr. Höfgen's request. Hans Miklas, come back here for a moment. *(Pause)* You see, it may be that I share your feelings about Mr. Höfgen. I too may have some doubts as to the authenticity of Mr. Höfgen's national-socialism.

MIKLAS: He was a communist.

(Josthinkel writes this down.)

JOSTHINKEL: A communist,...yes, well,...it's not

because he had a little flirtation with communism.... Many nazis, both humble and highly placed ones, had little flirtations with communism. But it's been said...there was a liaison with a prostitute,...a non-white....

MIKLAS: The whole theater knew about that. *(Miklas suddenly realizes that Josthinkel is writing down everything he says.)*

JOSTHINKEL: You see, Hans Miklas, if there was someone in this theater who could watch and warn me of any such...funny business, I would find that most helpful. What do you think?

MIKLAS: I don't know what you mean, Superintendant. Could we please discuss my wages?

JOSTHINKEL: You know, my boy, the sexual submissiveness some of our great German artists are showing before the erotic wiles of Jewish and Black women is giving us serious cause for concern.

MIKLAS: Superintendant, I'd like to discuss my wages.

JOSTHINKEL: That's why I'd like you to be my watchdog, my Moral Minister, as it were. Well? Do we have anything concerning Höfgen and his mistress that might serve to avenge you, my boy? Can we get him with some concrete evidence? I've said a great deal, Hans Miklas; it's your turn now.

MIKLAS: I don't look for my enemies in bed, Superintendant, nor on the lavatory pan.

JOSTHINKEL: What do you mean? I order you to make yourself clear.

MIKLAS: I mean that when I joined the party ten years

ago, Superintendant, it wasn't with the ambition of ending up as your spy or your peeping Tom. My ambition was to witness the triumph of the national-socialist revolution. I wanted to see the return of Germany's honor and the greatness of the German people reestablished. I hated the Jews because I was told: No more Jews, no more capitalism. But now I notice that a lot of Jews are leaving Germany, but capitalism is still rampant. I notice that there are no longer any Jewish professors at German universities, but there aren't any more boys from the working class than before. I notice that Jewish magistrates have been dismissed, but there's still one law for the rich and one law for the poor. It's still the rich who reap the benefits and the poor who receive the promises. And if that's not capitalism, then I wonder what capitalism is. And I wonder if we started our revolution to make Germany national-socialist or to fill the theaters with informers instead of actors. You've betrayed us. You've abused our anger. And now you want to dishonor me as well. Wretches that we are, poor, poor wretches. What have we done to deserve the horror of such masters?

(Lorenz comes running on. Miklas shoves him aside and runs out like a madman.)

JOSTHINKEL: *(recovering)* Follow him, Lorenz, and take all the measures necessary to keep him from doing something silly. Bolshevik propaganda has wormed its way into his mind and he's capable of anything. *(as Lorenz is about to go)* Take this, Lorenz. You may need it.

(Lorenz takes his weapon and goes.)

Scene Eighteen

(The Hamburg Theater. Miklas is on the stage, playing the violin. Mrs. Efeu and Knurr are at their usual places. Mrs. Efeu is playing the piano. Lorenz appears. In the wings, there are four shadows.)

MIKLAS: *(to Lorenz)* And now I'm even playing music written by the son of a Jew and a Gypsy.

KNURR: *(to Mrs. Efeu)* Come,...we had better leave.

(Mrs. Efeu is dragged off by Knurr. Miklas moves towards Lorenz. He is still playing the violin.)

Scene Nineteen

(The Railway Bridge. Myriam and Magnus. Magnus holds a letter.)

MYRIAM: So? This letter?

MAGNUS: Another reply. From the Little Theater in Dresden: "Honored to have qualified as a purely German theater for many years now—therefore impossible to consider your application. Should circumstances free you from the unfortunate attachments which hamper your career, would be pleased to hear from you again, and so on and so forth. Heil Hitler. What do you expect? They're idiots.

MYRIAM: Idiots. Idiots. Talk of the *schlemiel* calling the *schlemazel* black. Why can't you divorce me and take me back as your mistress? It'd be like that film that made me cry so much, *Back Street*.

MAGNUS: Myriam, we've broken too many dishes discussing that subject. There's no more to be said. But you mustn't worry, my dear, we'll pull through as we've always pulled through, with grace.

MYRIAM: Worried? Who's worried? The baker, maybe he's a little worried. The others won't give us any more credit, so why should they worry? He's a nice man, that baker, or maybe he's Jewish, how do I know? We'll leave him a little note of apology if something happens to us.

MAGNUS: If something happens to us you can't expect us to start worrying about the baker. But why do you want something to happen to us?

MYRIAM: Did I say I wanted something to happen to us? All I said was *if* something happened to us. If they...if we...that's all I said.

MAGNUS: Something could happen to me alone. Or something could happen to you alone. That would be awful.

MYRIAM: Yes, that would be awful. I think it's better if something happened to both of us at once. I understand, Magnus, I understand. But do you understand?

MAGNUS: I understand.

MYRIAM: Do you really understand?

MAGNUS: Do you want me to understand something in particular?

MYRIAM: Do I want him to understand something in particular, he asks. When you say to someone: "do you understand," it's always because you want them to understand something in particular. Otherwise, you wouldn't have to insist so much, would you? I mean, do you understand that I've understood, or don't you?

MAGNUS: I understand, Myriam; don't get irritable.

MYRIAM: Irritable! Who's getting irritable!... *(Pause)* Is your shirt clean?

MAGNUS: Yes.

MYRIAM: And your underpants. What about your underpants? Are they clean?

MAGNUS: Myriam!

MYRIAM: Myriam. Why Myriam? My mother always used to say: "Myriam, my daughter, if you had an accident and your underpants were dirty, think what a disgrace it would be to the family."

MAGNUS: Myriam, I'm as bright as a button.

MYRIAM: Good. I feel better now. *(Silence)* We've had a good life, Magnus.

MAGNUS: Yes, but it was useless. We couldn't stop anything.

MYRIAM: We did what we could, Magnus. Who can say our life was useless? Maybe one day in 20, 30, 50 years, somebody will hear that a German actor by the name of Gottchalk killed himself rather than repudiate his wife the way they asked him to. And they'll say: "There's a man who said no in his own way." And for a minute, they'll think about us. And for that minute, we'll live again.

MAGNUS: Yes. Perhaps.

(They hold hands. They are sitting on the rail. A train whistles in the distance.)

Scene Twenty

(Thomas Brückner's house. The Verandah. Sebastien, Erika, Ludwig, Emelyne.)

SEBASTIEN: You really think we should leave, Ludwig?

LUDWIG: Yes, Mr. Sebastien. You must leave Germany. Both of you. Especially Miss Erika. Because of her Bolshevik cabaret.

SEBASTIEN: And our father?

LUDWIG: Let him stay in Switzerland. He can extend his holiday. Miss Erika, please listen to me when I tell you to go as quickly as you can. If they catch up with you....

SEBASTIEN: It's all right, Ludwig, we're going. Stop worrying. Go and prepare my things.

(Ludwig is going out.)

ERIKA: Ludwig? Who told you it was a Bolshevik cabaret?

(Ludwig stops, looks at her, doesn't answer, and goes. Emelyne stays.)

ERIKA: Emelyne?

EMELYNE: Yes....Erika?

ERIKA: What are you thinking?

EMELYNE: Ludwig's been working for them for several years. He used to tell them everything that went on in this house. But he's fond of you, so now he's telling you what is being planned there. What'll happen to me? I'm his wife. They'll turn him into a mad dog. He's already like that sometimes. They'll make monsters out of all of us.

ERIKA: Come with us, Emelyne. We'll take you to America.

EMELYNE: No, Miss Erika, you can't take all of Germany into exile. You'll have to leave me here. I'll pack your case.

ERIKA: I'll take one small bag.

SEBASTIEN: This nightmare can't last.

EMELYNE: Yes, Sir. It will last.

(The telephone rings.)

ERIKA: Hello? Father! Sebastien, it's the Magician.

(Emelyne indicates the telephone might be bugged and they must be careful.)

Yes, yes, Father. No, no, rest there for a few more days. In fact, we were thinking of coming to see you for a little while. Tomorrow? No, absolutely not. The house is in a frightful mess. It is, Father....Father....

SEBASTIEN: *(takes the telephone)* Hello, Father? It's raining, too. We're having a dreadful March. It's snowing, actually. *(to Erika)* He says the weather's bad in Switzerland. Listen to me, Father, listen, there are storms on the way. No, they're not spring storms. *(to Erika)* He says he doesn't care, he wants to come back.

ERIKA: Hello, Father? Listen to me. Don't come back. You're no longer safe in Germany. We're not either. Is that clear? We're leaving. There. Understood? We'll be with you day after tomorrow. Lots of love.

(She hangs up and goes, followed by Emelyne. Ludwig comes on with a suitcase. Sebastien takes two glasses of cognac. He serves Ludwig and himself.)

SEBASTIEN: It's the first time we drink together, isn't it, Ludwig?

LUDWIG: Yes, it's the first time.

SEBASTIEN: But it doesn't matter anymore, does it?

LUDWIG: No, it doesn't matter anymore.

SEBASTIEN: We didn't drink to anything. But what is there to drink to?

(Erika comes in with Emelyne.)

SEBASTIEN: It's time for us to go.

(He shakes Ludwig's hand and kisses Emelyne.)

LUDWIG: Have a good trip, Mr. Sebastien. And I wish you a bright future abroad, Miss Erika.

ERIKA: Have a bright future in Germany, Ludwig.

(Ludwig takes the suitcases out, followed by Emelyne.)

SEBASTIEN: It's time to go.

ERIKA: Just one more little moment. I feel as if I'd never seen this room before. When we're gone there won't be a living soul left here.

SEBASTIEN: My sister, my sister.

ERIKA: My orchard, my dear, my beautiful, my treasured orchard. My happiness, goodbye.

(Theresa comes in, carrying a suitcase.)

ERIKA: Theresa! We're leaving.

THERESA: So am I. The *gestapo* came and arrested Otto yesterday. Alex, too. I'm all that's left of the Peppermill.

ERIKA: And me. We'll take it with us, Theresa, we'll take it everywhere we go.

SEBASTIEN: And every word we write, every truth we utter, will do them harm, a little harm.

SCENE TWENTY-ONE

(The Hamburg Theater. Hendrik, playing Mephisto, takes a solo bow to tumultuous applause. Josthinkel brings a microphone onto the stage. He's in full evening dress and holds a telegram in his hand.)

JOSTHINKEL: *(to the audience)* Minister, General, ladies and gentlemen, it gives me the greatest pleasure this evening to commit an indiscretion. This telegram was not addressed to me. But a quasidiabolic intuition allowed me to guess its contents and authorized me to open it. This telegram is addressed to our great national-socialist actor, Hendrik Hofgen. I will, however, read it to you all forthwith.

(Applause)

"Fully aware of the services rendered by the actor Hendrik Hofgen and knowing how much the prestige of the theater of our Third Reich will be enhanced by his future successes, I have decided to name Hendrik Hofgen Administrator of all the theaters of Prussia. And it is signed...it is signed: Adolf Hitler. Our Fuhrer."

(Applause. Bows. Josthinkel brings Nicoletta from the wings and she stands beside her husband.)

JOSTHINKEL: *(reciting)* "Open the ball, divine couple, pair beloved of the gods, sovereign royalties of the nether regions, bewitching angels. Lead us to the depths of the earth, to the primeval caves oozing with blood, where the warriors make love and the lovers make war, and where the beauty of death entwines with the beauty of love in a sublime and unique feast."

(Applause. More bows. Suddenly, the theater is empty. Nicoletta and Hendrik remain alone. They're silent, frozen.)

NICOLETTA: Aren't you getting changed, Hendrik? They're waiting for us at the Grand Hotel.

HENDRIK: I don't want to go.

NICOLETTA: You have to go, Hendrik. The reception is in your honor. Don't forget Goering himself has come to Hamburg to embrace his dear Mephisto and drive him back all the sooner to Berlin. It's too late, Hendrik, you have to go. I'll wait for you in the foyer.

(She goes out. A figure appears on the gangway.)

HENDRIK: Who's that? Otto? Otto! My brother, my friend, you *are* here. They told me—*(He runs towards Otto.)* You've come at last. I'm saved! *(But he stops in front of a man who's staring at him in silence.)* Who are you? I've never seen you here before. Everyone's left the theater, you shouldn't be here. You have no right—

(The man comes forward, slowly. Hendrik tries to close the curtains but the man leaps onto the stage and reaches him in a few steps.)

HENDRIK: Don't touch me! Help! Knurr!

ALEX: No need to shout, Administrator, I've come to bring you Otto's greetings.

HENDRIK: I don't know who you're talking about.

ALEX: You don't remember Otto? Your friend, your brother, Otto. Otto is dead and sends you his greetings.

HENDRIK: Listen, my friend, I'm not afraid of you, but I should tell you that you're not safe here—

ALEX: Otto was beaten for nine days. In the end, he had no face left. His body was a mass of bleeding sores, broken bones, and all I could recognize of him were his eyes. But when they took him away for his last interrogation, Otto managed to say—it was difficult to understand him, his mouth was full of blood—he managed to say: "When you've reached this stage, you no longer make mistakes. I know now that we'll win. I'm sure of it in a way I never was before. We'll have to fight for a long time, but in the end, we'll win."

HENDRIK: Why are you telling me this?

ALEX: So that your friends in the government will learn about it. So that the scum you keep company with, those men who stink of urine, will hear of it from your own mouth. Otto died without revealing a single name. They threw his body from a third-floor window. I am now going to name the murderers so that they will be damned for the centuries to come: They were the S.A. Witske, the S.A. Kubik, the S.A. Moder. Listen carefully, Administrator: Witske, Kubik, Moder.

HENDRIK: How do you know all this?

ALEX: I shared Otto's cell. They transferred me after his death and I jumped from the lorry.

HENDRIK: Well, you didn't die, did you? You got yourself out of it; you let Otto down.

ALEX: I'm still alive, yes, unfortunately for you, Administrator. Unfortunately for all of you. But no, I'll never let Otto down. They wouldn't allow anyone at Otto's funeral, so do you know where his memorial service took place? In Dachau. They heard of his death through one of the prisoners' wives. And one night, a man started to sing. Then another joined him. And another. Six thousand prisoners sang for Otto and there was nothing anyone could do to stop it. No one will ever sing like that for you, Administrator.

HENDRIK: Don't come near me. I'll give you some money.

(Nicoletta comes on. Hendrik grabs her purse.)

Give me some money, quickly. This man's threatening me. He wants money.

NICOLETTA: No, Hendrik. He doesn't want your money. Good evening, Alex. You've come too late. There is nothing you can do for us anymore. I think you had better leave as soon as you can. The rot has set in and we are beginning to stink. Go. Go quickly.

HENDRIK: Get out or I'll call the police. Go to Hell!

(Alex goes. Hendrik nestles against Nicoletta and begins to cry.)

HENDRIK: What do they all want from me? Help me. Protect me.

NICOLETTA: Be quiet, Hendrik. We mustn't say anything. There is nothing left for us to do now but to go in mourning for ourselves. Get dressed. They're waiting for us.

HENDRIK: Why are they tormenting me? I haven't done anything. What can I do? I'm only an ordinary actor.

(The lights go down. The song and projection begin.)

UNSTERBLICHE OPFER

Unsterbliche Opfer ihr sanket dahin.
Wir stehen und weinen voll schmerz Herz und Sinn.
Einst aber, wenn Freiheit den Menschen erstand
Und all euer sehnen Enfühlung fand,
Dann weben wir künden, wie ihr einst gelebt
Zum Höchsten der Menschheit empor nur gestrebt.

Als Opfer seid ihr gefallen in Streit
In heiliger Liebe zum Volke
Ihr wart für die Menschheit zu geben bereit
Die Freiheit und Glück und das Leben.

IMMORTAL SACRIFICE (fragment)

Immortal victims, you have fallen,
We linger here and cry, our hearts and souls filled
  with pain.
But one day, when man is free
And all your hopes have been fulfilled,
We will herald the lives you led.
You who aspired to the highest of human values.

You have fallen, victims of the battle,
Because of your sacred love of the people
For humanity you were ready to offer
Your freedom, your joy, your lives.

—Translated by Margaret Glover

This poem by W.G. Archangelsky (1878) was set to music attributed to N.N. Ikonnikov and sung as a funeral march for the Russian revolutionaries who died in 1905. Resistance groups in Buchenwald, and probably in other Nazi concentration camps, sang it illegally in memory of their murdered companions.

THIS PLAY IS DEDICATED TO

HANS OTTO
actor, communist
tortured and assassinated by the Gestapo in Berlin
November 24, 1933

ERICH MÜHSAM
anarchist poet
tortured and hanged at the Oranienburg
  concentration camp
July 10, 1934

MADAME MÜHSAM
disappeared in the Soviet Union
most probably during Stalin's purges

CAROLA NEHER
actress
emigrated to the Soviet Union
deported by Stalin
disappeared in 1936

KURT TUCHOLSKY
pacifist writer and satirist
committed suicide in Sweden
December 21, 1935

ERNST LUDWIG KIRCHNER
painter
committed suicide in Switzerland
June 15, 1938

CARL VON OSSIETZKY
journalist, pacifist writer
died of starvation after three years of imprisonment
May 4, 1938

WALTER HASENCLEVER
playwright
interned at a camp at Milles, France
committed suicide
June 21, 1939

EGON FRIEDDELL
historian
committed suicide in Vienna
1938

ERNST TOLLER
poet
committed suicide in New York
May 22, 1939

CARL EINSTEIN
poet
interned at a camp at Gurs, France
committed suicide
July 3, 1940

WALTER BENJAMIN
writer, essayist
committed suicide in France at the Spanish border
September 26, 1940

RICHARD OEHRING
poet
committed suicide in Holland
1940

WILLI MÜNZENBERG
writer, editor, communist
excommunicated from the party
found dead in Grenoble
1940

HERWARTH WALDEN
writer, theoretician
disappeared in the Soviet Union
1941

JOACHIM GOTTCHALK
actor
committed suicide with his wife and son
November 1941

JAKOB VAN HODDIS
poet
interned near Koblenz
assassinated in a gas chamber
April 30, 1942

STEFAN ZWEIG
writer, pacifist
committed suicide in Rio de Janeiro
February 22, 1942

SHIMON DUBNOV
historian
assassinated in a Soviet concentration camp
1942

PAUL KORNFELD
playwright
assassinated in a concentration camp
1942

ERNST OTTWALT
communist writer
assassinated in a Soviet concentration camp
1943

ALFRED WOLFENSTEIN
poet, critic
committed suicide in Paris
January 22, 1945

ERIKA MANN
actress, pamphleteer
1905-1969

KLAUS MANN
writer
committed suicide in Cannes
May 21, 1949

∽